INTO ITALIAN WINE

The Italian Wine Professional Certification Course

SECOND EDITION

By Jack Brostrom
and Geralyn Brostrom

Published by
Italian Wine Central
Napa, California

Italian Wine Central is grateful for the cooperation
and assistance of the Italian Trade Commission

ITALIAN TRADE AGENCY
ICE - Italian Trade Commission

Date of information: February 2016

Please bring any typographical errors or content issues
to the attention of admin@italianwinecentral.com.

Second edition
First printing

Contents

Riomaggiore, one of the five seaside villages that make up the Cinque Terre in Liguria

Preface

Welcome to the world of Italian wine. It has been several years since an updated book about the broad palette of Italian wine—the denominations (wine place-names), grape varieties, styles, production methods, and wine laws—has been published, and in that time, many significant changes have taken place in Europe and Italy. Wine educators and specialists, ourselves included, for years have had to make do with well written but out-of-date books on the subject, Internet sources with conflicting information, and personal experience to keep on top of the shifting sands of Italian wine.

It was in that context that we conceived and launched the Italian Wine Central website, www.italianwinecentral.com, as an up-to-date and reliable resource. This was followed by the Italian Wine Professional (IWP) course, designed to help others get up to speed with a core knowledge of Italian wine. Now, with *Into Italian Wine,* we are proud to present the official course book for the Italian Wine Professional program.

This book should prove useful in a number of ways:

- as a good read for those who are interested in broadening their knowledge of Italian wine,
- as a reference book for anyone who works with or buys Italian wine,
- as a study vehicle for those wanting a solid foundation in Italian wine for its own sake, and
- as a stepping-stone for anyone looking to achieve the Italian Wine Professional certification or other advanced wine credentials.

The structure of *Into Italian Wine* mirrors that of the IWP course and covers the essential information that someone in a professional position should know with regard to Italian wine. The overall course is designed at an advanced intermediate level, meaning that it goes well beyond an introductory course in the number of grape varieties and denominations covered and the detail of the information, while reserving the more intricate subject matter for an expert-level program. The IWP program covers the full breadth of Italian wine, touching on all 20 regions and all the classic Italian grape varieties and denominations as well as many grapes and wine areas that have gained popularity recently or that are worthy of more attention by the wine community. The course puts all this knowledge in a context that makes it understandable and memorable. The scope of this information is categorized and presented for review in a summary of the course's learning objectives that appears before Unit 1.

The course material is divided into eight study units—although if you're reading the book for pleasure rather than pursuing the credential, you might want to mentally substitute the word *chapter* for *unit.* The opening unit sets the stage by providing much of the background information and terminology that is fundamental to the understanding of the other units—climate, geography, history, and the wine laws that prevail in Italy.

The next six units survey Italy's most important exported wine denominations and grape varieties in a format that is intentionally different from most wine books. Rather than progressing region by region around the country and covering each region's wines all at once, *Into Italian Wine* is organized first by wine style—red, white, sparkling, dessert—second by grape variety, and only then by region. While at first this might be an unfamiliar arrangement for those who have taken other wine courses, it is much closer to the way people choose wines and the way wine lists are typically written and is therefore a more practical way to approach Italian wines. It is also a more efficient way to study and learn about Italian wines since it gives the reader a solid base upon which to append new information as new denominations and wines enter the marketplace.

Units 2–4 cover red wines from the northern, central, and southern regions, respectively. The next two units describe Italy's white wines, starting with those of the peninsula and islands, an area where many crisp, seafood-friendly wines are produced to match with the bounty of the nearby Mediterranean Sea. Unit 6 discusses the wines of the northern regions, which are typically more full-bodied and richer. While this is by no means a hard-and-fast division in styles, it is a useful and thought-provoking way of considering wines of similar styles together rather than compartmented by political region. Each of these units addresses consumers' interest in engaging in truly local food and wine experiences, by grouping wines with the cuisines of relevant production zones.

Unit 7 covers the specialty wines and spirits of Italy, including the numerous sparkling wines, dessert wines, and grappa. The last unit then returns to a few of the most iconic Italian wine denominations to delve deeper. These classic areas and their wines have the widest distribution and often the most recognition in the market, and therefore wine professionals are expected to be more familiar with them than is necessary for many others.

In addition to the principal content about Italian wine in each unit, there is much additional information in the book to help put the wines in context, including custom maps created by Italian Wine Central, vivid photos, and an introduction to the Italian language, cuisine, and culture. Each unit also contains educational exercises that are strongly recommended for anyone using *Into Italian Wine* as a study aid. These exercises lead the reader to consider the book's information in a variety of different ways, thereby reinforcing an understanding of the material by engaging different learning styles. Completion of these exercises is essential to mastering the course content.

The back matter in this book contains several further resources that can be used as a quick reference that goes beyond the scope of the Italian Wine Professional course. The first of these is a synopsis of the primary rules—types of wine produced, grape variety percentages, aging requirements—for each of the denominations discussed earlier in the course. There is also a list of every Italian wine denomination, grouped by region and quality level. Answers to the end-of-unit exercises can be found in the back of the book as well, along with an index to the eight units to help locate specific references in the text.

Whatever your interest in the subject—as consumer, wine salesperson, culinary professional, or educator—we hope that you will find this book informative and a valuable guide to your enjoyment of Italian wines.

Study Checklist

This checklist is included for those who are studying for the Italian Wine Professional certification test or who, for their own purposes, want to measure their comprehension of the material against the course's learning objectives. The categories of information below represent the body of knowledge a person working in the wine industry with a specialty in Italian wine should be able to recall without referring to other resources. Those preparing for the IWP exam are advised to review each item in the checklist multiple times until they are comfortable with meeting the standards—for example, by turning each bullet point into a flashcard or by having another person quiz them on the study points. Combine this activity with the end-of-unit exercises to prepare for the test.

General

- Recall Italy's world ranking in grape growing, wine production, overall exports, and exports to the U.S.
- Recall basic Italian history of interactions with other countries that impacted the wine industry, including the ancient Greeks, the ancient Romans, other cultures during the Renaissance and later, and the European Union
- Know Italy's geographic position in Europe and its neighboring countries and seas
- Know Italy's most important topographical features
- Identify all 20 political/administrative regions in Italy on a map
- Know which regions
  - have the most denominations
  - produce the most wine
  - have strong non-Italian cultural influences
- Recall in which regions Florence, Milan, Naples, Rome, and Venice are located

Wine Label Terms and Wine Laws

- Understand the quality pyramid for Italian wine under both EU and national law
- Recall the general requirements a wine must meet to use a protected place-name on its label

- Know the labeling requirements for Italian wines
- Understand the relationship between the DOP, DOC, and DOCG designations
- Know the general relationship between DOPs and IGPs in terms of geographic areas, quality, and price
- Understand the meaning of common labeling terms, including *riserva*, *superiore*, and *classico*
- Know the minimum standard for labeling a wine as a varietal
- Understand the term *super* in the context of "super Tuscan" and similar wines

Viticulture and Vinification

- Understand the differences between making red wines and white wines
- Understand the differences between making table wines and sparkling wines
- Know the grape varieties most commonly used in Italy to make sparkling wines
- Understand basic sparkling wine terminology used in Italy
- Understand the differences between making table wines and sweet and/or fortified wines
- Understand basic dessert wine terminology used in Italy
- Understand the differences between making wine and grappa

Denominations

For the following denominations, know:
- the correct spelling
- in which region they're located
- what their quality level is (DOCG, DOC, IGP)
- what type(s) of wines they make (red, white, sparkling, dessert)
- what the primary grapes of their best-known wine(s) are
- whether their wines are blends, varietals, or 100%
- denominations with highest volumes of production

For the denominations covered in Unit 8, also know:
- grape varieties and percentages, aging requirements, styles, subzones, and primary communes of production

Piedmont: Alta Langa, Asti, Barbaresco, Barbera d'Alba, Barbera d'Asti, Barolo, Brachetto d'Acqui, Diano d'Alba, Dogliani, Dolcetto DOCs, Erbaluce di Caluso, Gattinara, Gavi, Ghemme, Langhe, Monferrato, Nizza, Ovada, Piemonte, Roero

Valle d'Aosta: Valle d'Aosta/Vallée d'Aoste

Lombardy: Bonarda dell'Oltrepò Pavese, Franciacorta, Garda, Lugana, Oltrepò Pavese, Oltrepò Pavese Metodo Classico, Valtellina denominations

Trentino–Alto Adige: Alto Adige/Südtirol, Trentino, Trento, Valdadige, IGP delle Venezie

Veneto: Amarone della Valpolicella, Asolo Prosecco, Bardolino, Bardolino Superiore, Bianco di Custoza, Conegliano Valdobbiadene Prosecco, Garda, Lugana, Prosecco, Recioto della Valpolicella, Recioto di Soave, Soave, Soave Superiore, Valpolicella, Valpolicella Ripasso, IGP delle Venezie, IGP Veneto

Friuli–Venezia Giulia: Collio, Friuli Grave, Prosecco, IGP delle Venezie

Emilia Romagna: Colli Bolognesi Pignoletto, Lambrusco DOCs, Pignoletto

Tuscany: Bolgheri, Brunello di Montalcino, Carmignano, Chianti and its subzones, Chianti Classico, Maremma Toscana, Morellino di Scansano, Rosso di Montalcino, Rosso di Montepulciano, Sant'Antimo, Vernaccia di San Gimignano, Vino Nobile di Montepulciano, Vin Santo, IGP Toscana

Marche: Castelli di Jesi Verdicchio Riserva, Cònero, Rosso Cònero, Rosso Piceno, Verdicchio dei Castelli di Jesi, Offida, Verdicchio di Matelica Riserva, Verdicchio di Matelica

Abruzzo: Cerasuolo d'Abruzzo, Montepulciano d'Abruzzo, Montepulciano d'Abruzzo Colline Teramane, Trebbiano d'Abruzzo

Umbria: Montefalco Sagrantino, Orvieto

Lazio: Cesanese del Piglio, Cesanese di Affile, Cesanese di Olevano Romano, Est! Est!! Est!!! di Montefiascone, Frascati, Frascati Superiore, Orvieto

Campania: Aglianico del Taburno, Falanghina del Sannio, Fiano di Avellino, Greco di Tufo, Taurasi, Vesuvio

Basilicata: Aglianico del Vulture, Aglianico del Vulture Superiore

Puglia: Castel del Monte denominations, Primitivo di Manduria, Primitivo di Manduria Dolce Naturale, Salice Salentino, IGP Puglia, IGP Salento

Calabria: Cirò

Sicily: Cerasuolo di Vittoria, Etna, Marsala, Pantelleria, Sicilia, IGP Terre Siciliane

Sardinia: Cannonau di Sardegna, IGP Isola dei Nuraghi, Vermentino di Gallura, Vermentino di Sardegna

Grape Varieties

For each of the following grape varieties, know:
- its color (red or white)
- whether it is an international or Italian variety
- with which region(s) it's most closely associated
- the correct spelling
- additional facts covered in the course (e.g., which are the most planted varieties, common alternative names) for a few varieties

Red: Aglianico, Barbera, Bombino Nero, Brachetto, Cabernet Franc, Cabernet Sauvignon, Cannonau, Carignano, Cesanese, Corvina, Croatina, Dolcetto, Frappato, Freisa, Gaglioppo, Grignolino, Lagrein, Lambrusco, Merlot, Monica, Montepulciano, Nebbiolo, Negroamaro, Nerello Mascalese, Nero d'Avola, Piedirosso, Pinot Nero, Primitivo, Raboso, Refosco, Rondinella, Sagrantino, Sangiovese/Brunello/Morellino/Prugnolo Gentile, Schiava, Syrah, Teroldego, Uva di Troia/Nero di Troia

White: Ansonica/Insolia, Arneis, Catarratto, Chardonnay, Coda di Volpe, Cortese, Erbaluce, Falanghina, Fiano, Friulano/Tai, Garganega, Glera, Grecanico Dorato, Grechetto, Greco, Grillo, Malvasia, Moscato, Nuragus, Passerina, Pecorino, Pinot Bianco, Pinot Grigio, Ribolla Gialla, Sauvignon Blanc, Traminer, Trebbiano, Verdicchio, Vermentino, Vernaccia, Zibibbo

Tasting Practice

A picture may be worth a thousand words, but when it comes to learning about wine, tasting is worth at least that much. This book and course provide a lot of information about Italian wine, but you can't expect to reach a professional level of knowledge about Italian wines without tasting them. The following list represents a recommended starter set of wines that would serve as a good introduction to the breadth of Italy's wines. Get to know as many of them as you can.

Unit 2: Northern Reds

- Dolcetto (Dogliani or Diano d'Alba)
- Nebbiolo (d'Alba, d'Asti, or Roero)
- Nebbiolo from northern Piedmont (Gattinara or Ghemme)
- Nebbiolo from Lombardy (Valtellina)
- Barbera (d'Asti or Nizza)
- Valpolicella DOC
- If available: Bardolino; Bardolino Chiaretto; Grignolino; Lagrein; Schiava; Teroldego; Valpolicella Ripasso

Unit 3: Central Reds

- Mid-priced Chianti (non-subzone)
- Chianti from Colli Senesi or Rufina
- Mid-priced Chianti Classico
- Varietal Montepulciano-based wine from Còne-ro, Offida, Rosso Piceno, or Montepulciano d'Abruzzo
- Morellino di Scansano
- Montefalco Sagrantino
- If available: Carmignano; Cerasuolo d'Abruzzo; Cesanese (del Piglio); Chianti Classico Riserva; dry, frizzante DOC-level Lambrusco (di Grasparossa, di Sorbara); Montepulciano d'Abruzzo; Vino Nobile di Montepulciano

Unit 4: Southern Reds

- Aglianico from Campania (Taurasi)
- Negroamaro (Salice Salentino)
- Primitivo from Puglia (di Manduria or IGP)
- Nero d'Avola from Sicily
- Cannonau (di Sardegna or IGP)
- Gaglioppo (Cirò)
- If available: Aglianico del Vulture; Frappato (Cerasuolo di Vittoria or IGP); Negroamaro rosato (Salice Salentino); Nerello Mascalese (Etna or IGP); Piedirosso (Vesuvio Rosso)

Unit 5: Peninsula & Island Whites

- Verdicchio from Jesi or Matelica
- Vermentino from Sardinia (di Gallura or di Sardegna)
- Vernaccia di San Gimignano
- Fiano di Avellino
- Greco di Tufo
- Pecorino (Offida)
- Pignoletto
- If available: Ansonica/Inzolia from Sicily; Carricante (Etna Bianco); Catarratto; Coda di Volpe (Vesuvio Bianco); Falanghina (del Sannio); Frascati; Grecanico Dorato; Grillo; Nuragus (di Cagliari); Passerina; Trebbiano d'Abruzzo; Vermentino from Liguria

Unit 6: Northern Whites

- Cortese (Gavi)
- Arneis (Roero)
- Garganega (Soave)
- High-end Pinot Grigio (Alto Adige, Collio, Oltrepò Pavese, Trentino)
- Friulano (Collio)
- Pinot Bianco from Trentino–Alto Adige
- Ribolla Gialla
- If available: Bianco di Custoza; Chardonnay, Gewürztraminer, Pinot Bianco, Sauvignon, and/or Riesling from Trentino–Alto Adige; Erbaluce (di Caluso); Lugana

Unit 7: Sparkling Wines, Dessert Wines, & Spirits

- Franciacorta Brut
- Mid-priced Prosecco DOC
- Conegliano Valdobbiadene Prosecco
- Moscato d'Asti
- Asti spumante
- Brachetto d'Acqui
- DOC-level Vin Santo (del Chianti Classico)
- Recioto della Valpolicella
- Grappa
- If available: Alta Langa or Oltrepò Pavese Metodo Classico; sparkling DOC-level Lambrusco; Pantelleria passito; Primitivo di Manduria Dolce Naturale; Recioto di Soave

Unit 8: Luxury Wines

- Amarone della Valpolicella
- Barbaresco
- Barolo
- Brunello di Montalcino
- Chianti Classico Gran Selezione
- Sangiovese-based Super Tuscan (Bolgheri, IGP Toscana)
- If available: Riserva of Amarone, Barbaresco, Barolo, or Brunello; single-vineyard versions of any of the above; "super" wine from a region other than Tuscany

Florence, Tuscany's capital, seen from the village of Fiesole

Introduction to Italy and Italian Wines

Vineyards cascade down the slopes beneath Barolo Castle in Piedmont.

Why is Italy important in the wine world?

For starters, it is the world's largest producer of wine. After a very poor harvest in 2014 reduced Italy's output to second after France, the 2015 harvest reestablished Italy in its customary position of making more wine than any other country. It is also perennially the world's largest exporter of wine by volume and the second largest exporter by value after France.

Furthermore, Italy has the third largest vineyard acreage of any country (after Spain and France) and is the largest source of imported wine in the United States by volume and by value.

Beyond the numbers, Italy has a key historical position in the establishment of vineyards throughout Europe, and it is the producer of many distinctive wines with no real equivalent outside Italy. And given the prominence of Italian cuisine in restaurants and kitchens around the world, the wines of Italy that developed alongside this food are constantly in demand.

The tricolore, *Italy's flag*

Learning Objectives

Unit 1 discusses the geography, history, and wine laws of Italy. The learning objectives for this unit—the fundamental information an Italian Wine Professional should know and the points most likely to be included on the exam—are:

- Italy's position in the world wine trade
- Italy's influence in establishing grapes and winemaking in Europe
- Location and influences of the Alps, Apennines, Po River, neighboring countries, and adjacent seas
- Location of all 20 regions and some major cities
- EU wine laws and the quality pyramid
- Italian implementation of EU wine law
- Italian wine labeling terms

Geography of Italy

The Italian peninsula resembles a boot anchoring southern Europe.

Italy is centrally positioned in Europe longitudinally (i.e., east–west). It has a southerly position in latitude, and extends into and dominates the central Mediterranean Sea.

The country's shape is instantly recognizable. The main peninsula resembles a boot, with two large islands to the southwest.

Italy is similar in length to California, but not as wide. It is also positioned farther north than California. The warmth of the Mediterranean relative to the Pacific Ocean keeps Italy's climate more temperate than its latitude would indicate, as shown below.

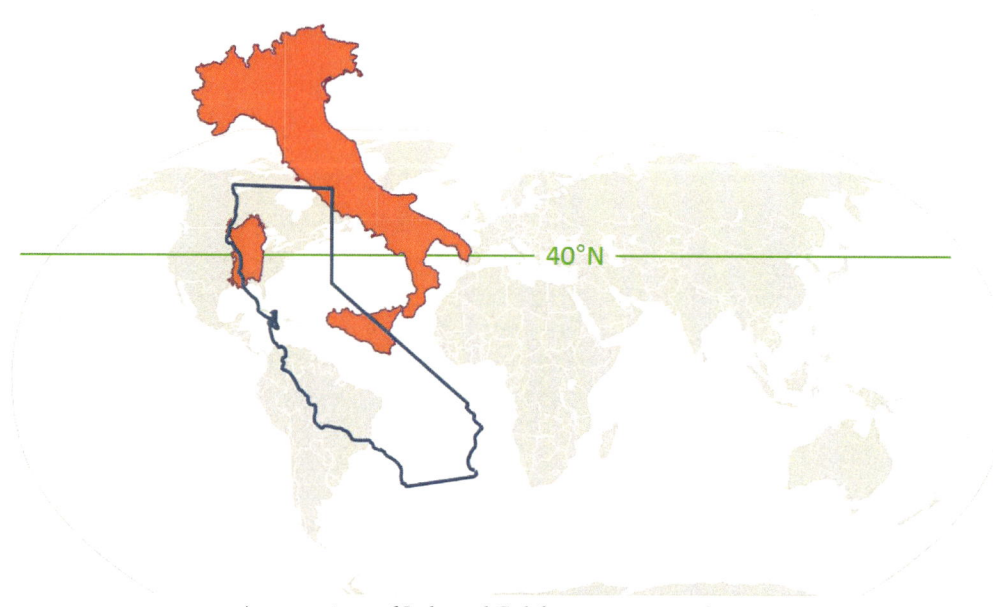

40°N

A comparison of Italy and California in terms of size and position relative to the 40th parallel of latitude

Italy borders on four countries:
- France
- Switzerland
- Austria
- Slovenia

plus two small principalities, San Marino and the Vatican City, which lie entirely within Italy's borders.

Everywhere else, Italy is surrounded by the Mediterranean Sea. Specific basins of the Mediterranean Sea go by various names. Around Italy are:
- The Adriatic Sea to the northeast of the peninsula
- The Ionian Sea to the southeast
- The Tyrrhenian Sea to the southwest
- The Ligurian Sea in the northwest above Corsica

The majority of Italy is covered with mountains, most of which are part of two ranges. The Alps run along the entire northern border. The Apennines run the length of the peninsula, from Liguria in a sweeping arc to the toe in Calabria. The islands are also covered with rugged mountains. The only large plains are located across the north end of the peninsula, formed in large part by Italy's largest river, the Po. There is also a smaller flat area running down the heel of the boot.

Climate of Italy

The two maps immediately below show the average high temperatures in Italy for the months of January and July.

As you might expect, the Alps and high Apennines are very cold in winter, but otherwise, the winter temperatures are normally above freezing and the south is fairly mild. In summer, the hottest places are the Po Valley, the Adriatic coast, and the islands.

The map at the bottom of the page shows the average annual rainfall totals experienced in Italy. The wettest areas are in the high elevations of the Alps and the west side of the Apennines. The driest areas are the same ones that have the highest temperatures: the Po Valley; the Adriatic coast, especially in the heel; and the islands.

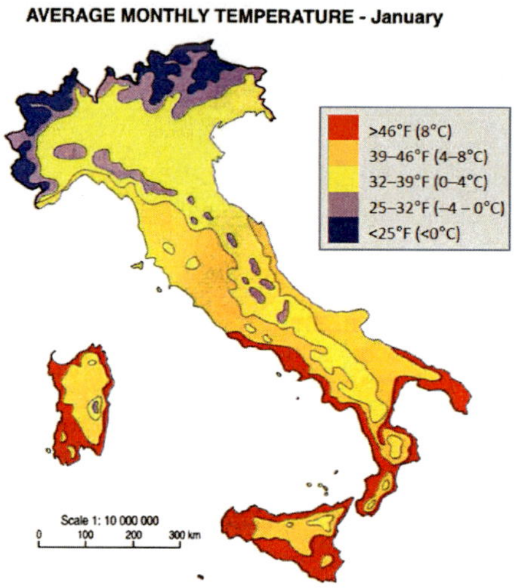

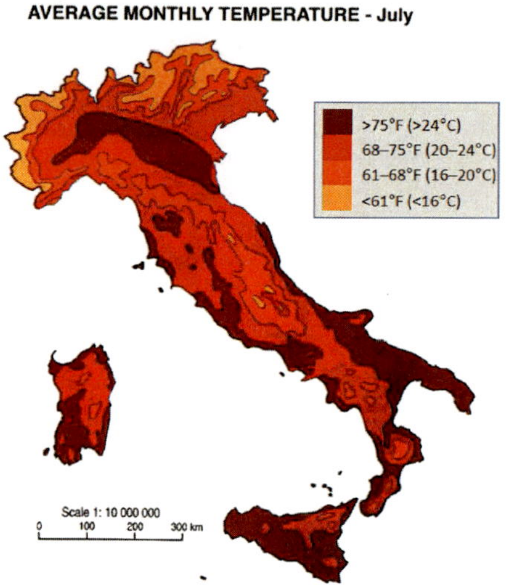

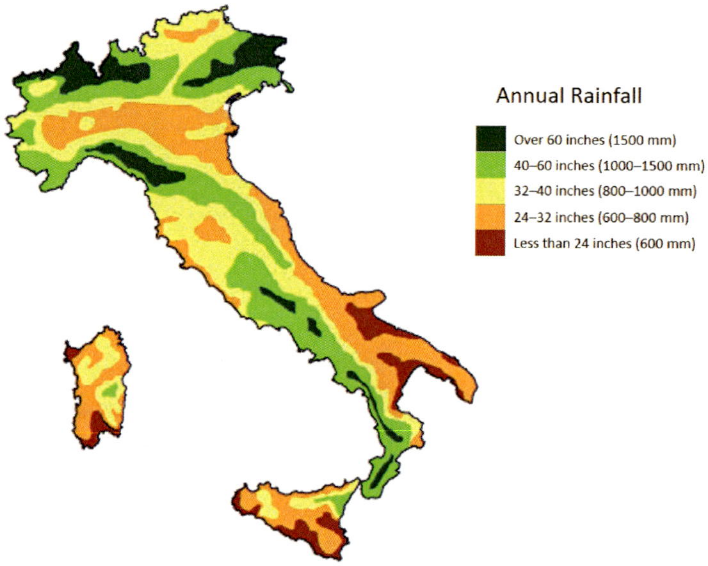

AVERAGE MONTHLY TEMPERATURE - January

- >46°F (8°C)
- 39–46°F (4–8°C)
- 32–39°F (0–4°C)
- 25–32°F (-4 – 0°C)
- <25°F (<0°C)

Scale 1: 10 000 000
0   100   200   300 km

AVERAGE MONTHLY TEMPERATURE - July

- >75°F (>24°C)
- 68–75°F (20–24°C)
- 61–68°F (16–20°C)
- <61°F (<16°C)

Scale 1: 10 000 000
0   100   200   300 km

Annual Rainfall

- Over 60 inches (1500 mm)
- 40–60 inches (1000–1500 mm)
- 32–40 inches (800–1000 mm)
- 24–32 inches (600–800 mm)
- Less than 24 inches (600 mm)

Putting this information together, Italy's climate can be simplified by organizing the country into a few climatic zones, as depicted in the map below :

- Alpine Zone: Cool, short summers; long winters with frequent snow
- Po Valley: Hot, humid summers; cold, foggy winters
- Ligurian and Tyrrhenian Coast: Hot summers and mild winters
- Apennines: Cool summers; cold, rainy winters
- Adriatic Coast: Hot summers and chilly winters
- Mediterranean Zone: Hot, dry summers; very mild winters

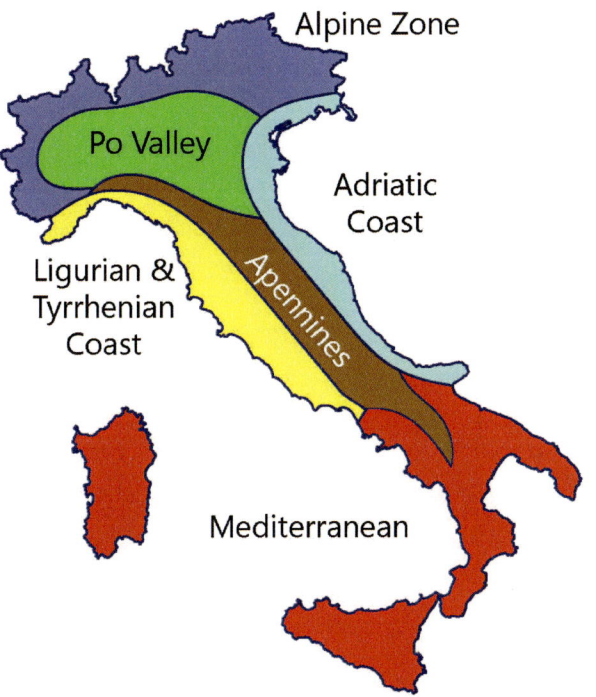

Top: *Snow-covered vineyards in Piedmont*
Bottom: *The resort beach at Termoli in Molise*

Political Geography of Italy

Italy has 20 official regions, or *regioni* in Italian. These are conceptually similar to states in the U.S. or provinces in Canada, and each has its own capital and regional parliament. Most regions have a few divisions called *provincia* or provinces, similar to counties.

The regions and provinces are usually based on historical boundaries of former states—kingdoms, duchies, republics, and so forth. Regional boundaries can mark significant cultural differences.

Within the regions and provinces are municipalities ranging from Rome (Roma)—the national capital, largest city, and Italy's center since the Roman Empire, located in Lazio—through smaller cities, suburbs, towns, villages, and hamlets. Besides Rome, Italy's most important cities include:

- Milan (Milano), the second largest city and major city of the north, located in Lombardy
- Naples (Napoli), the largest city of the south, located in Campania

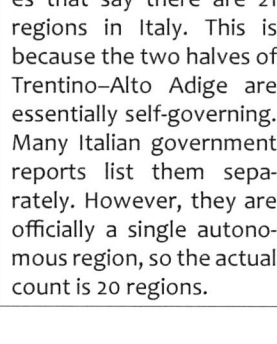

You may see some sources that say there are 21 regions in Italy. This is because the two halves of Trentino–Alto Adige are essentially self-governing. Many Italian government reports list them separately. However, they are officially a single autonomous region, so the actual count is 20 regions.

- Florence (Firenze), cultural heart of the Renaissance, located in Tuscany
- Venice (Venezia), another tourist favorite, located in the Veneto

In alphabetical order, the 20 regions are:

- Abruzzo
- Basilicata
- Calabria
- Campania
- Emilia Romagna
- Friuli–Venezia Giulia
- Lazio
- Liguria
- Lombardy
- Marche
- Molise
- Piedmont
- Puglia
- Sardinia
- Sicily
- Trentino–Alto Adige
- Tuscany
- Umbria
- Valle d'Aosta
- Veneto

Nation   Regions   Provinces

Valle d'Aosta

Piedmont

Lombardy

Trentino–Alto Adige

Friuli–Venezia Giulia

Veneto

Liguria

Emilia Romagna

Tuscany

Marche

Umbria

Abruzzo

Lazio

Molise

Campania

Puglia

Basilicata

Sardinia

Calabria

Sicily

Twenty Regions of Italy

History of Italian Wine

This segment describes the history of Italy as it relates to wine. Italians are very proud of their history, which still has tangible influences on modern Italian society. This is mostly just background information, but it does help give some perspective on why the Italian regions and their wines are so different from one another.

Early viticulture in Italy is credited to the Greeks, who colonized Sicily and the southern Italian peninsula. By 500 BC, there were numerous Greek outposts in the south. Rome was still a small city, fighting against other neighboring tribes. The Greeks introduced several grape varieties that were the ancestors of many southern Italian varieties grown today.

Rome began expanding after 500 BC, slowly but surely conquering and absorbing all the other cultures on the peninsula and the islands, including the Greek colonies, by about 200 BC. The Romans learned from their former enemies and absorbed their best technologies and ideas, including winemaking.

For the next four centuries, the Roman Empire continued to expand, eventually controlling all of southern and western Europe, North Africa,

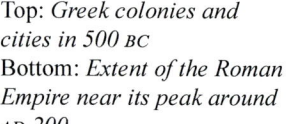

Top: *Greek colonies and cities in 500 BC*
Bottom: *Extent of the Roman Empire near its peak around AD 200*

and the Near East. Everywhere they went, the Romans planted grapevines, thereby establishing the basis for to-day's wine industry.

After the fall of the Roman Empire, economic conditions in Europe declined, and the former empire broke up into myriad constantly changing political entities. As a luxury, viticulture might have almost disappeared throughout Europe were it not for two things. First, water quality in much of medieval Europe, especially in the cities, was poor and unhealthy, whereas alcoholic beverages like wine were inherently more hygienic. Second, the Church required wine for sacramental purposes, so monks continued to pursue viticulture and improve on winemaking techniques. As the home of the popes, Italy was naturally one of the centers of winemaking in medieval Europe.

The Italian peninsula and the islands fell under control of various foreign rulers, popes, and local powers—families such as the Medici and Este. Parts of Italy were ruled or occupied by Byzantines, Lombards, Normans, Arabs, Germans, French, Spanish, and Austrians, all of whom had an influence on regional cuisine and viticulture.

For more than a thousand years after the end of the Roman Empire, grape growing was strictly a local affair, for local consumption or sacramental use. Grapevines mutated, cross-pollinated, and evolved into innumerable different varieties. Some variations proved more suitable for winemaking in a particular area and were cultivated, while less suitable ones died out or were removed. Throughout Europe, grape varieties became associated with the specific places where they produced the best wine, and appellations were born.

Because Italy was so fragmented by political boundaries, cultural rivalries, and mountainous terrain, hundreds of unique grape varieties developed in relative isolation throughout the country. The foundation was set for the vast array of wine appellations, styles, and varieties that exists today in Italy. In addition, in more recent times, a few grape varieties that were renowned in other countries were introduced into Italy, especially in the

The Italian islands, peninsula, and adjacent areas to the north were in constant turmoil in the centuries after the Fall of Rome, with complicated internal and external politics.

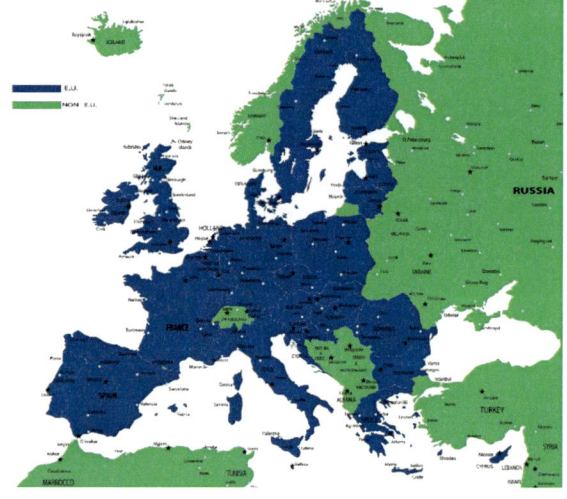

areas that had cultural or political ties with France, Spain, or the Germanic countries.

Unification of Italy as one country for the first time since the Roman Empire came about in the 19th and early 20th centuries. In 1861, most of modern Italy reunited as the Kingdom of Italy. Later additions were Veneto and Friuli (1866), Lazio (1870), and Trentino–Alto Adige (1919).

The monarchy lasted until the end of World War II. In 1946, the Italian kingdom became a republic, and in 1957, Italy became a founding member of the European Economic Community. Important dates in Italy's recent wine history include 1963, when the first Italian national wine law was established, and 1992, when a major overhaul of the 1963 wine law was passed.

In 1993, the European Union was created out of the European Economic Community to more closely coordinate politics and economics across Europe. That coordination came to the wine industry in 2008, when the EU established a wine law that began to shift control of wine from individual countries to the European government.

And that leads to the final subject for this unit: wine law.

Top: *Map of the states existing in modern-day Italy after the Congress of Vienna in 1815, with a red line indicating the territory that comprised the Kingdom of Italy when it was established in 1861*
Bottom: *The member nations of the European Union* (blue) *as of 2015*

EU Wine Law

It is important to understand that the laws relating to wine in Europe now come from the EU. However, each country is responsible for interpreting and enforcing the law—meaning that there are still differences in the way wine is handled from country to country. In order to comprehend Italian wine law, we must first start with the system that governs the wine industry in Italy, France, Germany, and every other EU country.

Under EU wine law, which controls Italian wine law, there are three quality levels recognized for wines. You can think of these conceptually as Good, Better, and Best. As you move

up in quality from Good to Better to Best, this will usually go hand in hand with more legal restrictions on how the wine is made, a lower volume of production, and of course higher prices.

Most often, these levels are depicted as what is known as a quality pyramid, illustrating the idea that there is a broad base of everyday wine that builds up to a pinnacle of top-quality wines. The official English-language terms for the three quality levels are:

- Wine ("Good")
- Protected Geographical Indication, or PGI ("Better")
- Protected Designation of Origin, or PDO ("Best")

PDOs have existed for years for cheeses, meats, olives, and many other agricultural items, but were established at the EU level for *wine* only in 2008. To qualify as a PDO, the highest level, a wine must meet a long list of requirements that govern, among other things:

- Where the grapes were grown
- How the vineyard was planted and managed
- When the grapes were picked
- What types of grapes go into making the wine and, for blends, in what proportions
- Methods used in making the wine
- Flavor, aroma, color, and sweetness of the finished wine
- Alcohol content and other chemical components
- Length of aging and whether barrel aging is required
- Labeling and packaging

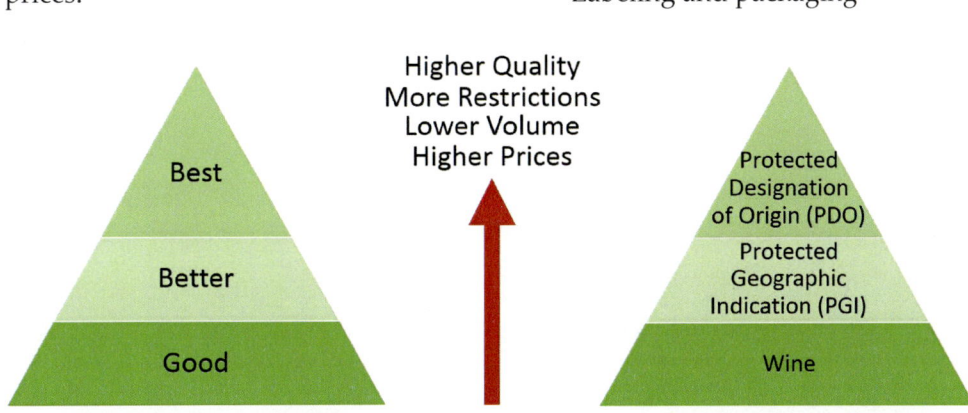

Higher Quality
More Restrictions
Lower Volume
Higher Prices

The wine quality pyramid in the European Union

The purpose of PDOs is:
- To tie a specific agricultural product to the place where it was created or developed over time
- To prevent producers in other places from taking advantage of and perhaps damaging a traditional product's reputation
- To ensure that items for sale are typical of that product and meet consumer expectations

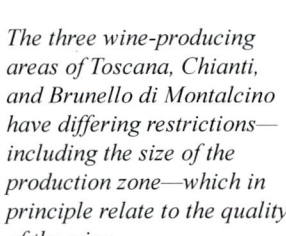

The middle tier, below the PDOs, is the PGIs. To qualify as a PGI, the requirements are similar to those for a PDO, but not as detailed or as difficult to achieve.
- The geographical area where the grapes can be sourced is usually bigger than for PDOs.
- More grape varieties are usually allowed to be used.
- Viticultural and winemaking requirements are less stringent.

To qualify as "Wine," the bottom tier, there are few requirements.
- The grapes can be sourced from anywhere in the EU.
- Any grape varieties can be used.
- Viticultural and winemaking requirements are minimal.

❧

To show how these quality levels are applied in reality, consider three protected wine areas in Tuscany and their requirements.

Wine from the PGI "Toscana"
- Can be made anywhere within Tuscany
- Can be white, rosato, or red
- Can use any proportions of more than two dozen grape varieties

Wine from the PDO "Chianti"
- Can be made anywhere within a large area in the middle of Tuscany
- Must be red wine
- Must contain a minimum of 70% Sangiovese
- Must meet more and stricter requirements than the PGI

Wine from the smaller PDO "Brunello di Montalcino"
- Can only be made around the village of Montalcino
- Must be red wine
- Must contain 100% Sangiovese
- Must meet still stricter requirements than the Chianti PDO

❧

This section has described the way EU wine law has been defined throughout the Union. But as noted earlier, each country is responsible for interpreting and enforcing the law. The next section will look at how Italian wine law puts the EU law into action.

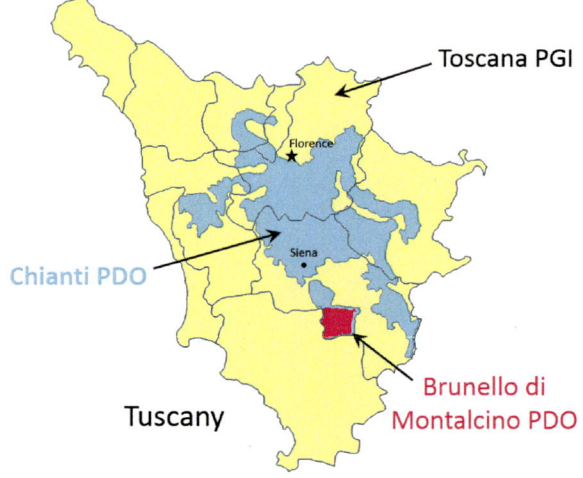

The three wine-producing areas of Toscana, Chianti, and Brunello di Montalcino have differing restrictions—including the size of the production zone—which in principle relate to the quality of the wine.

Italian Wine Law

In the Italian language, PDO is translated as Denominazione d'Origine Protetta or DOP. PGI is Indicazione Geografica Protetta or IGP.

These terms are used in official EU documents and may appear on Italian wine labels, *but*—and here's where it can get a bit confusing—EU wine law allows countries to continue to also use traditional quality terms that existed in their national wine law before 2008.

Italy's national wine law has not one but *two* quality levels that equate to the EU's PDO level:

- Denominazione d'Origine Controllata (DOC) is the main category at the PDO level.
- Denominazione d'Origine Controllata e Garantita (DOCG) is a higher level that is based on higher production standards and therefore, in principle, better quality.

Italy's traditional term for PGI is Indicazione Geografica Tipica (IGT). Wineries can use either the traditional term or the official EU term on their labels.

Because the DOCG level is more difficult to achieve, it is more prestigious than DOC, so wines that qualify for a DOCG appellation will likely continue to use that term instead of DOP on the label. However, because of the many variables involved, DOCG wines are not always superior to DOC wines. There is less incentive to continue using DOC and IGT on wine labels, but many wineries prefer the traditional terms, so both the old and new terms will be seen on labels.

Important points to remember about both EU and Italian wine law:

- Wine names that are protected as PDOs or PGIs represent defined geographical areas and cannot be used for wines from any other region within the EU or, through trade agreements, in most other countries.
- The grapes used to make wines labeled with a protected name (PDO or PGI) must be harvested within the geographic boundaries of that area (100% of the grapes for PDOs, 85% for PGIs).
- Each PDO or PGI sets rules for the styles and characteristics of wines that use its name.

EU Terms (in Italian) / Traditional Italian Quality Terms

EU Terms (in Italian)	Pyramid	Traditional Italian Quality Terms
Denominazione d'Origine Protetta (DOP)	DOCG	Denominazione d'Origine Controllata e Garantita (DOCG)
	DOC	Denominazione d'Origine Controllata (DOC)
Indicazione Geografica Protetta (IGP)	IGP/IGT	Indicazione Geografica Tipica (IGT)
Vino	Vino	Vino da Tavola (VdT)

Italy's wine quality pyramid, aside from using Italian nomenclature, also adds a fourth level to the standard EU quality pyramid.

Italian Wine Labeling

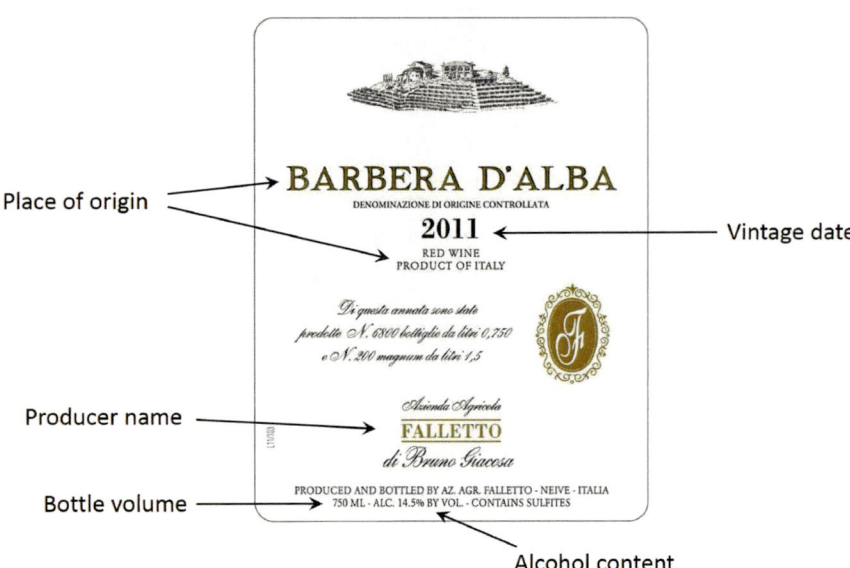

Place of origin → BARBERA D'ALBA

Vintage date →

Producer name → FALLETTO

Bottle volume →

Alcohol content

Neck bands for wines bottled before 2013 had different colors depending on the style of the wine—red, white, or sparkling—but did not distinguish between quality levels.

Neck bands being issued now have either golden edges for DOCG wines or blue edges for DOC wines, regardless of the wine's style. The bands are optional at the DOC level.

In Italy as in every country, there are various items that must be communicated to the consumer on the label of a bottle of wine. Typical labeling requirements include:

- Producer name
- Place of origin (denomination or country) and quality level
- Vintage date (year of harvest), unless a blend of multiple vintages
- Alcohol level
- Bottle volume
- Sulfite warning

At left is an example of an Italian wine label showing the required elements. The required elements are not necessarily all found on the main label; they may be on secondary labels or even embossed on the bottle itself.

A feature of Italian wines that is not seen in too many other countries is the *fascetta* or band that is seen on most bottles of DOP-level Italian wine (that is, DOCs and DOCGs), usually affixed around the bottle's neck *(left)*. These numbered ribbons show that the necessary taxes have been paid and that the winery is not producing more bottles than it has been approved to make. The bands are required for DOCG wines, but can be replaced with traceability serial numbers elsewhere on the bottle for DOCs.

In addition to the required label elements, there are a number of other terms that may be seen on the label, some of which are allowed only if the wine meets additional requirements, and others simply at the producer's discretion.

Some wines have the name of a grape variety on the label; this is called varietal labeling and is standard practice in the New World, but less so in Europe. Sometimes listing the grape variety is an option; other times, it is part of the denomination name. In either case, wines can be varietally labeled—that is, can name a single grape variety on a wine label—only if that variety comprises at least 85% of the grapes used to make the wine.

At right is an example of a wine label that lists a grape variety. Remember that this means there is at least 85% Nebbiolo in this wine. It *may* contain 100% Nebbiolo, or it can have up to 15% of some other grapes blended in to add complexity and improve the wine's balance and flavor profile. The blending grapes, if any, must be on an approved list of options. This will become an important point in the discussion of Super Tuscan wines in Unit 3.

Another option is a proprietary name to make the wine more recognizable and marketable, or simply to identify one wine from similar ones from the same producer or area. "Centine" on the label at right is a proprietary name that is the brand or trademark name for this specific wine.

Most wines show a vintage date, which is the year the grapes were harvested. If the wine does not have a vintage date anywhere on the bottle, it probably means the wine is a blend of multiple vintages, as is often done with sparkling wines.

A label may list a vineyard name, provided that the grapes all came from a single vineyard. On the label at right, "Vigna Monticchio" indicates that the source of the grapes for this wine was the Monticchio vineyard. Also, note that this wine is labeled as a Riserva. Unlike in the New World, the word "Reserve," or *Riserva* in Italian, is a legally defined term, but the definition varies from denomination to denomination. It indicates longer aging than the standard (non-riserva) version of the same wine—at least two years total, sometimes longer. For white wines, it also usually indicates some amount of barrel aging.

Grape variety

Proprietary name

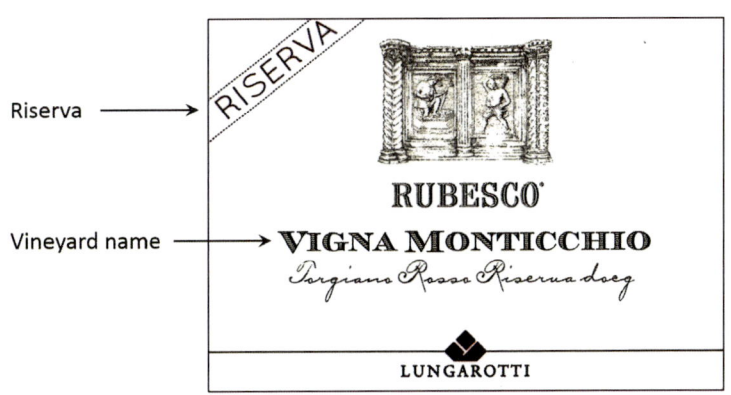

Riserva

Vineyard name

There are other "style" descriptors on some labels referring to such characteristics as:
- Color
- Effervescence
- Quality amplifying terms

And, in some denominations, certain vineyards may be located in a sub-zone or a "Classico" area, which may show up on the label.

Here's one more label example, from the Soave area of the Veneto. On this label, the word Superiore, which means "higher," indicates a wine with higher minimum alcohol level than the standard (non-superiore) version of the same wine. The minimum alcohol level for a superiore wine is usually higher by either ½ or 1 percentage point. This typically translates into wines made from riper grapes than the basic version.

In addition, Soave is one of the denominations that has a subzone called the Classico ("Classic") area. When Classico is used with the name of a denomination, it means that the grapes came from the most historic and respected part of the region. Only about two dozen denominations have a classico zone.

Introduction to the Italian Language, Part 1

As an Italian Wine Professional, it is important to be able to pronounce Italian names and common words properly. Therefore, this course includes some practice with the Italian language so you can be more confident and professional when discussing Italian wines, place-names, and other simple terms. This unit introduces the pronunciation of the letters of the alphabet as they are spoken in the Italian language.

Vowels

First, the vowels:
- a = *ah,* as in car   (Napoli, pasta)
- e = *ay,* as in age or ray   (Venezia, Nero, Barbera)
- i = *ee,* as in eat   (Italia, Primitivo)
- o = *oh,* as in owe or toe   (Roma, Barolo)
- u = *oo,* as in boot   (Friuli)

Consonants

Most consonants are pronounced the same as they usually are in English. Exceptions include:
- c followed by e or i is pronounced *ch*   (Ciao, Montepulciano, Dolcetto)
- c followed by a, o, or u is pronounced *k*   (Bianco, Calabria, Greco)
- g followed by e or i is pronounced *j*   (Sangiovese, Giorgio, gelato)
- g followed by a, o, or u is pronounced as hard *g*   (Garganega, linguine, Gorgonzola)
- q followed by u is pronounced *kw*   (Acqui)
- s is sometimes pronounced like *z*   (Lasagna)
- z is often pronounced like *dz* or *tz*   (Venezia, Lazio, grazie, zero)

Sometimes the pronunciation of consonants depends on the letter that follows. Doubled consonants—bb, cc, etc.—generally sound the same as the single consonant but are held longer, as if pronouncing *both* letters in turn (Brunello, pizza, grappa, mozzarella). Most other consonant pairs are the same as in English, with the following notable exceptions:
- ch is pronounced *k*   (Chianti, Marche, Verdicchio)
- gh is pronounced as a hard *g*   (Spaghetti, Bolgheri)
- gl is pronounced *lyi*   (Tagliatelle, Aglianico, Puglia)
- gn is pronounced *ny*   (Lasagna, Prugnolo)
- sc followed by e or i is pronounced *sh*   (Prosciutto)
- sc followed by a, o, or u is pronounced *sk*   (Lambrusco)

Unit 1 Exercises

The exercises that follow are designed to provide practice and familiarity with the material taught in the Italian Wine Professional course.

The purpose of the exercises is to provide different ways of approaching the information presented in the units so as to help in understanding the material and recalling it later—whether in taking the IWP exam, in performing one's job, or in looking over a wine list or a store shelf. By doing these and subsequent units' exercises, you will quickly see which topics are familiar to you and which are less so. For any subject matter that you find difficult to master, you should reread the relevant text and then develop additional ways of practicing your knowledge of that area, such as repeatedly writing out the information, using flashcards, creating personalized maps or tables, or asking a friend to drill you on the content. An answer key is provided in the back of the book, and additional copies of the exercise maps are available at http://italianwinecentral.com/exercise-maps.

Geography

1. Study the map of Italy, focusing on the country's shape and size. Take a blank sheet of paper and, without looking at the map again, draw the outline of Italy, including its two major islands. Compare your drawing with the actual map.
2. List the countries Italy borders.
3. On the outline of Italy (Fig. 1), show where it borders its neighboring countries. Label the seas around the Italian peninsula.
4. On the outline of Italy, shade in the most mountainous areas of Italy. Label the two primary mountain ranges. Draw in the Po River. Compare your results with the topographic map.
5. List the 20 political regions of Italy.
6. Study the map of Italy, focusing on the 20 political regions. On the outline of Italy, without looking at the map again, draw the boundaries of the regions. The exact shapes and curves are not important, but be as accurate as possible about sizes, positions, and which regions border on other regions, countries, or seas. Compare your drawing with the actual map.
7. Looking at the map of Italy, list the political regions you encounter in order starting from the northwest and following the coastline around the entire peninsula to the northeast. Try it again in the opposite direction without looking at the map.
8. List the political regions of Italy that have no coastline.
9. Without a map, list the political regions of Italy that you encounter in order starting from the west and following the northern border of Italy eastward.

10. On the map showing Italy's regions (Fig. 2), mark the locations of the following cities from memory: Florence, Milan, Naples, Rome, Venice. Check your work.

History

11. Who is credited with bringing the first grapevines to Italy and establishing viticulture on the Italian Peninsula?
12. How did the Roman Empire contribute to the wine world as we know it today?
13. What other non-Italian cultures contributed to Italy's viticultural diversity?

Wine Law and Labeling

14. How many levels does the EU wine quality pyramid have? How many levels are there on the Italian wine quality pyramid? What accounts for the difference?
15. Draw the EU wine quality pyramid. Label the segments with the appropriate English-language term. Now add labels for the Italian-language equivalents.
16. In the EU wine quality pyramid, which segment on average has the highest quality wines? The highest production quantities? The lowest prices? The least restrictions on the types of wines a winery can produce?
17. Write out the full Italian terms for DOCG, DOC, DOP, IGP, and IGT. Check your spelling. Now say them aloud until you can say them smoothly and feel relatively comfortable with the pronunciation.
18. Define the following Italian label terms:
    - Classico
    - Riserva
    - Superiore

Figure 1. Outline of Italy
Download a pdf of this image at http://italianwinecentral.com/exercise-maps

Figure 2. Outline of the Regions of Italy
Download a pdf of this image at http://italianwinecentral.com/exercise-maps

Lake Como in Lombardy

Northern Italian Reds

Regions of Northern Italy

The regions covered in this unit are:

- Piedmont
- Liguria
- Valle d'Aosta
- Lombardy
- Trentino–Alto Adige
- Friuli–Venezia Giulia
- Veneto

What do these regions have in common, and what are their differences?

One characteristic the northern regions have in common is that all seven regions are connected by the Alps. However, only Trentino–Alto Adige and Valle d'Aosta are entirely Alpine, and Liguria is also mountainous throughout (partly Alps, partly Apennines). The other four regions have large areas of lowland plains, especially the Po River Valley. Four regions are landlocked; the other three have Mediterranean coastline.

This satellite image of northern Italy shows how the snowcapped Alps form a natural boundary with the rest of Europe in the north. The broad Po Valley and lowlands of the northeast coast stand out in brown.

Another thing all seven regions have in common is that they border on other countries. Piedmont, Valle d'Aosta, and Liguria border France and/or the French-speaking part of Switzerland and have a long history with and significant cultural influence from the French. Lombardy, Trentino–Alto Adige, Veneto, and Friuli–Venezia Giulia border the Germanic part of Switzerland and/or Austria and have a long history with and significant cultural influence from the Austrians. Friuli–Venezia Giulia also shares a border with Slovenia.

Additional features of northern Italy include:

- The northern regions are more affluent and business oriented than the rest of Italy.
- Temperatures in summer are moderate in the hills, but hot on the plain.
- These regions have the coldest temperatures in Italy during the winter.
- There is more humidity, more clouds, and less sunshine here than in the peninsula and islands.
- Cooler temperatures and less sunshine in the hills lead to wines with high acidity and moderate alcohol, but normally with full phenolic ripeness.

Learning Objectives

Unit 2 introduces the red wines of northern Italy, from the Nebbiolos and Barberas of Piedmont to the Corvinas and international varieties of the northeast. Pay particular attention to the following learning objectives in this unit:

- Geography and cultural history of the regions
- Major red grape varieties of the regions and where they are concentrated
- Commercially significant denominations
  - Which region are they located in?
  - Red wines only, or other styles as well?
  - Primary grape variety or varieties
  - Single-variety (100%), varietal (85+%), or blend (85% of one variety not required)?

Red Grape Varieties of Northern Italy

The most prestigious grape of northern Italy is Nebbiolo, grown mainly in the northwest in Piedmont and Lombardy. However, Barbera is the most prevalent red grape in this area. Other well-known red varieties in the northwest include Dolcetto, Grignolino, Freisa, and Croatina.

In the Veneto, the most prized red grape is Corvina, which usually is blended with Rondinella. Native Italian grape varieties of the northeast include Raboso in the Veneto, Refosco in Friuli–Venezia Giulia and Veneto, and Schiava, Lagrein, and Teroldego in Trentino–Alto Adige.

Several international red grape varieties are widespread in the northern regions as well, especially Merlot, along with Cabernet Sauvignon, Cabernet Franc, and Pinot Noir, known in Italy as Pinot Nero. Note that many Italian denominations allow wines to be labeled just "Cabernet" whether they contain Cabernet Sauvignon or Cabernet Franc or both.

We'll begin this unit with an overview of the red grape varieties that are prominent in northern Italy.

As you will see over the next few units, most of Italy's hundreds of grape varieties are localized in one or another part of the country—with only a few exceptions that are more widespread, including the so-called international varieties that have been brought to Italy from other countries. In this unit and the next two, the focus is on red grape varieties only.

For the rest of this unit, we will examine the northern regions more or less independently, looking at the grape varieties that are most closely associated with those regions.

Barbera vines

Key indigenous red grape varieties of northern Italy

Barbera: Native to Piedmont, but now widespread in Italy and internationally. Low in tannin, high in acidity, and deeply purple in color. *Aromas & flavors:* Tart red fruit (cherry, raspberry), dried herbs, lavender, underbrush, spices. *Best DOPs:* Barbera d'Asti, Nizza.

Brachetto: Aromatic red variety. Light bodied. *Aromas & flavors:* Sour red cherry, raspberry, strawberry, baking spices (cinnamon, nutmeg), floral notes.

Corvina: Thick skin, ideal for air-drying. Light in color and tannin. *Aromas & flavors:* Violet, blackberry, red cherry, herbs. Believed to be a descendant of both Marzemino and Refosco dal Peduncolo Rosso; distinct from Corvinone.

Croatina: Frequently called, but unrelated to, Bonarda, Uva Rara, or even Nebbiolo. High in color and tannin. *Aromas & flavors:* Red fruit (ripe black cherry, raspberry). *Best DOP:* Bonarda dell'Oltrepò Pavese.

Dolcetto: Low in acidity and high in tannin. Earlier ripening than Barbera or Nebbiolo. *Aromas & flavors:* "Grapey," blueberry, black currant, violet, orange peel, black tea. *Best DOPs:* Dogliani (most floral and powerful), Dolcetto d'Alba (fullest bodied), Diano d'Alba (in between); in Liguria, Ormeasco di Pornassio.

Freisa: High in acidity and tannin; can be bitter. *Aromas & flavors:* Strawberry, sour red cherry, sandalwood, earth. *Best DOP:* Freisa d'Asti. *Best biotype:* Freisa di Chieri. Close relation of Nebbiolo.

Grignolino: High in acidity and tannin; light in body and color (usually with an orange or garnet tinge). *Aromas & flavors:* Fresh flowers, red berries (cranberry), spices (white pepper), sometimes bitter almond. *Best DOPs:* Grignolino d'Asti, Grignolino del Monferrato Casalese.

Lagrein: Full bodied, darkly colored, with sometimes harsh, bitter tannins. *Aromas & flavors:* Blackberry, black plum, black tea, orange peel, cocoa. Offspring of Teroldego.

Nebbiolo: Aka Spanna in northern Piedmont, Chiavennasca in Lombardy, and Picotener in Valle d'Aosta. Italy's greatest native grape. Garnet with a telltale orange hue. High in acidity, tannins, and alcohol. Enormous aging potential. *Aromas & flavors:* Flowers (red rose, violet), sour red cherry, cranberry, tea, tobacco, licorice, sandalwood, truffle. Three main biotypes: Lampia (the "real" Nebbiolo), Michet (a high-quality version of Lampia with fanleaf virus), & Rosé (parent or offspring of Lampia; lighter in color, highly perfumed).

Raboso: Two related varieties: Raboso Piave (aka Friularo) and its offspring Raboso Veronese. Very high in acid, tannins, and anthocyanins (but loses color quickly). *Aromas & flavors:* Strawberry, black cherry, violet, tobacco, black pepper. *Best DOPs:* Piave, Piave Malanotte, Bagnoli Friularo.

Refosco: Group of unrelated varieties, of which the most significant are:
- *Refosco dal Peduncolo Rosso:* Rough tannins. *Aromas & flavors:* Dried red cherry, herbs, almond, flowers (lavender, geranium, violet). *Best DOP:* Friuli Colli Orientali.
- *Refosco Nostrano:* More acidic and less (but smoother) tannins. *Aromas & flavors:* Flowers (lavender, iris, rose), red licorice, spices (cardamom, cinnamon, marjoram).

Rondinella: Most reliable and least problematic of the Valpolicella varieties. Ruby red color; low in tannin. *Aromas & flavors:* Neutral, somewhat herbal.

Schiava: Group of unrelated varieties, most significantly Gentile, Grossa, and Grigia—typically interplanted and blended together as "Schiava." Aka Vernatsch (Südtirol), Trollinger (Austria, Germany). Light to medium bodied, pinkish, high in acid. *Aromas & flavors:* Intense strawberry, cherry, cranberry, almond, violet, red currant, pomegranate. *Best DOPs:* Lago di Caldaro, Santa Maddalena (subzone of Südtirol).

Teroldego: Darkly colored; soft tannins. *Aromas & flavors:* Red cherry, quinine, ink, tar, herbs. *Best DOP:* Teroldego Rotaliano. Related to Pinot Nero.

Piedmont

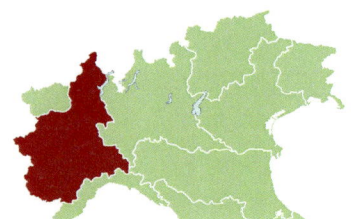

Our discussion of Italian regions begins in the northwest with Piedmont.

Piedmont, as it's known in English, is called Piemonte in Italian, meaning "foot of the mountain." It has more DOCGs (17) and more DOCs (42) than any other region. However, it has no IGPs.

Many denominations in Piedmont require 100% of a grape variety, which is uncommon elsewhere.

The primary red grape varieties in Piedmont are:

- Barbera, the most widely planted variety
- Dolcetto, the variety for everyday wines
- Nebbiolo, the most respected variety

Other red varieties include:

- Brachetto (mainly for sweet dessert wines)
- Freisa
- Grignolino

Piedmont's most famous red wine denominations are:

- Barolo DOCG
- Barbaresco DOCG
- Barbera d'Asti DOCG

The red wines in Piedmont have a definite hierarchy. Nebbiolo produces the greatest, longest-lived wines and is given the best vineyard sites. Barbera produces good, full-bodied wines that are ready to drink before the Nebbiolos. Dolcetto produces lighter red wines that are ideal for everyday drinking. We'll talk about these three grape varieties in turn, beginning with Nebbiolo.

Nebbiolo-Based DOPs

Nebbiolo is the great grape variety of Piedmont, where the majority of it grows, but it is also prominent in Lombardy. Its lofty status is recognized with several denominations dedicated solely to Nebbiolo-based wines, including seven DOCGs.

Barolo and Barbaresco are two small villages in southern Piedmont that make some of Italy's greatest wines. Both villages give their names to DOCGs that produce only red wine made from 100% Nebbiolo. Barolo and Barbaresco will be discussed in detail in Unit 8, Luxury Wines.

Besides Barolo and Barbaresco, five other DOCGs make varietal (i.e., at least 85%) Nebbiolo wines. Three are in Piedmont *(see map below)*:

- Roero, another small area in southern Piedmont better known for its white wines
- Gattinara and Ghemme, twin villages in northern Piedmont that make only Nebbiolo-based varietal wines

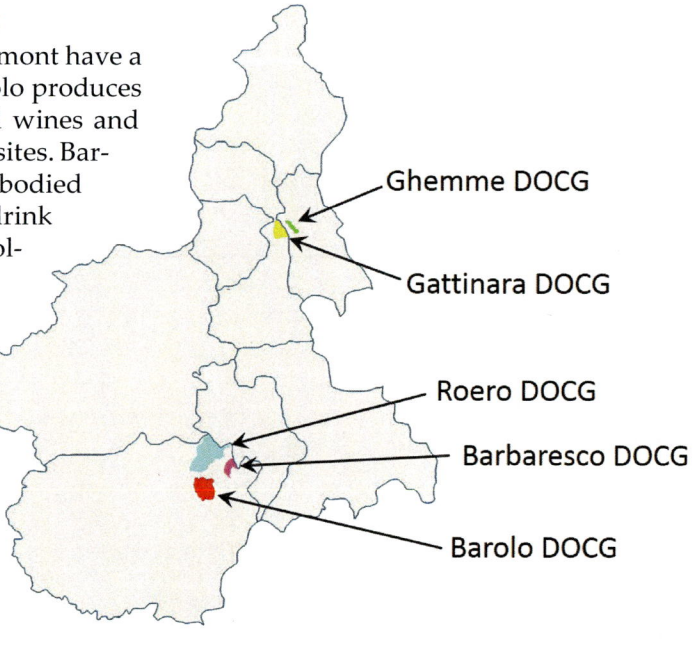

The other two Nebbiolo-based DOCGs are Valtellina Superiore and Sforzato di Valtellina in Lombardy *(right)*.

Several other denominations at the DOC level, almost all in Piedmont, also make Nebbiolo-based wines.

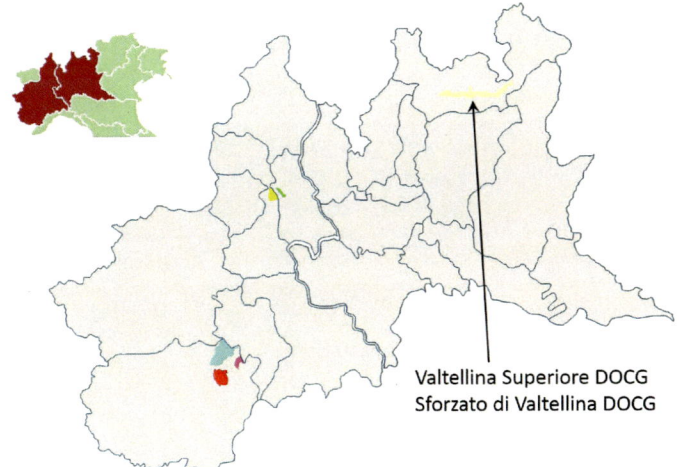

Valtellina Superiore DOCG
Sforzato di Valtellina DOCG

Barbera-Based DOPs

Barbera is among the most planted varieties in Italy, but about two thirds of it grows in Piedmont. It is planted in most of the same general areas as Nebbiolo, but usually Nebbiolo is given the more favorable vineyard sites.

Barbera is the primary grape in the red wines of several DOPs in Piedmont. The most prominent is Barbera d'Asti DOCG, a varietal Barbera wine from an area around the town of Asti.

Within the Barbera d'Asti denomination is Italy's most recently created DOCG, Nizza. Nizza wines are considered by many to be the best expression of Barbera and possibly among Italy's greatest wines.

Another large production region for Barbera is Barbera d'Alba DOC, from around the neighboring town of Alba.

Barbera-based wines are made in other DOCs throughout Piedmont and into Lombardy.

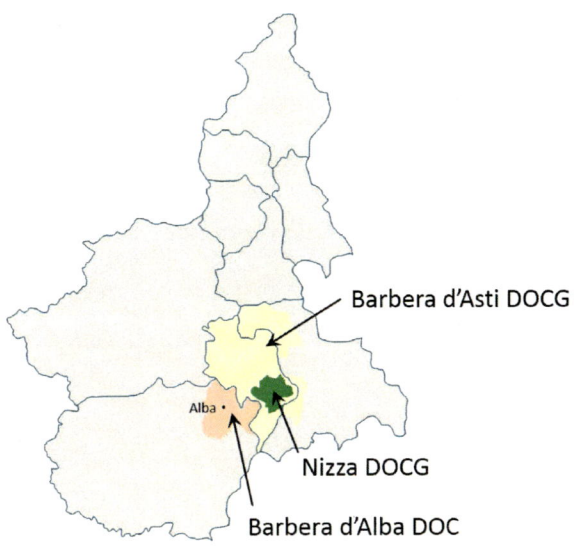

Barbera d'Asti DOCG

Alba

Nizza DOCG

Barbera d'Alba DOC

Dolcetto-Based DOPs

As is the case for both Nebbiolo and Barbera, there are several DOPs in Piedmont devoted specifically to the region's third most important red grape, Dolcetto. There are three DOCGs for Dolcetto, all making 100% varietal Dolcetto wines:

- Dogliani
- Diano d'Alba (aka Dolcetto di Diano d'Alba)
- Ovada (aka Dolcetto di Ovada Superiore)

In addition, there are four DOCs devoted solely to Dolcetto:

- Dolcetto d'Alba
- Dolcetto d'Asti
- Dolcetto d'Acqui
- Dolcetto di Ovada

The largest amount of Dolcetto wine is made in the Dolcetto d'Alba DOC.

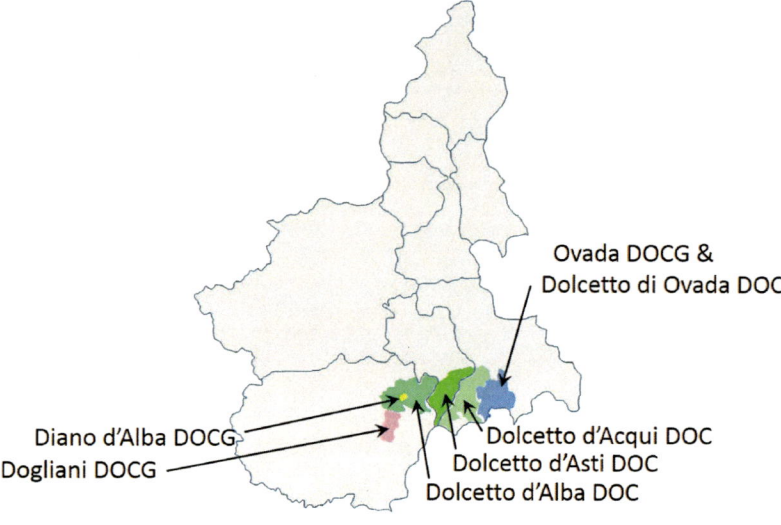

Ovada DOCG & Dolcetto di Ovada DOC

Diano d'Alba DOCG
Dogliani DOCG

Dolcetto d'Acqui DOC
Dolcetto d'Asti DOC
Dolcetto d'Alba DOC

Large Multipurpose DOCs in Piedmont

Piedmont has three overarching denominations that encompass numerous other DOPs.

- The Langhe DOC covers a broad zone of rolling hills that includes the Barolo, Barbaresco, and Roero DOCGs.
- The Monferrato DOC lies east of the Langhe and is centered on Asti.
- The Piemonte DOC is the largest denomination in the region, covering almost all of the wine-producing areas in Piedmont and incorporating both the Langhe and Monferrato.

These blanket denominations allow winemakers to blend grapes from different vineyards spread over a wider area. They also act as alternative or fallback denominations for most of the region's growers, meaning that if their grapes do not reach the standards required for one of the more renowned denominations, they can fall back to a less demanding one. In this way, they fill the role played by IGPs in most other regions, but with somewhat higher minimum standards.

The Langhe, Monferrato, and Piemonte DOCs all permit a range of wine styles, including several white and red varietals. They sometimes offer excellent value with wines approaching the quality of top wine areas but at a fraction of the cost.

Piemonte DOC

Monferrato DOC

Langhe DOC

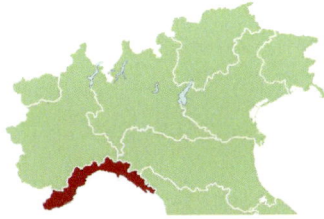

Liguria

Leaving Piedmont, we'll first briefly touch on two neighboring regions whose wines are less frequently seen in wine shops in the U.S. before returning to more familiar territory.

Liguria is the narrow region south of Piedmont. It consists of the Italian Riviera along the coast and a mountainous interior that includes the last vestige of the Alps and the beginning of the Apennine range.

Liguria has very little land suitable for significant agriculture, so it has the second smallest wine production of any region in Italy. Less than a third of its production is red wine, and very little is exported. The primary red grape varieties in Liguria are Rossese and Dolcetto.

Above: *Manarola village in Cinque Terre, Liguria*
Below: *Morgex, Valle d'Aosta*

Valle d'Aosta

The next region, just to the north of Piedmont, is Valle d'Aosta. It borders France and the Francophone part of Switzerland and is known as Vallée d'Aoste among its many French speakers.

Valle d'Aosta is the smallest region in Italy in terms of size, population, and wine production. The only significant habitable area is a broad, sheltered, glacial valley in the Alps.

This region has only one DOC, called Valle d'Aosta or Vallée d'Aoste. It has no DOCGs or IGPs. Valle d'Aosta's export volume is very small, although its wines can be found with a little looking. Despite its Alpine location, Valle d'Aosta makes more red wines than white. Its main red varieties are Petit Rouge, Nebbiolo, and Pinot Nero (Pinot Noir).

Lombardy

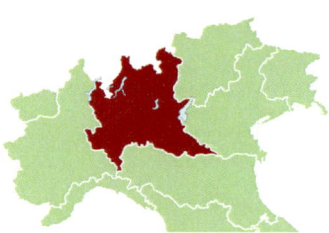

The next major region of northern Italy is Lombardy, home of the beautiful lake country south of Switzerland. In Italian, Lombardy is Lombardia. Milan (Milano), its capital, is Italy's second largest city. Lombardy has 5 DOCGs, 22 DOCs, and 15 IGPs.

The primary red grape varieties of Lombardy are:

- Barbera and Croatina, which are often blended together but also made as varietals
- Nebbiolo
- Pinot Nero, used mainly for sparkling wines

Lombardy's most famous red wine areas are Oltrepò Pavese and Valtellina, both of which have multiple denominations.

Oltrepò Pavese is the southern tip of Lombardy between Piedmont and Emilia Romagna. It has the largest volume of wine production in Lombardy. Several DOPs are named for the region, collectively producing

a wide range of wine styles. Red wines of Oltrepò Pavese include blends and varietals from Barbera, Cabernet Sauvignon, Croatina, and Pinot Nero. The largest-production denomination in this area is Bonarda dell'Oltrepò Pavese DOC, a varietal Croatina wine.

The Alpine valley of Valtellina, as noted in the discussion of Piedmont, is the center for Nebbiolo in Lombardy. Three denominations—two DOCGs and a DOC (Valtellina Superiore DOCG, Sforzato di Valtellina/Sfursat di Valtellina DOCG, and Valtellina Rosso DOC)—are named after the valley, all producing only varietal Nebbiolo wines.

Another denomination of this region is the Garda DOC. It lies partly in Lombardy and partly in Veneto—one of a very small group of denominations that are shared between regions. The Garda DOC includes areas on both the east and west sides of Lake Garda on the Veneto-Lombardy border. It produces primarily varietal wines, both white and red, from international and native grape varieties common in the Veneto. In addition, this area makes some of the best rosato wines in Italy, which are called *chiaretto* from the word for clear or light, referring to the wines' light red color.

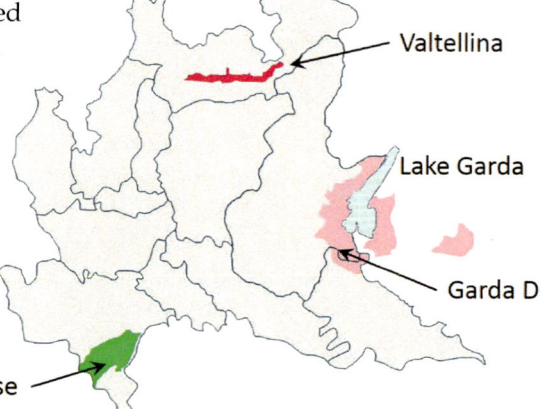

Top: Menaggio on Lake Como in Lombardy

Trentino–Alto Adige

Trentino–Alto Adige consists of two similar-looking but culturally distinct provinces: Italian-speaking Trentino in the south, and the largely German-speaking Alto Adige in the north—where it is more often called Südtirol (South Tyrol). Trentino–Alto Adige has no DOCGs, but it has 8 DOCs and 4 IGPs.

Trentino–Alto Adige is primarily white wine territory, with about one-fourth of its production being red or rosato. Its most important native red grape varieties are:

- Schiava, the region's most planted red grape variety, found mainly in Alto Adige
- Teroldego, Trentino's signature variety
- Lagrein, also mostly in Alto Adige

International red varieties that are significant here include Pinot Nero (for both red/rosato wine and sparkling wine) and Merlot.

The entire region is in the Alps, so viticulture is confined to the hillsides and floor of the valley the Adige River and its tributaries.

Most wines in Trentino–Alto Adige use one of the large provincial or regional denominations:

- Trentino DOC, for the growing areas of the southern province
- Alto Adige or Südtirol DOC, for the growing areas of the northern province
- Valdadige DOC ("Valley of the Adige"), covering most of the Trentino and Alto Adige DOCs as well as a bit of Veneto

All three denominations allow an array of types and styles, including whites and reds. Varietal wines, labeled with the variety's name, are common in these denominations.

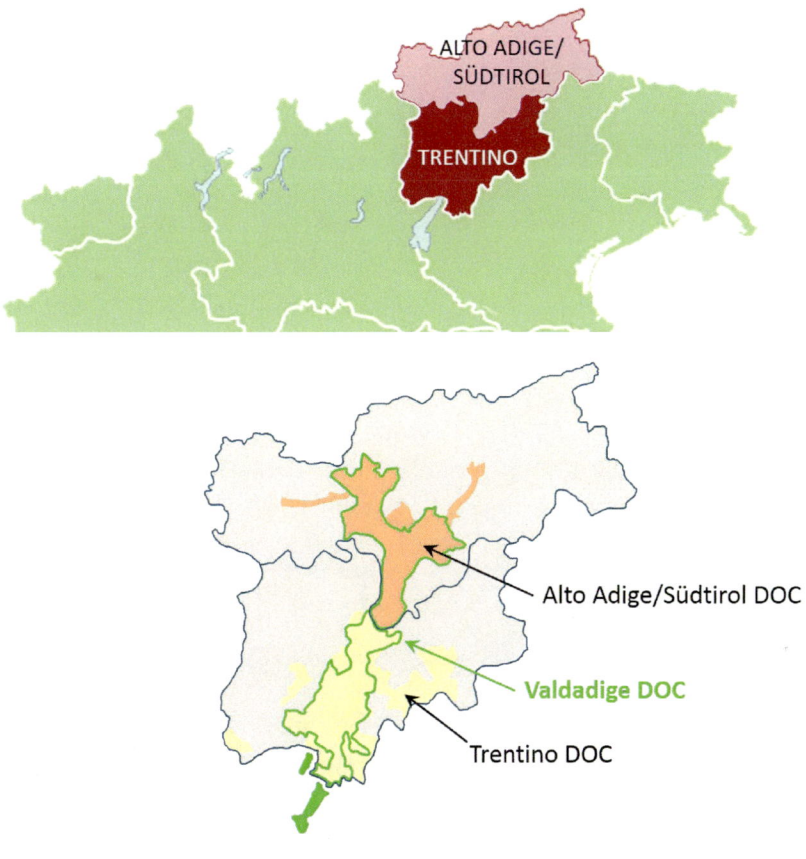

Top: *Vineyards in autumn in Valle Isarco, Alto Adige*

Veneto

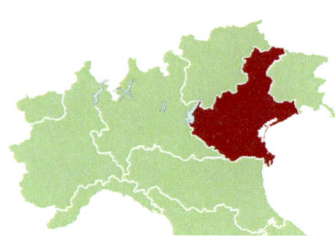

V eneto, the land of the Venetians, is arguably the most important wine region in Italy. It produces far more DOP-level wine, and far more wine overall, than any other region. Veneto has 14 DOCGs, 28 DOCs, and 10 IGPs.

Two thirds of Veneto's production is white wine, including a lot of sparkling wine. In terms of red wine, the primary grape varieties in Veneto are Merlot, Corvina, and Cabernet (both Franc and Sauvignon). Other important red varieties include:

- Rondinella
- Raboso
- Refosco

Corvina-Based DOPs

Veneto's most famous red wine denominations are the Bardolino and Valpolicella DOPs, a group of denominations whose wines are based primarily on Corvina.

Bardolino is next to Lombardy on the shore of Lake Garda. Valpolicella

lies just east of Bardolino, farther from the lake's influence. Both areas make red wines from a blend of traditional grape varieties. Corvina is the dominant variety, and Rondinella is a required minority component. Other grapes may be used but are not required.

Bardolino produces lighter red wines in two denominations:

- Bardolino DOC
- Bardolino Superiore DOCG

Bardolino is another source for excellent chiaretto (rosato) wines, as well.

Valpolicella produces fuller-bodied red wines in three denominations:

- Valpolicella DOC, the area's standard
- Amarone della Valpolicella DOCG, an intense full-bodied wine made with dried grapes
- Valpolicella Ripasso DOC, an intermediate style between Amarone and regular Valpolicella

In addition, there is a sweet red wine from the same area: Recioto della Valpolicella DOCG. Recioto della Valpolicella will be covered in Unit 7 with the dessert wines, while Amarone della Valpolicella will be discussed in detail in Unit 8, Luxury Wines.

Top: *The Grand Canal is the main thoroughfare of the magical city of Venice.*

IGPs of the Northeast

In addition to DOP wine, Veneto produces a large volume of IGP wine in many types and styles. One of the largest IGPs in Italy in terms of wine production is IGP Veneto, which includes the whole region.

Another significant IGP on the export market is IGP delle Venezie, which allows winemakers to blend wines or grapes not only from anywhere in the Veneto but also from Friuli–Venezia Giulia and the Trentino province of Trentino–Alto Adige.

Most grapes for IGP wine production are grown in the lower-elevation plains rather than in the hills closer to the Alps. Exported IGP wines are often varietals made with international varieties. For red wine production, Veneto has the most Cabernet Franc, Cabernet Sauvignon, and Merlot in Italy.

IGP Veneto

IGP delle Venezie

Friuli–Venezia Giulia

Our last stop on this tour of northern Italy is Friuli–Venezia Giulia, the northeasternmost region, which borders Austria and Slovenia.

The name of this region is often shortened to just Friuli, which is nearly as accurate from a wine standpoint because Venezia Giulia refers primarily to the small tail in the region's southeast around the city of Trieste, which is not really significant in wine production.

Friuli has 4 DOCGs, 10 DOCs, and 3 IGPs and is best known for white wine. There are no denominations in Friuli–Venezia Giulia that make red wine exclusively, but several of the key denominations such as Friuli Grave DOC, Friuli Colli Orientali DOC, and Collio Goriziano DOC produce red blends and varietals in addition to white wines. Merlot is the most planted red grape variety in the region, and Cabernet Franc and Refosco are also represented.

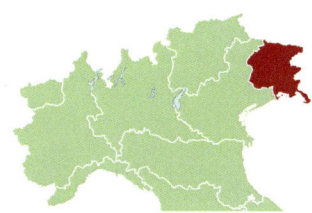

Northern Italian Cuisine

Top: *Fonduta*
Middle: *An appetizer platter of sliced prosciutto*
Bottom: *Pesto pasta*

That concludes this unit's survey of northern Italian red wines, but when it comes to Italy, you should never talk about wine without talking about food, so let's take a quick look at the cuisine of northern Italy. In principle, these are some of the foods that the wines discussed in this unit were created to drink with.

Meal starters in northern Italy include antipasti of speck—a fully boned ham, lightly smoked, typical of Alto Adige, where it is an IGP—and San Daniele prosciutto—a prosciutto DOP in Friuli, made using pig thighs and sea salt.

Fonduta is a classic Swiss-style fondue that is also traditional in Valle d'Aosta and Piedmont. The pot can contain either a mix of cheeses in which bread is dipped or simmering oil for cooking meat. Bagna càuda is a "hot bath" of garlic, olive oil, anchovies, and sometimes butter, cream, or chopped walnuts that is served like a fondue for dipping vegetables. It is typical of Piedmont in the fall.

Pasta is not nearly as common in northern Italy as in the rest of the country. When pasta is served, stuffed pastas like tortellini and agnolotti with white, butter, or brown sauces are more typical than strings with red sauce. Pesto is a pasta sauce that originated in the city of Genoa in Liguria and traditionally consists of crushed garlic, basil, and pine nuts blended with olive oil and cheese such as Parmigiano Reggiano.

Instead of pasta, risotto is often served. Risotto consists of top-quality rice cooked in a meat, fish, or vegetable broth to a creamy consistency. It may contain butter, wine, or onion. Risotto is made all over Italy, but is most common in the north. It may be a course of its own or a side dish.

Another typical side dish in the northern regions is polenta—cornmeal boiled into a porridge and then eaten as is or baked, fried, or grilled.

For main dishes, game is very popular, including venison, rabbit, and pheasant. A classic beef entree is the Milanese favorite ossobuco. Another northern specialty is vitello tonnato: cold, sliced veal covered with a creamy sauce flavored with tuna, served chilled or at room temperature.

An exotic delicacy that is prized in Piedmont and throughout the world is the truffle. White Alba truffles are the most sought-after species of truffle. They are found mainly in the Langhe and Monferrato areas, conveniently close to some of Italy's best wines. Truffles are astronomically expensive, but a little goes a long way, so truffles find their way into all sorts of dishes in season in the north.

Pictured (clockwise from top center): *Ossobuco alla milanese with risotto, roast pheasant, rabbit stew, white truffles, vitello tonnato*

Introduction to the Italian Language, Part 2

This unit's taste of the Italian language covers a few of the words that you might see on a wine label. These are not legal labeling terms, but just some prepositions, articles, and a few other words that can sometimes help make sense of a wine. You may see them in the names of denominations, wineries, individual wines, or vineyards, among other places.

Prepositions

di & **d'** = of
- *Examples:* Dolcetto di Ovada, Barbera d'Asti
- *Pronunciation:* dee, d- (letter *d* added to the following vowel)

a = to, at, in
- *Example:* Badia a Coltibuono
- *Pronunciation:* ah

su = on
- *Pronunciation:* soo

Articles

The choice of which article to use depends on the gender of the noun and whether or not it starts with a vowel.

il, la, & **l'** = the (singular)
- *Examples:* Il Poggione, La Morra
- *Pronunciation:* eel, lah, l- (letter *l* added to the following vowel)

i, le, & **gli** = the (plural)
- *Example:* Le Marche
- *Pronunciation:* ee, lay, lyee

Prepositions + Article

del, della, dell', dei, delle, & **degli** = of the
- *Examples:* Barbera del Monferrato, Amarone della Valpolicella, IGP delle Venezie
- *Pronunciation:* dell, *del*-lah, dell- (added to the following vowel), day, *del*-lay, *day*-lyee

al, alla, all', ai, & **alle** = to/at/in the
- *Example:* Guado al Tasso
- *Pronunciation:* ahl, *ahl*-lah, ahl- (added to the following vowel), eye, *ahl*-lay

sul, sulla, & **sulle** = on the
- *Pronunciation:* sool, *sool*-lah, *sool*-lay

Conjunction

e = and
- *Example:* Isole e Olena
- *Pronunciation:* eh

Common Name Elements

Colle, Collina, Poggio, Bricco, & **Ronco** = Hill
- *Example:* Friuli Colli Orientali
- *Pronunciation:* kohl-lay, kohl-*lee*-nah, *poh*-joh, *breek*-koh, *rohn*-koh

Valle & **Val-** = Valley
- *Examples:* Valle d'Aosta, Valtellina, Valdadige
- *Pronunciation:* *vahl*-lay, vahl

Terre = Lands, territory, area
- *Example:* Terre Siciliane
- *Pronunciation:* *tehr*-ray

San, Santa, Santo, & **Sant'** = Saint, holy
- *Examples:* San Gimignano, Vin Santo, Sant'Antimo
- *Pronunciation:* sahn, *sahn*-tah, *sahn*-toh, sahnt- (added to the following vowel)

Azienda, Cantina, Cascina, Fattoria, Podere, & **Tenuta** = Winery or wine estate
- *Pronunciation:* ah-*zyen*-da, kahn-*tee*-nah, kah-*shee*-nah, faht-*toh*-ree-ya, *poh*-deh-ray, tay-*noo*-tah

Unit 2 Exercises

1. Write down the seven Italian regions that touch on the Alps. Check your spelling.
2. In the list above, indicate the foreign country or countries that each region borders.
3. Fill in the blanks in the following table. (There may be more than one correct answer in some spaces.)

Denomination	Level	Primary Red Grape Variety	Region
Amarone della Valpolicella	DOCG		
Barolo	DOCG		
Dogliani	DOCG		

4. Where is Oltrepò Pavese?
5. On an outline map of the regions of Italy (Fig. 2 on p. 22), write the following grape varieties in the region or regions where they are most commonly found. (You can match the layout of the graphic from the unit or just write them anywhere in the region or regions.) Check your spelling. Save your work for use in Unit 3.
   - Barbera
   - Corvina
   - Croatina
   - Dolcetto
   - Freisa
   - Grignolino
   - Lagrein
   - Nebbiolo
   - Refosco
   - Rondinella
   - Schiava
   - Teroldego
6. Name at least three DOPs that make Dolcetto-based wine.
7. Name at least two IGPs in northern Italy and what region(s) they are in.
8. Which region has more DOCGs than any other? More DOCs?
9. In Barbaresco, what is the minimum percentage of its primary grape? And what is that grape?
10. Fill in the blanks in the following table. (There may be more than one correct answer in some spaces.)

Denomination	Level	Primary Red Grape Variety	Region
Alto Adige		Various	
	DOC	Dolcetto	
Friuli Grave		Various	
Gattinara			Piedmont
Roero			Piedmont
Valpolicella		Corvina	

11. Name three denominations in Trentino–Alto Adige.
12. What is the most prestigious red grape variety of Piedmont? Of Veneto?
13. In which region are the towns of Alba and Asti located? The city of Verona?
14. Fill in the blanks in the following table. (There may be more than one correct answer in some spaces.)

Denomination	Level	Primary Red Grape Variety	Region
		Barbera	Piedmont
		Various	Lombardy and Veneto
		Various	Trentino–Alto Adige and Veneto
		Nebbiolo	Lombardy

15. On the map of Piedmont (Fig. 3), draw in the main Nebbiolo-based denominations. With a different color pen or pencil if possible, draw in the main Barbera-based denominations on the same map. Do the same with the Dolcetto-based denominations. (If this is too complicated, use three separate Piedmont maps and then compare them side by side.)
16. Name at least three DOCGs that make Nebbiolo-based wine.
17. What is the capital and largest city of Lombardy?
18. Give alternative names/spellings for:
    • Alto Adige
    • Lombardy
    • Piedmont
    • Valle d'Aosta
19. Name the red grape variety with the most acreage in Trentino–Alto Adige.
20. Which region makes the most wine of all the Italian regions?
21. What is Collio and where would you find it?

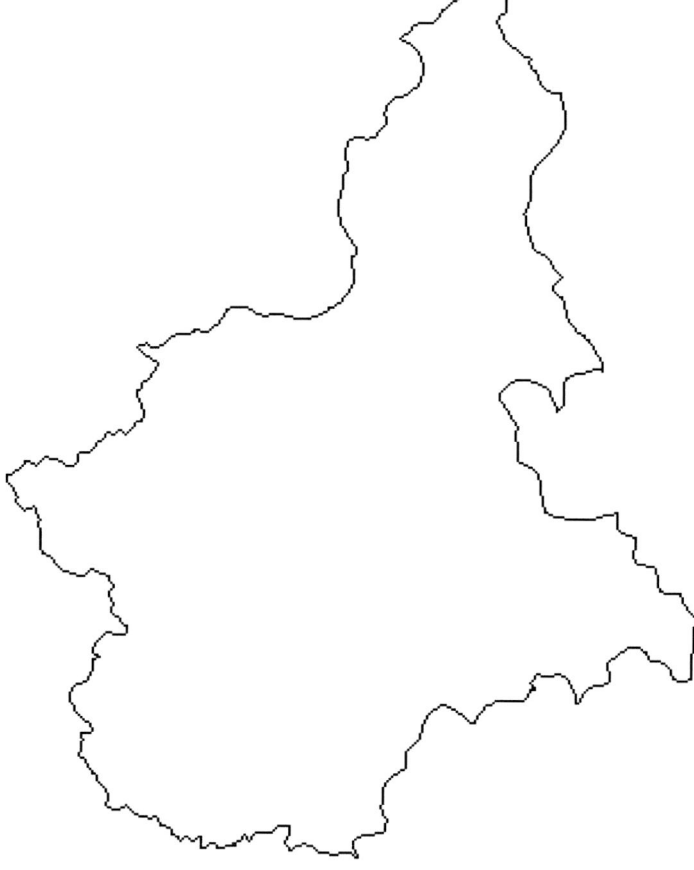

Figure 3. Outline of Piedmont
Download a pdf of this image at http://italianwinecentral.com/exercise-maps

Trevi Fountain, Rome

Unit 3
Central Italian Reds

Regions of Central Italy

The regions to be covered in this unit are those of the upper Italian peninsula:

- Emilia Romagna
- Tuscany
- Lazio
- Umbria
- Marche
- Abruzzo
- Molise

These central Italian regions have several features in common. For example, as shown in the topographic map below, all seven regions are connected by the Apennine mountains, which are too high and rugged for viticulture. Even the areas that are not in the mountains tend to be very hilly.

Temperatures in summer are quite warm, although not as hot as the south except perhaps in the Po Valley. Temperatures in winter fall into the range between the cold north and the mild south. These moderate temperatures and ample sunshine lead to wines with moderate acidity and moderate to high alcohol.

Some of the differences among the central regions are:

- Emilia Romagna is a transitional region between north and central, more like the northern regions economically and climatically.
- Tuscany, Umbria, and Lazio have a more Mediterranean climate, with little rain in the summer and relatively mild winters.
- The regions on the Adriatic coast, northeast of the Apennines, get more rain in the summertime and have colder winters.
- Umbria is landlocked.
- Tuscany, Emilia Romagna, and Lazio are more populated and have larger economies compared with the other four central regions.
- Marche, Umbria, Abruzzo, and Molise are more rural and relatively less affluent.

The topographic map below shows that, except for the lower Po Valley in Emilia Romagna and a few small coastal areas, central Italy is entirely mountainous. The Apennines paint a broad swath down the peninsula, while isolated hilly areas cover most of Tuscany and Lazio.

Red Grape Varieties of Central Italy

Central Italy is quite a bit simpler than either the north or the south when it comes to grape varieties, especially red grape varieties. Without a doubt, the primary red grape of central Italy is Sangiovese.

Sangiovese is the most planted grape variety in Italy overall, red or white. While it is grown in many regions of Italy, most of it is here in central Italy.

The map on the left below shows which regions focus most on Sangiovese. Darker colors indicate that Sangiovese is a higher percentage of that region's grapes. As you can see, the region most devoted to Sangiovese is Tuscany, where two thirds of the vineyards are planted with Sangiovese. Much of the rest is in the neighboring regions of Emilia Romagna, Marche, and Umbria, along with Puglia in the south.

The other principal grape variety of central Italy is Montepulciano. Montepulciano is the second most planted red grape variety in Italy and is grown in every region, but its home is the Adriatic coast of central Italy, as

shown below. The majority of Italy's Montepulciano is in Abruzzo, along with the other Adriatic regions of Marche, Molise, and Puglia.

There are only a few other significant red varieties in central Italy, most notably Lambrusco in Emilia Romagna, Sagrantino in Umbria, and Cesanese in Lazio.

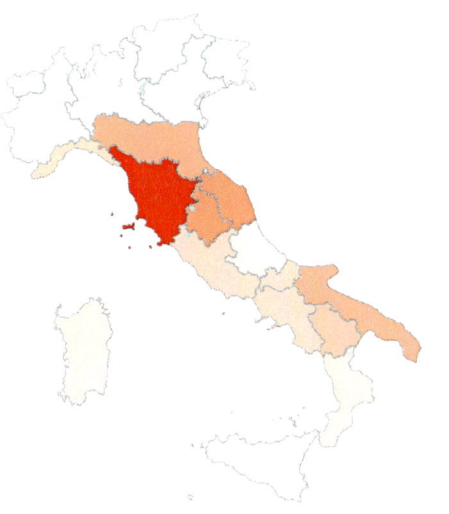

Sangiovese

Montepulciano

Concentrations of plantings of Sangiovese (left) and of Montepulciano (right). Darker reds indicate higher percentages of each grape variety in the region's vineyards.

Key indigenous red grape varieties of central Italy

Cesanese: Two distinct varieties—Cesanese Comune and Cesanese di Affile (the latter considered better). Moderate color and tannin. *Aromas & flavors:* Red cherry, spices (cinnamon, white pepper), rose petals.

Lambrusco: A family of about 8 related varieties, one of Italy's oldest. Primary family members:

- *Lambrusco Grasparossa (di Castelvetro):* Bigger, fuller bodied; considered the best.
- *Lambrusco di Sorbara:* Lightest, most floral.
- *Lambrusco Salamino:* Happy medium between Grasparossa and Sorbara.
- *Lambrusco Maestri: Aromas & flavors:* Plum, black cherry, chocolate, violet, bubblegum.
- *Lambrusco Marani:* Tannic. *Aromas & flavors:* Violet, iris, peony, black currant, red cherry.

- *Lambrusco Viadanese:* Aka Lambrusco Mantovano.

Montepulciano: Light to full bodied; soft tannins. *Aromas & flavors:* Red cherry, herbs.

Sagrantino: Italy's most tannic wine. *Aromas & flavors:* Black fruit, herbs.

Sangiovese: Several biotypes, including Brunello, Morellino, Nielluccio, Prugnolo Gentile, Sangiovese Grosso di Lamole, Sangiovese Marchigiano, Sangiovese Montanino, Sangiovese Romagnolo. Light in color. *Aromas & flavors:* (In warmer areas) sweet red cherry, plum, herbs; (in cooler areas) sour red cherry, red berries, licorice, violet, tea; (with age) underbrush, leather, tobacco.

Sangiovese vines

Learning Objectives

Unit 3 introduces the red wines of central Italy, home of Lambrusco, Sangiovese, and Montepulciano wines. The learning objectives for this unit are:

- Geography and cultural history of the regions
- Major red grape varieties of the regions and where they are concentrated
- Commercially significant denominations
    - Which region are they located in?
    - Red wines only, or other styles as well?
    - Primary grape variety or varieties
    - Single-variety (100%), varietal (85+%), or blend (85% not required)?

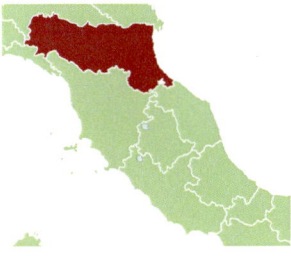

Emilia Romagna

The first region to be covered in this unit is Emilia Romagna, a region with one foot in the north and one in central Italy. This region includes much of the vast agricultural area in the Po River Valley.

Emilia Romagna is a major wine region even though it doesn't have a high profile in the export market. It produces more wine than any other Italian region except Veneto. There are 2 DOCGs and 19 DOCs in Emilia Romagna, along with 9 IGPs. The primary red grape varieties grown in the region are Lambrusco and Sangiovese.

The most famous red wine denominations in Emilia Romagna are three DOCs that feature the Lambrusco grape variety. From north to south, they are:

- Lambrusco Salamino di Santa Croce
- Lambrusco di Sorbara
- Lambrusco Grasparossa di Castelvetro

All three produce varietal Lambrusco wines—that is, wines that are made from at least 85% Lambrusco grapes—that are always either frizzante or fully sparkling. The method of production will be described further in Unit 7 in the context of sparkling wines. Lambrusco wines can be red or rosato, dry or sweet.

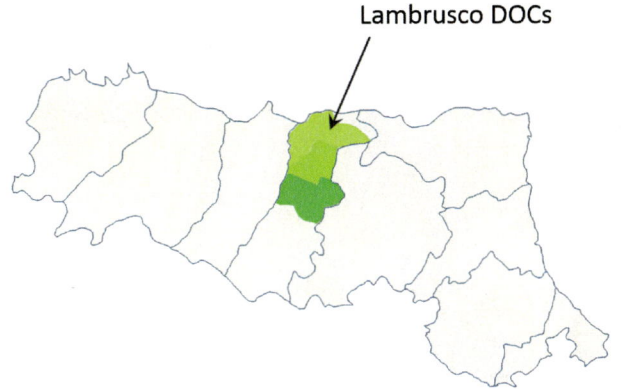

Lambrusco DOCs

The broad, flat Po Valley plains are Italy's breadbasket, producing crops of all sorts, including winegrapes.

Tuscany

The next destination is probably the most famous Italian region of all—Tuscany, or Toscana in Italian. It has more DOPs—11 DOCGs and 41 DOCs—than any other region except Piedmont. It also has 6 IGPs.

Red wine dominates production in Tuscany, accounting for nearly 90% of the wine, and Sangiovese dominates all other grape varieties. Other important red varieties include Cabernet Sauvignon, Merlot, and Syrah.

Sangiovese grapes on the vine

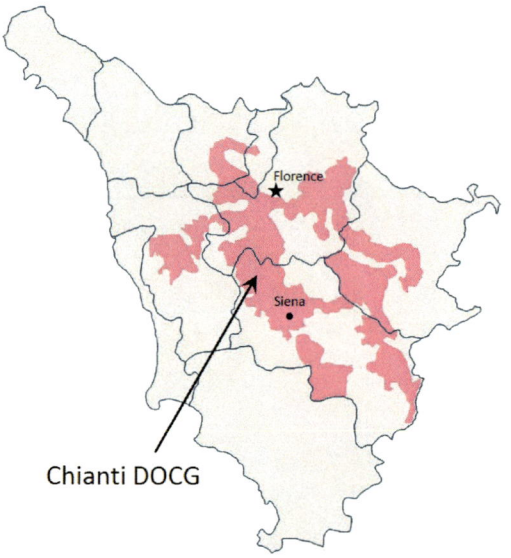

Chianti DOCG

Sangiovese-Based DOPs

Almost all of the famous red wines of Tuscany are based on the Sangiovese grape variety, and by the same token, almost all the well-known wines made from Sangiovese are from Tuscany. The most renowned Sangiovese-based DOCGs are:

- Brunello di Montalcino
- Carmignano
- Chianti
- Chianti Classico
- Morellino di Scansano
- Vino Nobile di Montepulciano

Among the most familiar DOCs that make Sangiovese-based wines are Rosso di Montalcino and Rosso di Montepulciano.

Chianti

In the discussion of Sangiovese-based wines, it's appropriate to start with one of the oldest wine regions in Italy, Chianti. Chianti is one of the most famous red wines in the world—practically everyone has heard of it. References to Chianti wine date back to the 14th century, and it has always enjoyed a substantial percentage of Italian wine exports.

Chianti has traditionally been made primarily from Sangiovese, but blended with other grape varieties. Only in recent times has it become permissible to make Chianti from Sangiovese alone. For centuries, Chianti was expected to contain small amounts of other varieties such as Canaiolo Nero and the white varieties Trebbiano and Malvasia. The requirement to contain white grapes has now been dropped (although they are still allowed), and Cabernet Sauvignon and Cabernet Franc have been added as permissible blending varieties. Nevertheless, the reliance on Sangiovese remains. Current statutes require a minimum of 70% Sangiovese in Chianti DOCG wines, so they are not necessarily varietal Sangiovese wines.

Chianti DOCG is a large region, ranking among the highest volume producing denominations in Italy. It is subdivided into seven subzones whose names may appear on the label. These subzones are:

- Colli Aretini
- Colli Fiorentini
- Colline Pisane
- Colli Senesi
- Montalbano
- Montespertoli
- Rufina

Of those, the ones that are most likely to be seen on an exported Chianti label are Colli Senesi, which means the "Hills of Siena" and includes the area around the city of Siena as well as Montalcino and Montepulciano, and Rufina, a small but esteemed district east of Florence.

Chianti Classico

The original production zone of Chianti is known as Chianti Classico. It was this territory that for centuries would have been called "Chianti." Much later, after the Chianti production zone spread to cover far more ground, Chianti Classico became the central subzone of the Chianti denomination. Eventually, however, the historic area split off and became the distinct and non-overlapping Chianti Classico DOCG.

Because of its longer pedigree, Chianti Classico is considered the more prestigious of the two Chianti denominations, and it puts a lot of effort into maintaining that reputation. Seeking to simultaneously separate itself from the wines of the extended Chianti zone and improve quality, Chianti Classico tinkered with the three-century-old Chianti formula, raising the required amount of

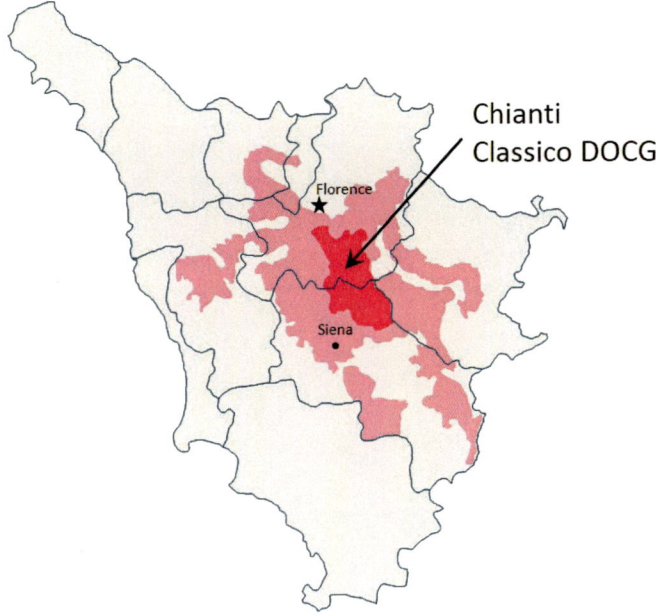

Chianti Classico DOCG

Sangiovese to 80% and banning the use of white grapes.

Chianti Classico recently took another innovative step, creating a new quality designation above riserva called *gran selezione*. Chianti Classico Gran Selezione is intended to elevate the area's best wines to prominence above the Chiantis of ordinary quality and position these wines again among Italy's greatest wines. Their progress toward this goal will be discussed further in Unit 8, Luxury Wines.

Carmignano, Montalcino, and Montepulciano

Three towns within the Chianti region have their own DOCG-level wines: Carmignano, Montalcino, and Montepulciano.

Carmignano has a DOCG for Sangiovese-based wines that, based on long tradition, are required to contain a small amount of Cabernet.

The DOCG of Montalcino is called Brunello di Montalcino. It is made from 100% Sangiovese, which here is called Brunello. Brunello di Montalcino is one of Italy's most expensive wines and one of its greatest, and it

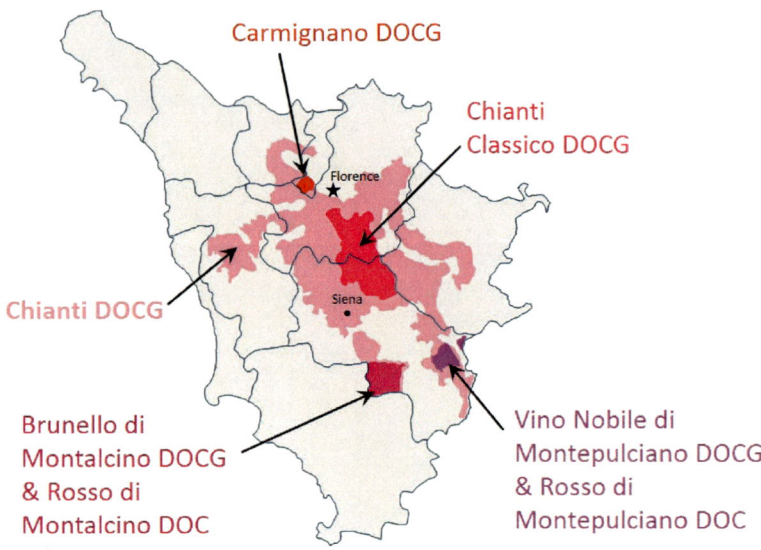

Carmignano DOCG

Chianti Classico DOCG

Chianti DOCG

Brunello di Montalcino DOCG & Rosso di Montalcino DOC

Vino Nobile di Montepulciano DOCG & Rosso di Montepulciano DOC

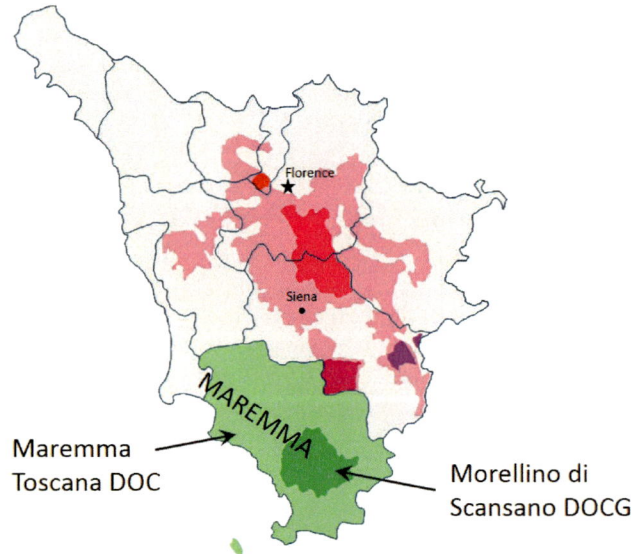

Maremma Toscana DOC

Morellino di Scansano DOCG

will be discussed further in Unit 8, Luxury Wines. A simpler wine from the same area, also 100% Sangiovese, is called Rosso di Montalcino DOC.

Another of Italy's historic wines is Vino Nobile di Montepulciano DOCG, from the village of Montepulciano. It is primarily Sangiovese, but not 100%—like Chianti, the minimum here is 70%. In this area, Sangiovese is called Prugnolo Gentile. Again, a similar but simpler wine from the same area is called Rosso di Montepulciano DOC.

Maremma and Morellino di Scansano

There's still more Sangiovese in the coastal area of southern Tuscany called the Maremma. This area is renowned for both Sangiovese-based wines and red wines made from international varieties. Maremma Toscana DOC covers the whole district and produces various styles of wine, including several white and red varietals, both international and indigenous. Within the Maremma, the most famous denomination is Morellino di Scansano DOCG, a varietal wine made from Sangiovese—going by yet another synonym, Morellino.

Coastal Tuscany is best known, however, not for Morellino di Scansano but for a category of wines known as Super Tuscans.

Super Tuscans

Tuscan wines originally became world famous for Sangiovese-based red wines, especially Chianti. In modern times, however, some producers decided they wanted to make wines that did not fit the Chianti formula—usually by adding international varieties—but there was no denomination for such wines. When they made great wines that could not be labeled with any denomination, the wines were dubbed "super Tuscans."

The same "super" terminology has been used for a few similarly unconventional wines in other regions—for example, you may hear a wine called a "super Venetian" or "super Calabrian"—but most such wines are Tuscan in origin. Super Tuscan is not an official term, so you won't see a wine labeled that way, and people may disagree on which wines to include in the category. In general, the term indicates a very high quality wine that does not meet (or originally did not meet) the requirements for a prestigious DOP.

With no denomination they could qualify for, Super Tuscans were once labeled as vino da tavola, the lowest quality level. This irrational situation is the major reason that the IGT level—now, IGP—was created in 1992, to give the super Tuscans some recognition above the everyday table wines. IGP Toscana, which covers the entire region of Tuscany, is one area that allows many different styles of wine, giving winemakers more freedom to experiment than is allowed by most DOC rules.

More recently, DOCs have been established with rules that allow or even encourage the production of these untraditional wines. These might be considered "Super Tuscan DOCs," even though that's sort of a contradiction in terms.

One of the most renowned examples is the Bolgheri DOC, on the coast just north of the Maremma. Bolgheri is the little town where the first super Tuscans were created, and this denomination still has the reputation of being a hotbed of innovation and excellence. Bolgheri is best known for red wines based on Cabernet Sauvignon and/or Merlot, usually blended with Sangiovese and/or Syrah, some of which are considered among Italy's

greatest wines. Bolgheri is the third Tuscan region that will be discussed further in Unit 8, Luxury Wines.

Maremma Toscana DOC, as already mentioned, is another area that produces a lot of wines from international varieties at a range of price points. Another denomination created for Super Tuscan–type wines is Sant'Antimo DOC, which covers roughly the same area as Brunello di Montalcino and Rosso di Montalcino and allows producers in the Montalcino commune to make wines that are not 100% Sangiovese.

Sassicaia was one of the first wines recognized as a "Super" Tuscan

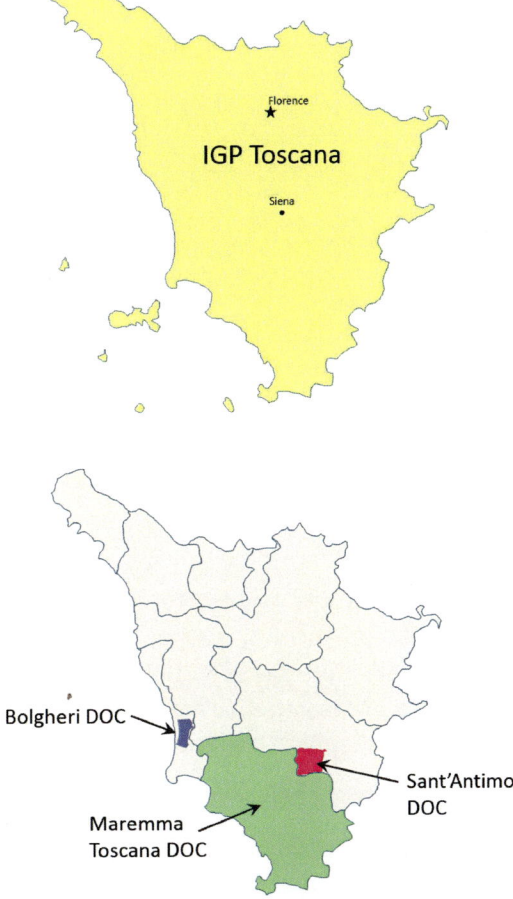

Lazio

Welcome to Lazio, where the Roman Empire was founded. Lazio is the region where Rome (Roma), the nation's capital and largest city, is located. Lazio is sometimes called Latium in English (and Latin), although that name is not used as often as Lazio.

The region has 3 DOCGs, 27 DOCs, and 6 IGPs. Lazio is known primarily for white wines, and its production of red wine is relatively small. The most-planted red grape varieties in Lazio are Merlot and Sangiovese, but its signature red grape is Cesanese, a variety that is becoming more familiar on export markets.

Cesanese production is centered in the hills east of Rome, where there are three denominations specifically for varietal Cesanese. The most important of these is the Cesanese del Piglio DOCG. Adjacent to it are two DOCs, Cesanese di Affile and Cesanese di Olevano Romano.

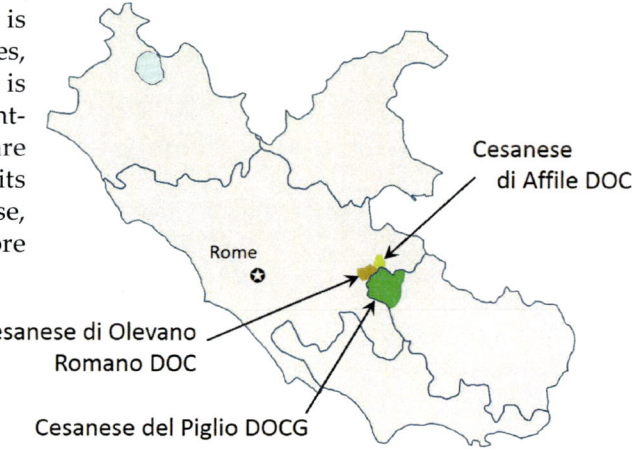

Cesanese di Affile DOC

Rome

Cesanese di Olevano Romano DOC

Cesanese del Piglio DOCG

Umbria

To the east of Tuscany and north of Lazio in the Apennines is the lovely hill country of Umbria. Umbria has a relatively small production volume of wine, roughly equally split between white and red wines. There are 2 DOCGs, 13 DOCs, and 6 IGPs.

As in Lazio, Umbria's primary red grape varieties are Sangiovese and Merlot, but it has another variety that it is best known for: Sagrantino, Italy's most tannic variety. The region's most famous red wine denomination is Montefalco Sagrantino DOCG, a red wine made around the town of Montefalco from 100% Sagrantino.

Montefalco Sagrantino DOCG

Marche

Crossing over to the Adriatic coast, Le Marche, or simply Marche, is the next region south from Emilia Romagna.

"Le Marche" translates to "The Marches" in English, although that name is rarely used. The Marches is a medieval term referring to a frontier or border area ruled over by a marquis or, in Italian, a *marchese*. In a sense, this is still a frontier, where Sangiovese and Montepulciano meet. These two varieties share the dominant position among red grape varieties in Marche, with a little more Sangiovese grown than Montepulciano.

Overall, Marche has a fairly small wine output, with slightly more red wine than white produced. It has 5 DOCGs, 15 DOCs, and a single IGP.

The most famous red wine denominations of Marche are:

- Rosso Cònero DOC and Cònero DOCG, both from the same area and both producing solely varietal Montepulciano wines

- Offida DOCG, another region for varietal Montepulciano wines, although it also makes white wine
- Rosso Piceno, a large DOC that produces only red wines from Montepulciano and Sangiovese—either as varietals or blends

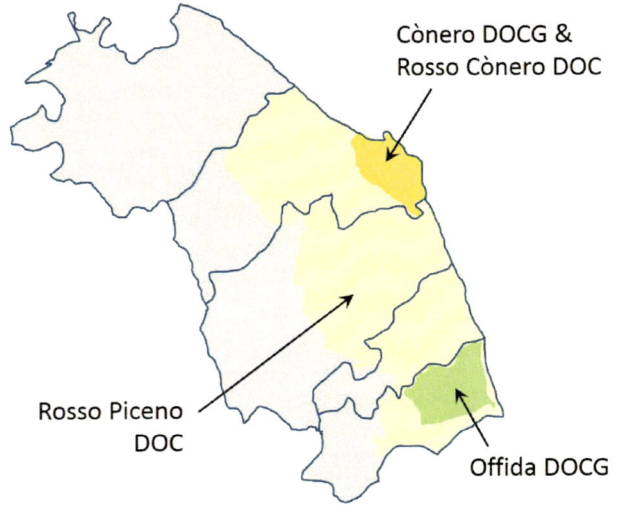

Vineyards on the coast near Ancona, Marche

Abruzzo

Down the Adriatic coast from Marche, east of Lazio, lies the region of Abruzzo. Note that the name is Abruzzo—not Abruzzi, a former name that was changed in the 1960s. Abruzzo is quite mountainous, but has a broad belt of foothills and lower terrain along the Adriatic Sea where most of the vineyards are.

The region has 1 DOCG, 8 DOCs, and 8 IGPs and produces more red wine than white. This is the heartland of Montepulciano, which is the predominant grape variety of Abruzzo.

The most important denomination in Abruzzo is Montepulciano d'Abruzzo DOC. As the name suggests, this is a varietal Montepulciano wine from a large area that includes most of the Abruzzo region suitable for grape growing. Montepulciano d'Abruzzo DOC has the highest wine production volume of any red wine DOP in Italy. Montepulciano d'Abruzzo Colline Teramane is a former subzone of the Montepulciano d'Abruzzo DOC that now has DOCG status.

Cerasuolo d'Abruzzo DOC is the denomination for rosato wines from the same area as the Montepulciano d'Abruzzo DOC. It produces *only* varietal rosato wines from Montepulciano, considered the best rosatos of central Italy.

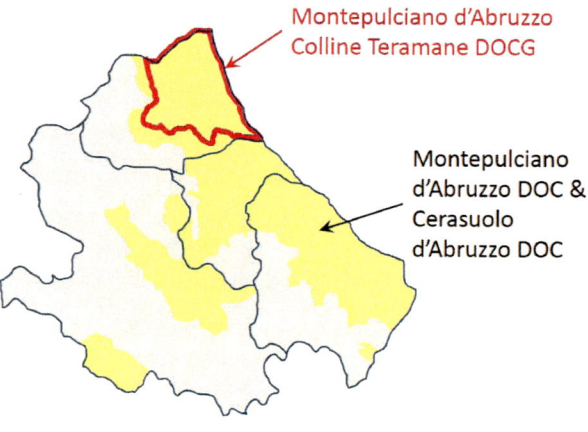

Montepulciano d'Abruzzo
Colline Teramane DOCG

Montepulciano
d'Abruzzo DOC &
Cerasuolo
d'Abruzzo DOC

Molise

The Montepulciano vineyards do not stop in Abruzzo, and indeed Montepulciano is again the predominant grape variety in this unit's final region, Molise.

Molise is the second smallest Italian region in size and consequently has a small production volume of wine. It has no DOCGs, 4 DOCs, and 2 IGPs, and its wines are not often seen in the export market.

A Tale of Two Montepulcianos

When it comes to Montepulciano, don't confuse the *town* of Montepulciano *(above)* with the Montepulciano grape variety *(right)*. Vino Nobile from the village of Montepulciano in Tuscany is a Sangiovese-based wine. Wines made from Montepulciano grapes come mainly from regions on the Adriatic coast, not Tuscany.

Montepulciano-Based DOPs

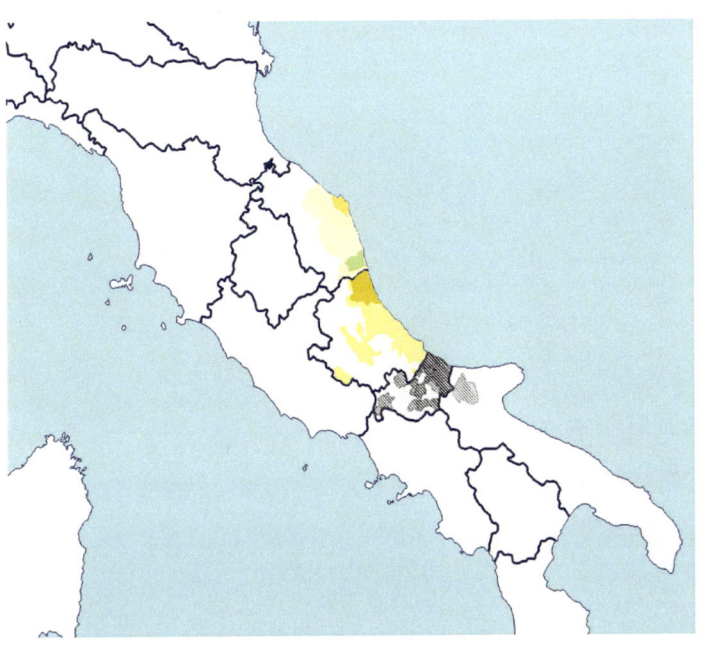

The map at left shows how important Montepulciano is on the Adriatic Sea coast. DOPs that feature Montepulciano form a continuous band along the coast from northern Marche to southern Abruzzo and beyond into Molise and the northern part of Puglia.

Central Italian Cuisine

Now let's take a look at the foods of central Italy that might be paired with the wines we've been talking about.

Any discussion of central Italian cuisine has to start with Emilia Romagna. The products of this region are legendary:

- Parma ham, aka Prosciutto di Parma
- Parmesan cheese, aka Parmigiano reggiano
- Balsamic vinegar from Modena
- Salami from Bologna

Tuscany is also renowned for fine food such as:

- Bistecca alla Fiorentina—a specialty of Florence, this is a thickly cut and very large T-bone steak, grilled over a wood or charcoal fire, seasoned with salt and olive oil; it is traditionally served very rare, often accompanied by Tuscan beans as a side dish
- Wild boar and other game such as rabbit and duck
- Ribollita—a hearty Tuscan stew made with cannellini beans, vegetables, and leftover bread; the name literally means "reboiled"

Pictured (clockwise from above): *Balsamic vinegar being extracted from its aging barrel, finely sliced prosciutto di Parma, ribollita, tortellini bolognesi, ravioli, spaghetti ai funghi (spaghetti with mushrooms)*

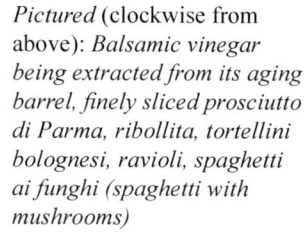

Although polenta and risotto from the north are still found in central Italy, pasta is more typical—spaghetti, tagliatelle, pappardelle, tubes, and stuffed pasta with all types of sauces. Filled pastas such as ravioli and tortellini, strings like spaghetti and fettuccine, wide noodles such as lasagna, and various shapes like penne, rigatoni, and orzo are all popular here.

Sauces for pasta include:

- Amatriciana—a traditional sauce in Roman cuisine, based on guanciale (cured pork cheek), pecorino cheese, and tomato; it is named for the town of Amatrice in Lazio
- Arrabbiata—a spicy sauce made from garlic, tomatoes, and red chili peppers cooked in olive oil; the name means "angry," referring to the heat of the peppers
- Bolognese—*ragù alla bolognese* is made with a soffritto of onion, celery, and carrot; finely chopped beef and possibly pork such as pancetta; wine; and a small amount of tomato concentrate
- Carbonara—another Roman specialty, this sauce is made with eggs, Pecorino Romano or Parmigiano Reggiano cheese, bacon (guanciale or pancetta), and black pepper
- Simple oil or butter with garlic, salt, and pepper

A regional specialty from the Marche is olive ascolane—stuffed olives from Ascoli Piceno that have DOP status. The olives are filled with ground seasoned pork or beef, coated with breadcrumbs, and deep fried.

Both white and black truffles are found in the Apennines, especially Umbria.

In addition, various Pecorino sheep's-milk cheeses are made throughout central Italy.

Top: *Rigatoni amatriciana*
Center: *Olive ascolane*
Bottom: *Black truffles from Umbria*

Italian Language: Conversational Basics

Here are a few words and phrases of polite conversation in Italian. Even if you don't know any other Italian vocabulary, these words will go a long way in breaking the ice with Italian speakers.

1. Hello (informal) = Ciao (*chow*)

2. Good morning or good day = Buongiorno (bwohn-*jor*-no)

3. Good evening = Buonasera (bwoh-na-*say*-ra)

4. How are you? (informal singular) = Come stai? (koh-may *sty*)

5. How are you? (formal singular) = Come sta? (koh-may *stah*)

6. Goodnight = Buonanotte (bwoh-na-*noh*-tay)

7. Good-bye, farewell = Ciao, addio, arrivederci (*chow*, ah-*diyo*, ah-reev-eh-*dair*-chee)

8. See you later = Ci vediamo (chee vay-dee-*yah*-mo)

9. Until next time = A la prossima (ah lah *prohs*-see-ma)

10. Please = Per favore (pair fah-*voh*-ray)

11. Thank you = Grazie (*graht*-zee-yay)

12. Sir = Signore (see-*nyoh*-ray)

13. Madam = Signora (see-*nyoh*-ra)

14. Miss = Signorina (see-nyoh-*ree*-na)

15. Sirs or "Ladies and Gentlemen" = Signori (see-*nyoh*-ree)

Pronunciation Practice: Tuscan Producers

Below are some well-known wine producers and brand names from Tuscany, along with the phonetic pronunciation of their names. Some, like Antinori, are not too hard to pronounce correctly, while others such as Cecchi and Luce can easily be mispronounced if they are not familiar. Review the vowel and consonant sounds from Unit 1 and then practice saying these names aloud.

1. Altesino (ahl-tay-*zee*-no)
2. Antinori (ahn-tee-*noh*-ree)
3. Avignonesi (ah-vee-nyoh-*nay*-zee)
4. Badia a Coltibuono (bah-*dee*-ya ah kohl-tee-*bwoh*-no)
5. Barone Ricasoli (bah-*roh*-nay ree-*kah*-zoh-lee)
6. Bibi Graetz (bee-bee *gratz*)
7. Capezzana (kah-pay-*tzah*-na)
8. Castellare (kah-stell-*lah*-ray)
9. Castello di Volpaia (kah-*stell*-lo dee vohl-*pie*-yah)
10. Cecchi (*chehk*-kee)
11. Col d'Orcia (kohl *door*-chah)
12. Folonari (foh-loh-*nah*-ree)
13. Frescobaldi (fress-koh-*bahl*-dee)
14. Il Poggione (eel poh-*joh*-nay)
15. Isole e Olena (*ee*-soh-lay eh oh-*lay*-na)
16. Luce (*loo*-chay)
17. Nozzole (*noht*-tzoh-lay)
18. Ornellaia (or-nell-*lie*-ya)
19. Poggio Scalette (*poh*-joh ska-*layt*-tay)
20. Querciabella (kwehr-cha-*bell*-la)
21. Ruffino (roof-*fee*-no)—different from the Chianti subzone Rufina (*roo*-fee-na)
22. Sassicaia (sahss-see-*kie*-ya)
23. Tignanello (tee-nyah-*nell*-lo)

Unit 3 Exercises

Note: These exercises are not limited to central Italy and in some cases refer back to information discussed in Units 1 and 2.

1. Beginning from the toe of the boot, write down the names of the six Italian regions on the western coast of the peninsula from south to north.
2. Name the two most important red grape varieties of central Italy. Which of those is number one?
3. One of the central Italian regions produces the second highest volume of wine of all the regions. Which region is it, and which region produces more wine?
4. Describe the relationship between DOC, DOP, and DOCG.
5. On an outline map of the regions of Italy (Fig. 2 on p. 22), for each region discussed in this unit, put an S in all the regions where Sangiovese is the most important red variety, an M in the regions where Montepulciano is more important, and both letters in the one region where they are equally important.
6. On the same map as above, write the following grape varieties in the region or regions where they are most commonly found.
    - Corvina
    - Dolcetto
    - Freisa
    - Lagrein
    - Lambrusco
    - Nebbiolo
    - Sagrantino
    - Schiava
7. One of the central Italian regions has the second most DOPs of all the regions. Which region is it, and which other region has the most?
8. In your own words, define and describe a "Super Tuscan."
9. Name three red-wine denominations in Marche.
10. Fill in the blanks in the following table. (There may be more than one correct answer in some spaces.)

Denomination	Level	Primary Red Grape Variety	Region
Morellino di Scansano			
Lambrusco Grasparossa di Castelvetro			
Valtellina Superiore	DOCG		
Carmignano			
Langhe		Various	
Cerasuolo d'Abruzzo			

11. Name at least four DOCGs that make Sangiovese-based wine.
12. Give alternative names/spellings for Tuscany and Le Marche.
13. What is the capital and largest city of Lazio?
14. Name the only Italian region in central Italy with no coastline. What is its most significant denomination for red wine?

15. In which region are the cities of Bologna and Parma located?
16. Fill in the blanks in the following table. (There may be more than one correct answer in some spaces.)

Denomination	Level	Primary Red Grape Variety	Region
	DOCG	Cesanese	
	DOCG	Dolcetto	
		Petit Rouge, Nebbiolo, Pinot Nero	Valle d'Aosta
	DOC	Sangiovese	Tuscany
	DOC	Cabernet, Merlot, Syrah	
	DOCG	Montepulciano	

17. What are the boundaries of IGP Toscana?
18. Write the names of the seven Chianti subzones. Check your spelling. Which of these subzones are most commercially important?
19. Name the primary red grape of Molise.
20. On a map of Tuscany (Fig. 4), draw in a rough outline of the Chianti and Chianti Classico denominations. Now add the other main Sangiovese-based denominations.
21. What denomination is the most prestigious one available for grapes grown in Montalcino? If a winemaker in Montalcino decides to make a second-label wine that is not at the DOCG level, what other protected place-names are available for the label (there are at least three)?

Figure 4. Outline of Tuscany
Download a pdf of this image at http://italianwinecentral.com/exercise-maps

Temple of Poseidon, Paestum, Campania

Southern Italian Reds

Regions of Southern Italy

The regions covered in this unit are those of the lower Italian peninsula, plus the two island regions:

- Campania
- Puglia
- Basilicata
- Calabria
- Sicily
- Sardinia

One thing these southern regions have in common is that they are mostly mountainous, as can be seen in the topographic map below. They are also generally less affluent and less developed than other Italian regions. Their historical lack of infrastructure and remoteness brought about the evolution of unique local grape varieties.

This topographic map of southern Italy shows how little flat land there is in the South outside of Puglia. The Apennines take up much of the peninsula down to the tip of the toe, and the islands are quite mountainous as well. Note the circular cone of 11,000-foot Mount Etna in northeastern Sicily, the highest point in Italy south of the Alps.

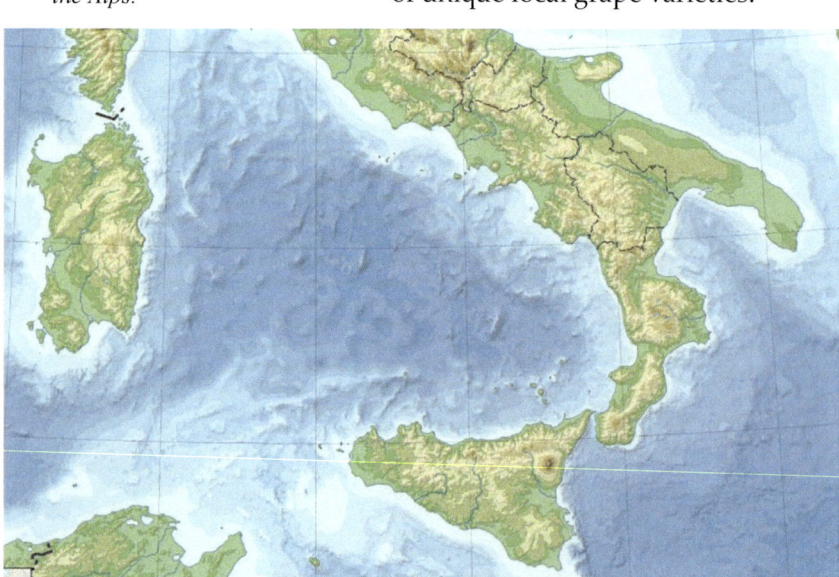

Winters in the south tend to be mild except at higher elevations. Summers are hot, dry, and usually cloud free. The high temperatures and continuous sunshine in summertime lead to wines with low to moderate acidity, depending on the variety, and high alcohol.

Differences among the southern regions include:

- Sicily and Sardinia are islands with substantially different political and cultural histories from both the mainland and each other.
- Campania is the most densely populated Italian region, while Basilicata and Sardinia are among the most sparsely populated.
- Puglia has areas of open plains that are ideal for large-scale agriculture.
- Campania and Calabria get more rain than the other regions—but primarily in winter, not during the growing season.

Next we'll turn to these unique and often unfamiliar local grape varieties.

The western coast of Basilicata

Red Grape Varieties of Southern Italy

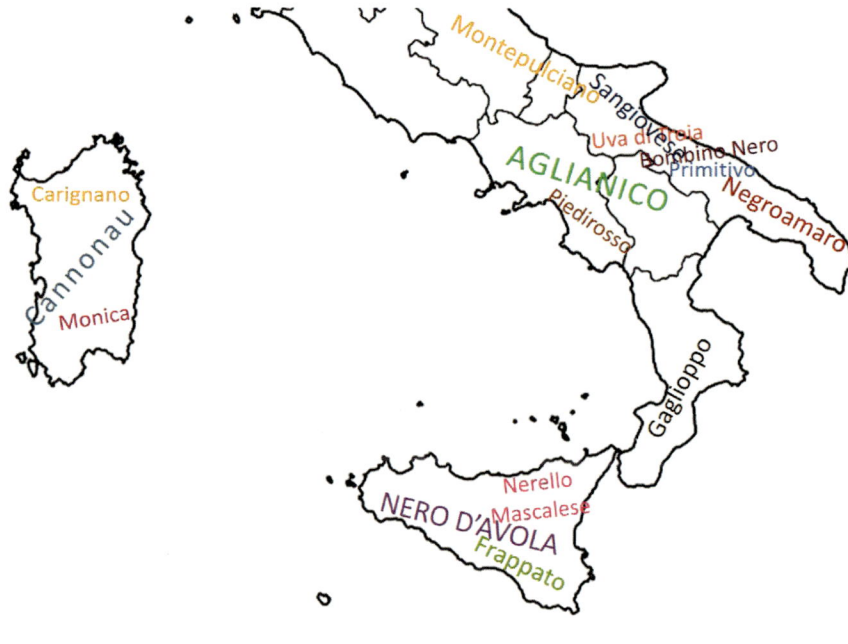

Unlike in central Italy, there is no dominant grape variety for the south generally. However, with the exception of Puglia, each region does have one dominant red variety. Only a couple of varieties are found in any abundance in more than one southern region.

Two of the more familiar grape varieties found in southern Italy are Sangiovese and Montepulciano, which extend their range from central Italy into the top of Puglia. But when one thinks of Puglia, it's more likely to be Negroamaro or Primitivo that comes to mind. These would be considered Puglia's signature grape varieties—major varieties that are uncommon anywhere else in Italy and help define the region's reputation. Other important grapes in this major growing region include Uva di Troia and Bombino Nero.

The leading variety of both Campania and Basilicata is Aglianico. Piedirosso is another variety associated with Campania.

The primary grape of Calabria is Gaglioppo.

Sicily's signature grape is Nero d'Avola, although the island is home to a number of other notable varieties not found elsewhere in Italy such as Frappato and Nerello Mascalese.

Sardinia, too, has many varieties that are rare elsewhere in Italy. Cannonau—which is essentially the same as the grape known as Grenache or Garnacha in other countries—is Sardinia's leading variety. Other red grapes associated with Sardinia include Carignano and Monica.

In the rest of this unit, we'll look at each of the southern regions in more detail, focusing on the red wines they are known for.

Learning Objectives

Unit 4 describes southern Italy's red wines, from Campania south to Sicily. The learning objectives for this unit, as for the previous red-wine units, are:

- Geography and cultural history of the regions
- Major red grape varieties of the regions and where they are concentrated
- Commercially significant denominations
  - Which region are they located in?
  - Red wines only, or other styles as well?
  - Primary grape variety or varieties
  - Single-variety, varietal, or blend?

Key indigenous red grape varieties of southern Italy

Aglianico: One of Italy's three greatest grape varieties and one of its oldest. Best vineyards are in volcanic soils on mountainous slopes. Taurasi, Taburno, and Vulture have separate biotypes. Very high acidity and prominent minerality. Usually quite tannic. *Aromas & flavors:* Floral (rose), sour cherry, plum (esp. from Vulture), leather and herbs (esp. from Taburno), smoke. Capable of long aging.

Bombino Nero: Thin skinned, so better for rosato than rosso. Usually added to Negroamaro wines. High acidity; light to medium bodied. *Aromas & flavors:* Red berries, floral, citrus. *Best DOP:* Castel del Monte Bombino Nero.

Bovale: Two distinct grape varieties: Bovale Grande and Bovale Sardo. Bovale Grande is similar or identical to Carignano, Bovale Sardo to Spain's Graciano. Sardo is considered the better of the two. Highly tannic and acidic; can produce deeply colored wines. *Best DOPs:* Campidano di Terralba and Mandrisolai.

Cannonau: Similar or identical to Garnacha (Grenache) and Tai Rosso. Light in color. *Aromas & flavors:* Floral, herbal. *Best DOP:* Cannonau di Sardegna, especially subzones Oliena, Jerzu, and Capo Ferrato.

Carignano: Transplanted from Spain centuries ago. Grows best on sandy soils, where it produces creamy wines with soft tannins. *Best DOP:* Carignano del Sulcis.

Frappato: Low in tannin, light bodied, and light in color. *Aromas & flavors:* Strawberry, violet, herbs.

Gaglioppo: Can have a red-orange color. High in acid with rough tannins. *Aromas & flavors:* Red berries, citrus zest, minerals, underbrush.

Monica: A group of similar but unrelated Sardinian varieties. Gently tannic. *Aromas & flavors:* Red berries, herbs, tar, tobacco.

Negroamaro: High in alcohol. *Aromas & flavors:* Black fruit, tobacco, shoe polish.

Nerello Cappuccio: Early ripening; darker in color but less tannic than Nerello Mascalese. *Aromas & flavors:* Ripe cherry, vanilla, coffee, minerals, slightly floral.

Nerello Mascalese: Light in color; tannic. *Aromas & flavors:* Sour cherry, tobacco, herbs, minerals.

Nero d'Avola: Officially called Calabrese. Often blended with Frappato. *Aromas & flavors:* Dark red cherry, herbs.

Piedirosso: Often blended with Aglianico to soften it. *Aromas & flavors:* Red berries, floral, tar, green herbal note.

Primitivo: Same as Zinfandel (Crljenak Kaštelanski or Tribidrag). One of earliest ripening varieties in Italy. High in alcohol. *Aromas & flavors:* Red cherry, strawberry jam, plum; sometimes tobacco, tar, herbs. *Best DOPs:* Gioia del Colle, Primitivo di Manduria.

Uva di Troia: Aka Nero di Troia. Blended with other Puglian varieties to give them finesse and freshness. Medium bodied; high in acid. Refined tannins. *Aromas & flavors:* Red cherry, red currant, black pepper, tobacco, underbrush.

Aglianico-Based DOPs

Aglianico, arguably the most important grape variety of southern Italy, is one of the few grapes with a significant presence in more than one southern Italian region. It is the most planted variety in both Campania and Basilicata. In both regions, Aglianico is mainly grown at higher elevations in the Apennines, and its best expressions come from volcanic soils.

In Campania, Taurasi DOCG, a varietal made from Aglianico, is considered by many to be the finest red wine of southern Italy. There are several other denominations throughout Campania that make varietal Aglianico wines, of which the best known is Aglianico del Taburno DOCG, which makes both red and rosato Aglianicos.

Farther southeast in Basilicata are two collocated denominations, Aglianico del Vulture Superiore DOCG and Aglianico del Vulture DOC, both of whose wines are made with 100% Aglianico.

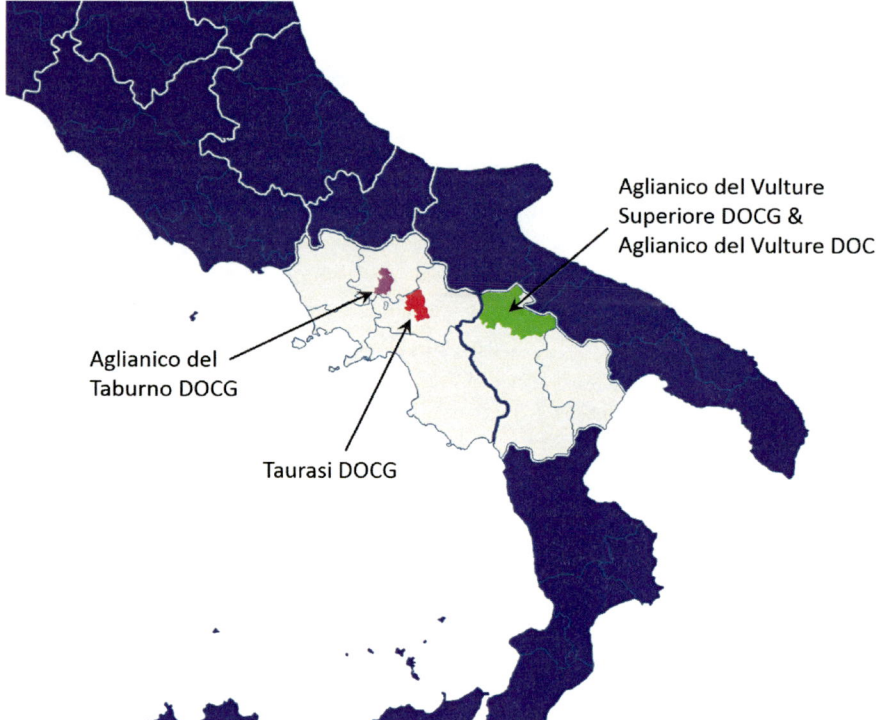

Aglianico del Vulture Superiore DOCG & Aglianico del Vulture DOC

Aglianico del Taburno DOCG

Taurasi DOCG

Basilicata

Basilicata is a rugged, sparsely populated region, with very small wine production. Red wine dominates production in Basilicata. It has 1 DOCG, 4 DOCs, and 1 IGP. More than half its vineyards are planted with Aglianico.

The most important denominations in Basilicata are the duo of Aglianico del Vulture DOC and its big brother Aglianico del Vulture Superiore DOCG. Both of these wines are pure Aglianico, grown in the north of Basilicata around an extinct volcano called Mount Vulture. (Be careful: the name may look like the English word *vulture*, but it's pronounced *vool*-too-ray.)

Campania

The gateway to southern Italy, in many ways, is Campania. This is the region where you'll find Naples (Napoli), the largest city in southern Italy and third largest overall. Among the regions of what we're calling southern Italy, Campania is the most populous, the closest to Rome (if not technically the northernmost), and the most touristed.

In terms of wine production, Campania has 4 DOCGs, 15 DOCs, and 10 IGPs. Although red wine is only slightly more prevalent than white wine in the region, the primary grape variety in Campania is Aglianico. Another notable Campanian red variety is Piedirosso.

The region's most famous red wine denomination is Taurasi DOCG, one of Italy's most esteemed DOPs. Taurasi is a varietal made from Aglianico (minimum 85%).

There are a number of other denominations in Campania that feature Aglianico as well, including one more DOCG: Aglianico del Taburno. This denomination produces varietal Aglianicos in both red and rosato styles.

The best-known denomination for Piedirosso is Vesuvio DOC. Its vineyards blanket the slopes of Mount Vesuvius (Vesuvio in Italian), the volcano that famously buried Pompeii near Naples two thousand years ago. Here, the red wines are a blend based primarily on Piedirosso; a small amount of Aglianico may be included in the blend. Vesuvio DOC also produces white wines, which will be covered in the next unit.

Mount Vesuvius presides over the Bay of Naples in Campania

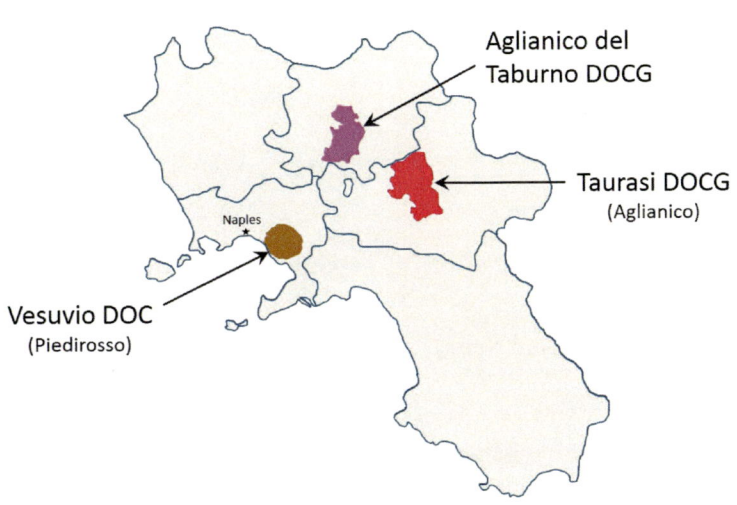

Aglianico del Taburno DOCG

Taurasi DOCG (Aglianico)

Naples

Vesuvio DOC (Piedirosso)

Puglia

Puglia forms the spur and heel of the Italian boot, stretching more than 200 miles from the Ionian Sea up the Adriatic coast. Its anglicized name is Apulia, but the Italian Puglia is heard more often.

Puglia has lots of sunny weather and contains most of the flat land in southern Italy, so it is a major source of agricultural products, including wine grapes. Not surprisingly, it is among the highest-volume regions for wine production in Italy.

Historically, much of this wine was intended to add some body and depth to lighter, thinner wines produced farther north and in other countries. More Puglian wines are being bottled in the region today, though, and quality has become more important than quantity. The region contains 4 DOCGs, 28 DOCs, and 6 IGPs and produces more red wine than white.

Puglia has not one but two signature grape varieties: Negroamaro and Primitivo. Many other varieties figure prominently in the region as well, primarily for non-DOP wines. Some are familiar varieties from central Italy such as Sangiovese, Lambrusco, and Montepulciano. Two uniquely Puglian varieties that feature in DOP-level wines are Uva di Troia, also known as Nero di Troia, and Bombino Nero.

The predominant grape varieties in Puglia change along the length of the region (*see map at left*). In the north, for example, Montepulciano is the primary grape variety for DOP wines, extending its influence from Molise and regions farther north. Quite a lot of Sangiovese is grown here, too. There are no particularly well-known denominations in this part of Puglia, however.

A little farther southeast, the main grape varieties are Uva di Troia and Bombino Nero. In this area is a

Vieste, on the Gargano Peninsula in Puglia

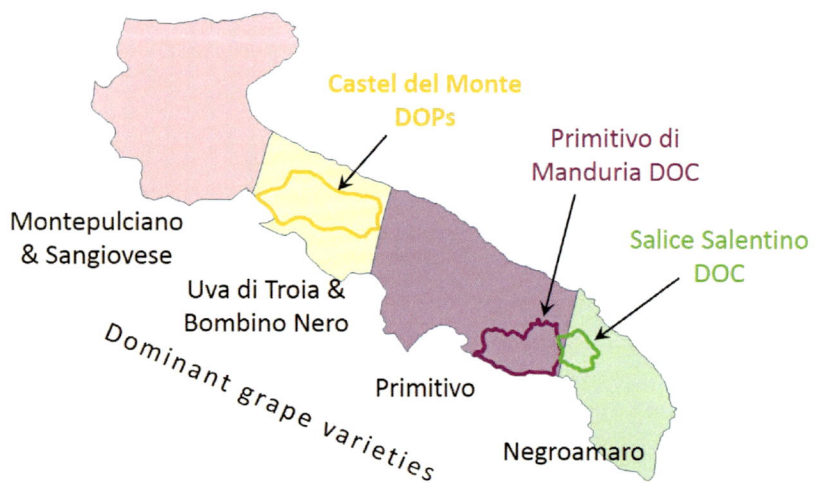

Castel del Monte DOPs

Primitivo di Manduria DOC

Salice Salentino DOC

Montepulciano & Sangiovese

Uva di Troia & Bombino Nero

Dominant grape varieties

Primitivo

Negroamaro

13th-century fortress called Castel del Monte, which gives its name to three DOCGs and a DOC, all producing wines in the same area based on one or both of those grapes. Three make reds based on Uva di Troia:

- Castel del Monte Nero di Troia Riserva DOCG (varietal)
- Castel del Monte Rosso Riserva DOCG (not necessarily varietal)
- Castel del Monte DOC, a more inclusive denomination that allows red wines from Aglianico and Cabernet as well as Uva di Troia, plus other styles of wine

The fourth denomination here is Castel del Monte Bombino Nero DOCG, a varietal wine from Bombino Nero—a grape so light in color that these wines naturally end up pinkish. This is one of only two denominations (with Cerasuolo d'Abruzzo DOC) devoted exclusively to rosato wines.

The next segment of Puglia is where most of Italy's Primitivo is found. While little Primitivo is grown elsewhere in the country, it is well known outside Italy under a different name—for all practical purposes, Primitivo is the same as California's Zinfandel grape. Primitivo di Manduria DOC is the only denomination in Italy specifically for dry Primitivo wines. Because the name of the grape variety is in the denomination name, it has to be a varietal. There's also a DOCG in the same location called Primitivo di Manduria Dolce Naturale DOCG that makes a *sweet* wine from Primitivo; it will be mentioned again with the dessert wines in Unit 7.

Negroamaro—sometimes spelled as two words, Negro Amaro—takes over in the southernmost part of Puglia. Several DOPs in this area make Negroamaro-based red and rosato wines. The best-known denomination is Salice Salentino DOC. Salice Salentino also makes other kinds of wine, but on export markets, its

Negroamaro-based (but not necessarily varietal) wines are its claim to fame. And for fans of rosatos, those made from Negroamaro may be southern Italy's best.

Alberobello, Puglia, a UNESCO World Heritage site for its more than 1,000 trulli (stone-roofed huts)

In addition to its traditional DOPs, Puglia produces a lot of wine from international varieties and from varieties more commonly associated with other regions in Italy such as Sangiovese. Much of this wine is still sold in bulk for blending with other places' wines, but increasingly it is being bottled as branded wines. IGP Salento, in the heel area, and IGP Puglia, covering the entire region, are two of the largest production volume IGPs in Italy—not only for red wines but for other styles as well.

IGP Puglia

IGP Salento

Calabria

Moving from heel to toe, the next region is Calabria. Calabria has only a small volume of wine production, of which there is five times as much red wine as white. There are no DOCGs, 9 DOCs, and 10 IGPs.

Calabria's primary red grape variety is Gaglioppo. Its most famous red wine denomination is the Cirò DOC, whose red and rosato wines are Gaglioppo based. The minimum content is 80% Gaglioppo, so they aren't always varietal wines. Cirò DOC also produces a white wine, which will be described in Unit 5.

Sicily

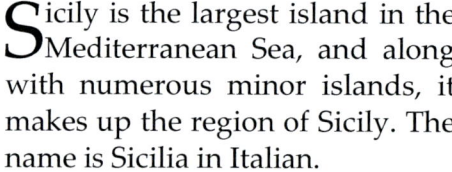

Sicily is the largest island in the Mediterranean Sea, and along with numerous minor islands, it makes up the region of Sicily. The name is Sicilia in Italian.

Sicily is one of the top four wine-producing regions in Italy. Puglia and Sicily (in one order or the other) are southern Italy's biggest wine producers. Like Puglia, Sicily used to send most of its prodigious wine output north to be blended into other regions' and countries' wines. Agricultural reforms of recent decades have reduced Sicily's volume and significantly improved the quality of its wines, which are now more likely to be bottled under a Sicilian label.

Perhaps surprisingly, Sicily produces more white wine than red. The primary indigenous red grape varieties in the region are:

- Nero d'Avola
- Nerello Mascalese
- Frappato

International varieties are also very prominent here, especially Syrah, Merlot, and Cabernet Sauvignon.

Sicily has 1 DOCG, 23 DOCs, and 7 IGPs. Its most famous red wine denominations are Etna DOC and Cerasuolo di Vittoria DOCG.

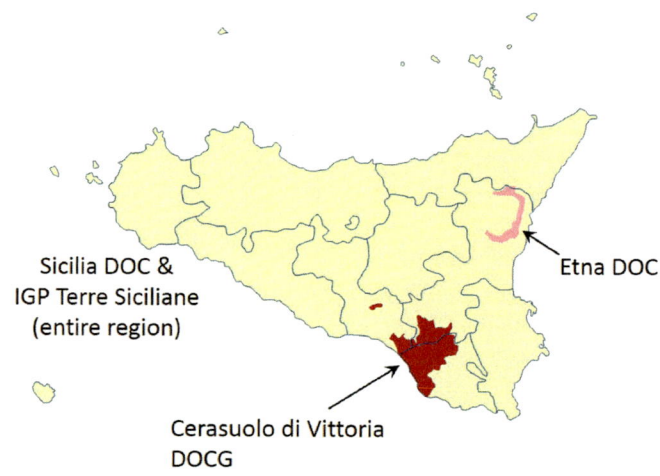

Two appellations cover the entire region of Sicily: Sicilia DOC and IGP Terre Siciliane. Sicilia DOC is among the highest-producing denominations, and IGP Terre Siciliane has the highest volume output of any IGP. Both allow many different styles of wines—reds, whites, and others—made from traditional Sicilian grapes or international varieties. Like IGP Puglia, they produce large quantities of blending wines, bulk wines, and branded wines.

Etna DOC is located on the slopes of the famous volcano Mount Etna (below). Its red wines are based on Nerello Mascalese (minimum 80%). Etna also produces white wines.

Cerasuolo di Vittoria is the only DOCG in Sicily. It makes exclusively red wines that are a blend of Nero d'Avola and Frappato. *Cerasuolo* is a dialectical word for cherry. Note that in Cerasuolo d'Abruzzo, the word

refers to the light cherry color of the rosato wine, while in Cerasuolo di Vittoria it refers to the aromas and flavors of this red wine.

Mount Etna is one of the most active volcanoes in Italy, erupting frequently and sometimes spectacularly.

Sardinia

Last but not least, we come to Italy's other island region, Sardinia. Sardinia is the second largest island in the Mediterranean, after Sicily. The Italian name for Sardinia is Sardegna.

Sardinia's production volume is relatively small, with more red wine production than white wine. The island has 1 DOCG, 17 DOCs, and 15 IGPs.

The primary red grape variety of Sardinia is Cannonau. Other notable red varieties are Carignano and Monica.

Sardinia does not have any particularly famous red wine

Cannonau di Sardegna DOC & IGP Isola dei Nuraghi

denominations, but its most important one is probably Cannonau di Sardegna DOC. Cannonau di Sardegna is a denomination for red and rosato varietal wines from Cannonau made anywhere in Sardinia.

Another appellation for Sardinian wines that you might see in the market is IGP Isola dei Nuraghi, which can be used for almost any style of wine made on Sardinia. The name means "Island of the Nuraghi," referring to prehistoric structures that are found all over Sardinia (singular: *nuragus*). Their purpose is unknown, but they are found only here.

Southern Italian Cuisine

Pictured (top to bottom): *Margherita pizza, braided mozzarella cheese, Sardinian gnocchetti, Calabrian handmade fusilli*

What comes to mind when you think of southern Italian cuisine? Perhaps it's Italy's most beloved export to the world: pizza.

Naples is considered the home of pizza, and Neapolitans (and many others) point to the Margherita pizza as the one true pizza, or *vera pizza napoletana*. It consists of three very specific toppings:

- Sauce made with San Marzano tomatoes
- Buffalo mozzarella cheese
- Basil

These three ingredients give it the colors of the Italian flag. The patriotic pizza was supposedly created in honor of Queen Margherita, the wife of King Umberto I of Italy, on the occasion of her visit to Naples in 1889 (although recent investigation seems to show that that story was invented in the 20th century). The art of Neapolitan pizzamaking has been nominated in 2016 for inclusion in UNESCO's list as part of the Intangible Cultural Heritage of Humanity.

The cheese featured on true Neapolitan pizza is mozzarella, made using the milk of a breed of water buffalo that has been in Italy since Roman times. Mozzarella cheese can be made anywhere in Italy, but the best comes from parts of Campania and Lazio where it is protected as Mozzarella di Bufala Campana DOP. Obviously, mozzarella has to some extent become a generic word and mozzarella cheeses are being made all over the world. However, these foreign ones are industrial versions made with cow's milk and lack the richness of true Italian mozzarella.

Pasta is found everywhere in the south. Puglia produces much of Italy's wheat for pasta. Tomatoes are grown in abundance in the south, so red sauces are common. The cloudless summers allow sun-drying of tomatoes and other fruits, as well.

Olives are grown everywhere in the peninsula, including the south, for eating on their own or use in preparations. Lemons feature in many recipes, too. And eggplant is a big ingredient in Sicilian cooking.

Calabria is famous for hot peppers, and they are put to many uses. 'Nduja, for example, is a Calabrian specialty: a spreadable pork sausage laced with lots of hot peppers.

Pictured (clockwise from top): *Olives for sale at the farmers market, lemons, sun-dried tomatoes from Basilicata, Calabrian hot chili peppers and 'nduja sausage*

Italian Language: Colors

Colors are useful vocabulary words because several of them occur in the names of grape varieties, denominations, and branded wine names—giving an immediate clue to the style of wine in question. You may come across others in an Italian-language wine description. Below are some of the more common ones with regard to wine.

1. Bianco (*byahn*-koh) = White
2. Rosato (roh-*zah*-toh) = Pink
3. Rosso (*rohss*-so) = Red
4. Nero (*nay*-ro) = Black
5. Grigio (*gree*-jo) = Gray
6. Ambra (*ahm*-brah) = Amber
7. Dorato (doh-*rah*-toh) = Golden
8. Giallo (*jahl*-lo) = Yellow
9. Rubino (roo-*bee*-no) = Ruby
10. Granato (grah-*nah*-toh) = Garnet
11. Porpora (*pohr*-poh-rah) = Crimson, purple
12. Viola (vee-*oh*-la), violetta (vee-oh-*let*-tah) = Purple, violet

Pronunciation Practice: Red Grape Varieties

Practice pronouncing the names of the red Italian grape varieties listed below with phonetic pronunciations. At the same time, think about where these grapes are found and in which denominations they are used.

1. Aglianico (ahl-*yah*-nee-ko)
2. Barbera (bar-*bay*-ra)
3. Bombino Nero (bom-*bee*-no *neh*-ro)
4. Brachetto (bra-*ket*-toe)
5. Cannonau (kan-no-*now*)
6. Carignano (kair-ee-*nyah*-no)
7. Cesanese (chay-zah-*nay*-zay)
8. Corvina (kor-*vee*-na)
9. Croatina (kro-ah-*tee*-na)
10. Dolcetto (dohl-*chet*-toe)
11. Frappato (frah-*pot*-toe)
12. Freisa (*fry*-za)
13. Gaglioppo (gahl-*yo*-po)
14. Grignolino (gree-nyo-*lee*-no)
15. Lagrein (la-*griyn*)
16. Lambrusco (lam-*broos*-koh)
17. Monica (*moh*-nee-kah)
18. Montepulciano (mon-tay-pool-*cha*-no)
19. Nebbiolo (neb-bee-*oh*-lo)
20. Negroamaro (neg-ro-ah-*mah*-ro)
21. Nerello Mascalese (neh-*rel*-lo mahss-kah-*lay*-zee)
22. Nero d'Avola (*neh*-ro *dahv*-oh-lah)
23. Piedirosso (pyed-ee-*rohs*-so)
24. Pinot Nero (*pee*-no *neh*-ro)
25. Primitivo (pree-mee-*tee*-vo)
26. Refosco (ray-*foh*-skoh)
27. Rondinella (rohn-dee-*nell*-la)
28. Sagrantino (sah-grahn-*tee*-no)
29. Sangiovese (sahn-jo-*vay*-zay)
30. Schiava (skee-*yah*-va)
31. Teroldego (teh-*roll*-deh-go)
32. Uva di Troia (*oo*-va dee *troy*-ya)

Unit 4 Exercises

Note: Some of these exercises refer back to information discussed in previous units.

1. Beginning from the heel of the boot, write down the names of the seven Italian regions on the eastern coast of the country from south to north. What is the country that borders the last of these regions, and what is the name of the body of water that all these regions touch?
2. On the map of Italy at right (Fig. 5), name each of the denominations shown. Do as many as you can without help, then use the DOP list on page 78 to identify the others.
3. Of the southern Italian regions, which produce the most wine? What two regions farther north produce more?
4. Fill in the blanks in the following table. (There may be more than one correct answer in some spaces.)

Denomination	Level	Primary Red Grape Variety	Region
Bardolino Superiore	DOCG		
Castel del Monte Nero di Troia	DOCG		
Etna			
Morellino di Scansano			
Offida			
Isola dei Nuraghi		Various	
Taurasi			
Valtellina Rosso	DOC		

5. On an outline map of the regions of Italy (Fig. 2 on p. 22), write the following grape varieties in the region or regions where they are most commonly found.
    - Aglianico
    - Barbera
    - Cesanese
    - Croatina
    - Gaglioppo
    - Lambrusco
    - Monica
    - Nerello Mascalese
    - Piedirosso
    - Primitivo
    - Teroldego
    - Uva di Troia
6. In which region are the cities of Florence and Siena located?
7. Give alternative names/spellings for Sardinia and Sicily.
8. For each of the following regions, name the red grape variety its reputation is based on and at least one denomination that features that variety.
    - Abruzzo
    - Basilicata
    - Calabria
    - Campania
    - Piedmont
    - Sardinia
    - Sicily
    - Umbria
    - Veneto

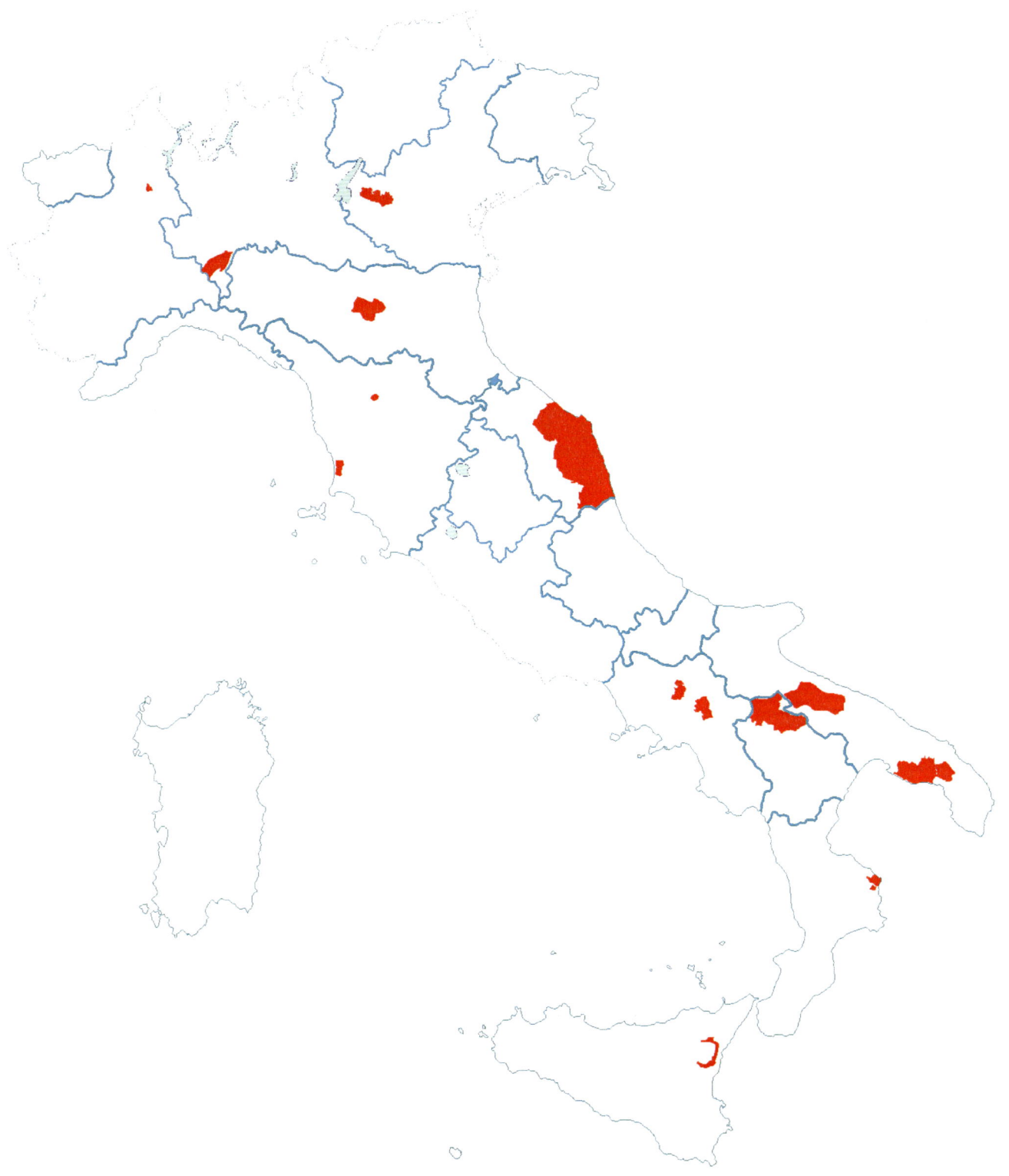

Figure 5. Miscellaneous DOPs

9. Name the three levels of the quality pyramid under EU (not Italian) wine law, in both English and Italian.
10. For each of the following grape varieties, write the region or regions where they are most commonly found.
   - Bombino Nero
   - Cannonau
   - Carignano
   - Frappato
   - Freisa
   - Grignolino
   - Negroamaro
   - Nero d'Avola
   - Rondinella
11. What is Apulia?
12. Fill in the blanks in the following table. (There may be more than one correct answer in some spaces.)

Denomination	Level	Primary Red Grape Variety	Region
		Nero d'Avola and Frappato	
	DOC	Barbera	Piedmont
			Basilicata
	IGP	Various	Sicily
		Negroamaro	
	DOC	Sangiovese	
		Primitivo	
	DOC		Sardinia

13. What is the largest city in southern Italy?
14. Write down three synonyms for Sangiovese that are used in certain parts of Tuscany. Where are those alternative names most often used?
15. When selecting a wine to serve with hearty Sicilian dish that calls for a red wine, what grape varieties would be obvious choices to consider?
16. Name at least two DOPs that can make Schiava-based wine.
17. What is Sicily's only DOCG? If a winemaker in that area makes a wine that does not meet the DOCG's requirements, what DOC might be available for the label?

List of DOPs shown in Figure 5

- Aglianico del Taburno
- Aglianico del Vulture
- Bolgheri
- Carmignano
- Castel del Monte
- Cirò
- Etna
- Gattinara
- Lambrusco Grasparossa di Castelvetro
- Oltrepò Pavese
- Primitivo di Manduria
- Rosso Piceno
- Salice Salentino
- Taurasi
- Valpolicella

Capo Vaticano, Tropea, Calabria

Unit 5
White Wines of the Peninsula & Islands

This unit and the next are devoted to Italy's white wines. The international phenomenon of Pinot Grigio notwithstanding, the white wines of Italy are largely under-appreciated. The focus tends to be on Italy's great red wines, yet there are many gems among the whites, as well.

This unit focuses on the Italian peninsula and islands—areas that are strongly influenced by the sea. Many of the white wines throughout this part of the country, by no accident, pair extremely well with dishes that feature seafood. Unit 6 will then cover the northern regions, where farming and hunting are more important.

For now, we will concentrate on still, mostly dry wines. Sparkling white wines and sweet dessert-style whites will covered separately in Unit 7.

Regions covered in Unit 5

Learning Objectives

In Unit 5, we turn to white wines, focusing on those made in the Italian islands and the regions of the Italian peninsula. The learning objectives for this unit are:

- Major white grape varieties of the regions and where they are concentrated
- Commercially significant denominations
  - Which region are they located in?
  - White wines only, or other styles as well?
  - Primary grape variety or varieties
  - Single-variety, varietal, or blend?

White Grape Varieties of the Peninsula & Islands

We'll begin with an overview of the primary white grape varieties that are covered in this unit.

First and foremost is Trebbiano. Trebbiano is Italy's most prevalent white variety. It is found in abundance down the Adriatic coast from Emilia Romagna to northern Puglia. Trebbiano is important in other regions as well, particularly in Tuscany, Lazio, and Sicily.

Some other significant varieties in central Italy include the "three V's." Verdicchio is the signature white grape of Marche. Vermentino is increasingly important in Tuscany, although its real home is on the island of Sardinia. It is also the primary grape in Liguria. The third V, Vernaccia, is a key white grape in red-heavy Tuscany.

Besides Verdicchio, Marche features two other interesting native varieties: Passerina and Pecorino, the latter extending its range down into Abruzzo. Grechetto is the quality white grape of Emilia Romagna and Umbria. And Malvasia, which often appears in sweet wines, makes a famous dry wine in Lazio.

Campania has a set of white varieties that are more or less unique to that region:

- Fiano
- Falanghina
- Greco
- Coda di Volpe

Sicily produces a considerable amount of white wine. Like Campania, the island has a portfolio of white grape varieties that are grown almost nowhere else, including:

- Ansonica
- Catarratto
- Grecanico Dorato
- Grillo
- Zibibbo

Besides these unique varieties, Sicily grows considerable amounts of Trebbiano and a number of international varieties. For example, it has the largest concentration of Chardonnay of any region in Italy.

Sardinia has an indigenous grape called Nuragus as its second white variety after Vermentino.

You may have noticed that there are no white grape varieties listed for the foot of the Italian peninsula. That's because there's not a lot of white wine made in Calabria, Basilicata, or the lower two thirds of Puglia. This is red territory.

In the remainder of this unit, we'll go through these regions and their white varieties again, more or less counterclockwise, to talk about some of the better-known denominations that use these varieties.

Key indigenous white grape varieties of the peninsula and islands

Ansonica: Aka Insolia, Inzolia. Naturally tannic white grape. Light to medium bodied in Sicily; fuller bodied in Tuscany. Golden color. *Aromas & flavors:* (Tuscany) Citrus; (Sicily) yellow apple, dried apricot. *Best DOP:* Elba.

Catarratto: Most-planted Italian white variety. Two biotypes: Comune (higher sugar, lower acid) and Lucido. Medium to full bodied. *Aromas & flavors:* Sage, thyme, banana, pineapple, citrus; somewhat bitter finish.

Coda di Volpe: Low in acidity; high in extract and color. Austere on volcanic soils; richer and softer elsewhere. *Aromas & flavors:* Peach, pineapple, papaya, honey. *Best DOPs:* Taburno, Sannio.

Falanghina: Group of at least two distinct varieties: Falanghina Beneventana and Falanghina Flegrea. Both high in acidity. *Aromas & flavors:* (Flegrea) Peach, yellow apple, apricot, cherry pit; (Beneventana) less fruity, more floral. Both have a green, leafy note. *Best DOPs:* (Flegrea) Falanghina del Sannio; (Beneventana) Benevento.

Fiano: One of Italy's greatest white varieties. Light to full bodied; very versatile. Best on volcanic soils. Steely, minerally; ageworthy. *Aromas & flavors:* Hazelnut, green apple, pear, honey.

Grecanico Dorato: A biotype of Garganega (*see Unit 6*).

Grechetto: Two unrelated varieties: Grechetto di Orvieto and Grechetto di Todi (aka Grechetto Gentile or Rèbola). Todi is the better of the two, but both are often mixed in Grechetto wines. Light bodied; high in acidity. *Best DOPs:* Colli Bolognesi Pignoletto, Colli Martani. *Aromas & flavors:* Lemon, white flowers, chamomile, lime, yellow apple, anise.

Greco: Group of a dozen unrelated varieties, including some red ones. Most important:
- *Greco:* Campanian variety. Wines are full bodied, oily, tannic; deep yellow. Ageworthy. *Aromas & flavors:* Yellow flowers, honey, peach, pear, tropical fruit. *Best DOP:* Greco di Tufo.
- *Greco Bianco:* Calabrian variety; reportedly same as Malvasia di Lipari. *Best DOP:* Greco di Bianco.

Grillo: Crossing of Catarratto and Zibibbo. Crisp acidity. *Aromas & flavors:* Lemony, herbal; similar to Sauvignon Blanc. *Best DOPs:* Contea di Sclafani, Alcamo, Delia Nivolelli, Monreale.

Malvasia: Group of mostly unrelated varieties—17 different "Malvasias" on official list, most white, some red, one rosa. Primary white varieties:
- *Malvasia Bianca di Candia:* Most-planted Malvasia. Light bodied; high in acidity. *Aromas & flavors:* White flowers, citrus, green or yellow apple, herbs.
- *Malvasia Bianca Lunga:* Primary ingredient (with or without Trebbiano Toscano) in vin santo. Low acidity.
- *Malvasia del Lazio:* Aka Malvasia Puntinata. Highest-quality Malvasia. *Aromas & flavors:* Yellow fruit (peach, mango, banana, passionfruit), sage. *Best DOP:* Frascati. Crossing of Zibibbo and Schiava Grossa.
- *Malvasia di Candia Aromatica:* High-quality variety, especially for sweet wines. *Aromas & flavors:* Aromatic; tropical fruit and spice. *Best DOPs:* Colli Piacentini, Colli di Parma.
- *Malvasia di Lipari:* Primarily used for passito wines. *Aromas & flavors:* Peach, apricot, honey, orange. *Best DOP:* Malvasia delle Lipari. Genetically same as Greco Bianco (of Calabria).
- *Malvasia Istriana:* Often used for "orange wines." Minerally. *Aromas & flavors:* Peach, apricot, pear, wisteria, (with age) diesel. *Best DOPs:* Carso, Collio, Friuli Isonzo.

Nuragus: Delicate aromatics. *Best DOP:* Nuragus di Cagliari.

Passerina: Multiple biotypes; may be a group of distinct varieties under the same name. High acidity. *Aromas & flavors:* Ripe citrus, tropical fruit. *Best DOPs:* Offida, Controguerra.

Pecorino: High-quality variety. High acidity; high alcohol. *Aromas & flavors:* Apple, pear, delicately herbal (sage, thyme, mint). *Best DOP:* Offida.

Trebbiano: Prolific group of several unrelated varieties, all white. Only related ones are (1) Abruzzese and Spoletino and (2) di Lugana and di Soave (which are Verdicchio). Primary varieties:
- *Trebbiano Abruzzese:* The highest-quality Trebbiano (not counting the ones that are actually Verdicchio). High acidity. *Aromas & flavors:* White flowers, peach, citrus.

- *Trebbiano Toscano:* The most-planted Trebbiano. Same as Ugni Blanc, the grape of Cognac. High in acidity. *Aromas & flavors:* Generally neutral; can be delicately herbal and lemony.

Verdicchio: One of Italy's greatest white varieties. Aka Trebbiano di Lugana, Trebbiano di Soave. High acidity; ageworthy. *Aromas & flavors:* Floral, delicately fruity, almond. *Best DOPs:* Castelli di Jesi Verdicchio Riserva, Verdicchio di Matelica Riserva.

Vermentino: Biotypes include Liguria's Pigato and Piedmont's Favorita. *Aromas & flavors:* Citrus, tropical fruit, acacia, rosemary, thyme; saline finish.

Vernaccia: Group of several unrelated varieties, some red. Primary ones:

- *Vernaccia di Oristano:* Sardinian variety. *Aromas & flavors:* Apricot, hazelnut, almond, white chocolate, herbs. *Best DOP:* Vernaccia di Oristano.
- *Vernaccia di San Gimignano:* Tuscan variety. *Aromas & flavors:* Relatively neutral. *Best DOP:* Vernaccia di San Gimignano.

Zibibbo: Aka Moscato di Alessandria (Muscat of Alexandria), an offspring of Moscato Bianco and member of the large Muscat family of varieties. *Aromas & flavors:* Apricot, orange blossom, lily of the valley, ginger, dried herbs; (sweet wines) orange jam, caramel, fig, raisin. *Best DOP:* Pantelleria.

Trebbiano

Trebbiano is one of just a handful of grape varieties that are truly widespread in Italy. It is the most planted white grape variety in Italy, second only to Sangiovese overall. Trebbiano is found in nearly every region, but is most abundant in the peninsula, especially in Emilia Romagna, Puglia, and Abruzzo.

The fact of the matter, however, is that Trebbiano as such doesn't exist. There are actually several different grapes called Trebbiano that are not closely related. The trouble is that they are not always specifically identified, so the entire Trebbiano family is often treated as a single variety. The differences among the various Trebbianos are significant, however, and are worth learning more about.

Although Trebbiano is a native of Italy, there is four times as much of it growing in France, where it is known as Ugni Blanc and is used primarily for making Cognac and Armagnac. Small amounts are found in several other countries (mainly Argentina and Uruguay).

It is often used as bulk wine or for blending, and only rarely as a varietal. Nevertheless, Trebbiano is used as a varietal or blending partner in dozens of denominations, some of which will be mentioned later in this unit.

Trebbiano vines in the Falerio DOC in Marche

Vermentino-Based DOPs

Vermentino is one of the few white grape varieties that have a strong association with more than one region.

It is the most important white variety of Sardinia and the most important variety, white or red, of Liguria. In addition, it makes some of the best white wines of Tuscany.

Vermentino is even more widespread under other guises. In Liguria, the variety known as Pigato is actually a biotype of Vermentino, meaning that it is genetically the same as Vermentino but differs somewhat in performance. Likewise, a white grape called Favorita in Piedmont is also genetically Vermentino, as is Rolle in Corsica (the big French island that lies between Liguria and Sardinia).

Among the well-known denominations for Vermentino wines are:

- Vermentino di Gallura DOCG (Sardinia)
- Vermentino di Sardegna DOC (Sardinia)
- Bolgheri DOC (Tuscany)

Liguria

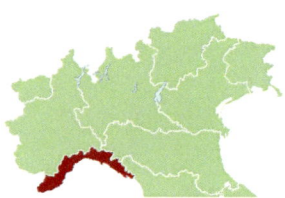

If you are lucky enough to make it over to the Italian Riviera, the wine you will be served as you bask in the sun on a clifftop perch overlooking the azure waters will likely be white and probably made from Vermentino.

More than 40% of Liguria's wine is made from Vermentino—either under that name or the local name Pigato. Of course, the region's production is very small—second smallest of all the regions—and the tourists are very thirsty, so not much Ligurian wine gets exported. Denominations you might find at a specialty wine shop include Colli di Luni DOC and Riviera Ligure di Ponente DOC.

Sardinia

Two thirds of Italy's Vermentino is planted on the island of Sardinia, where it is the number one white grape variety. In fact, Sardinia's sole DOCG is dedicated to Vermentino.

There are two main DOPs for Vermentino on the island. Vermentino di Sardegna DOC is one of the large denominations on Sardinia that allows producers to make varietal wines from anywhere on the island. Vermentino di Gallura DOCG, also a varietal wine, comes from a more specific area on the northern tip of Sardinia.

A second white variety of note in Sardinia is Nuragus, a variety unique to this region. There is a denomination for this variety: Nuragus di Cagliari DOC, named after the regional capital city Cagliari. It encompasses the southern half of the island.

Recall from Unit 4 that a *nuragus* is one of those iconic prehistoric structures found all over Sardinia, after which this grape may be named. Those structures are also referenced in the name of the catchall IGP Isola dei Nuraghi. However, don't be confused into thinking that IGP Isola dei Nuraghi is named after the grape variety; there are many varieties besides Nuragus, white and red, that can be used in the wines of that IGP (as is true of almost all IGPs). But yes, there is such a thing as an IGP Isola dei Nuraghi Nuragus wine.

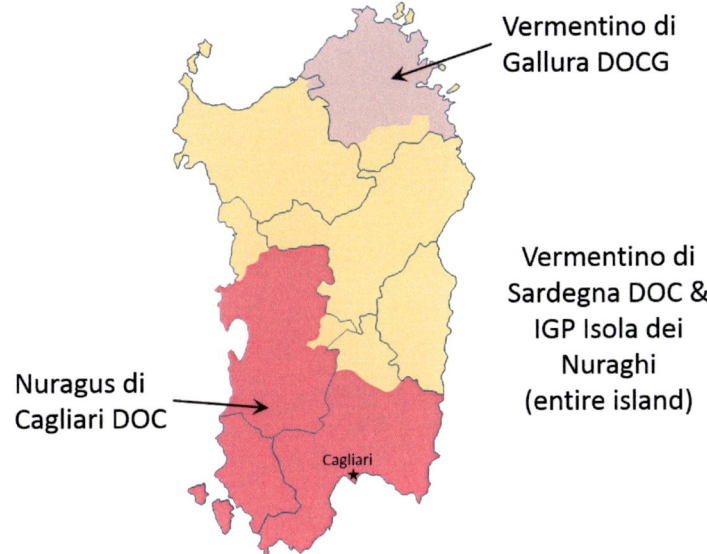

Vermentino di Gallura DOCG

Vermentino di Sardegna DOC & IGP Isola dei Nuraghi (entire island)

Nuragus di Cagliari DOC

Cagliari

A nuragus stands watch on a lonely islet as it has for millennia.

A seaside vineyard in Sardinia

Tuscany

Tuscany should not be your first choice of regions to visit if you're not a fan of red wines—almost 90% of Tuscany's production is red or rosato. Nonetheless, the region does have a few notable white wines.

The most planted white grape variety in Tuscany is Trebbiano; in fact, the most common member of the Trebbiano family is called Trebbiano Toscano. However, Trebbiano Toscano wines—with the exception of some sweet ones—are rarely distinguished.

More interesting are Tuscany's Vermentinos, which come from vineyards along the coast. One denomination that produces Vermentino is Bolgheri DOC, which in addition to its famous red wines allows both Vermentino- and Sauvignon Blanc–based white wines. Other sources of Vermentino include Maremma Toscana DOC, the island of Elba, and vineyards farther north close to Liguria.

Inland, the go-to white wine is Vernaccia. Vernaccia's home is the hill town of San Gimignano, which lies

San Gimignano, Tuscany

just within the Chianti area. Vernaccia di San Gimignano, with a history as long as Chianti's, is Tuscany's only DOCG for white wine.

Given the relative lack of white wine denominations, many Tuscan white wines are labeled at the IGP level—especially IGP Toscana, which covers the whole region and permits many kinds of wines, white as well as red.

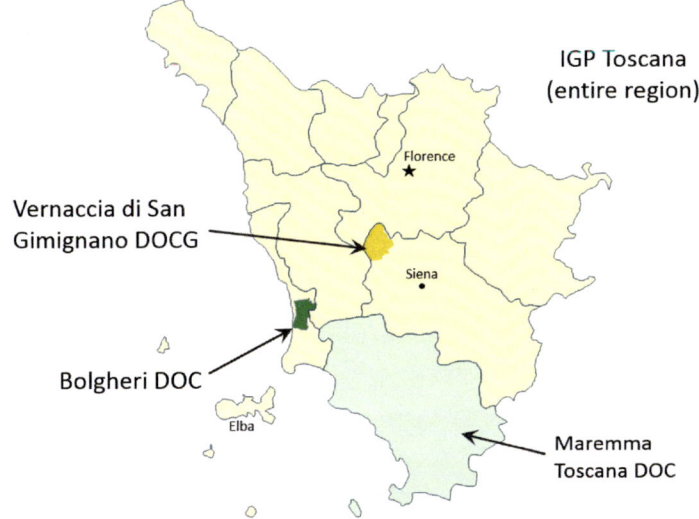

IGP Toscana
(entire region)

Florence

Vernaccia di San
Gimignano DOCG

Siena

Bolgheri DOC

Elba

Maremma
Toscana DOC

Grechetto-Based DOPs

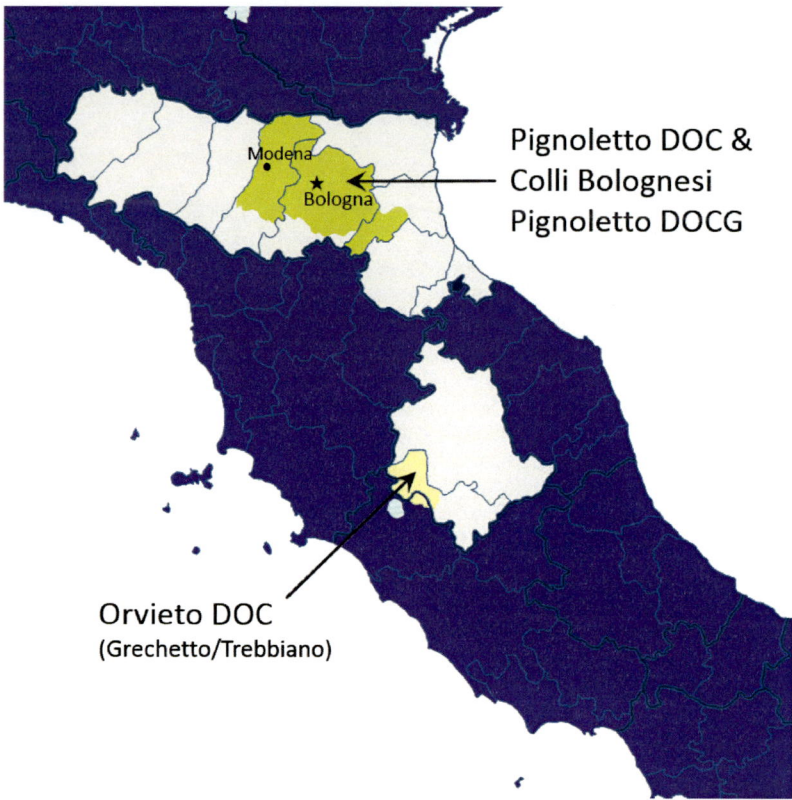

Pignoletto DOC &
Colli Bolognesi
Pignoletto DOCG

Orvieto DOC
(Grechetto/Trebbiano)

An important white grape variety of central Italy is Grechetto. It has long been associated with Umbria, but was also a prominent grape of Emilia Romagna under a different name. Only recently has DNA analysis determined that the variety known as Pignoletto in Emilia Romagna was in fact the same as Umbria's Grechetto.

This caused some concern in Emilia Romagna, where they are proud of their Pignoletto wine and didn't want its identity to be lost if producers in Emilia Romagna were forced to label their wines as Grechetto or if producers in other areas decided to call their Grechetto-based wines Pignoletto. The answer was to create a new denomination, the Pignoletto DOC, to preserve the name and restrict its use to the local area. This is one of Italy's newest denominations. There is also a DOCG, Colli Bolognesi Pignoletto, that covers the same area as the DOC—with more stringent viticultural requirements, of course. Both Pignoletto DOC and Colli Bolognesi Pignoletto DOCG produce only varietal Grechetto wines.

Pignoletto notwithstanding, the denomination most closely associated with Grechetto is probably Orvieto DOC. This denomination around the town of Orvieto lies mostly in Umbria, but also partly in Lazio. It is a relatively high-volume DOC that produces only white wines, the best of which are based on Grechetto. However, Orvieto wines can be based on Grechetto and/or Trebbiano and can in fact be 100% Trebbiano, so there can be significant variation from one producer to the next.

Lazio

Just south of Umbria is the region of Lazio. Lazio is the mirror image of Tuscany in that it has one of the highest percentages of white wine compared to red wine of any Italian region. Roughly four of every five bottles of wine from Lazio are white.

As previously noted, a sliver of the Orvieto DOC, with its mix of Grechetto and Trebbiano, lies in Lazio. But Lazio's reputation rests more on two other storied white wine areas that are entirely within Lazio.

One is right next to Orvieto DOC, around Lake Bolsena, a crater lake from an ancient volcano in northern Lazio. This denomination goes by the improbable name of Est! Est!! Est!!! di Montefiascone DOC. The name comes from an entertaining if dubious tale about a bishop traveling to Rome who was something of a wine aficionado. The bishop sent one of his assistants ahead to scout out inns to see if their wine was any good, with instructions to write "Est" ("It is") on the door if the wine was decent. In the town of Montefiascone, the assistant was so impressed with the local wine that he wrote Est on the door three times.

This wine—which is usually shortened to Est! Est!! Est!!!—is a blend based primarily on Trebbiano Toscano and can be either sweet or dry. How many Ests the assistant would write today is unclear, but it's a good story.

Once that bishop arrived in Rome—just like the modern tourist—he would probably have been served a wine from Frascati. This area in the Alban Hills not far from Rome has been slaking the thirst of the metropolis of Rome for two thousand years. Frascati Superiore DOCG and Frascati DOC both produce only white wines based on Malvasia. The wines can be

sweet or dry. Frascati's reputation was damaged a few decades ago by overproduction, but the denominations are undergoing a revival as the remaining producers are reducing yields and starting to replant with a superior type of Malvasia (Malvasia del Lazio).

Orvieto DOC
(Grechetto/
Trebbiano)

UMBRIA

Est! Est!! Est!!! di
Montefiascone DOC
(Trebbiano)

Rome

LAZIO

Frascati DOC &
Frascati Superiore DOCG
(Malvasia)

Campania

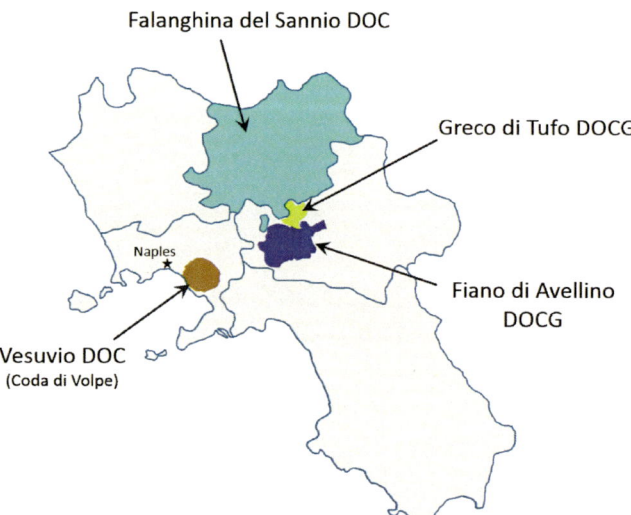

Falanghina del Sannio DOC

Greco di Tufo DOCG

Naples

Fiano di Avellino DOCG

Vesuvio DOC
(Coda di Volpe)

Top: *The Amalfi Coast south of the Bay of Naples is one of Campania's—and Italy's—most treasured vistas.*

Campania is well known for its white wines, which make up almost half of its production.

The white grape varieties associated primarily with Campania are:

- Fiano, one of Italy's most respected white grape varieties
- Greco, so named because it is believed to have been brought to Italy by the ancient Greeks
- Falanghina
- Coda di Volpe, which translates as "Foxtail," which is what the grape clusters' shape reminded people of

Campania has two DOCGs for white wines: Fiano di Avellino, a varietal wine from Fiano, and Greco di Tufo—you guessed it—a varietal wine from Greco. The primary denomination for Falanghina is Falanghina del Sannio DOC. All three of these denominations are located in the hills and higher elevations of the Campanian Apennines.

As for Coda di Volpe, its claim to fame is being a key part of the white blend for the Vesuvio DOC. In Unit 4, this denomination was mentioned for its red wines based on Piedirosso. The Vesuvio DOC encircles Mount Vesuvius, which towers over Naples and Pompeii, the town it buried intact two thousand years ago. Now dormant, Vesuvius is the very essence of volcanic soil, which suits Coda di Volpe just fine.

Vesuvio DOC has a unique category of wine called Lacryma (or Lacrima) Christi, the "Tears of Christ." This traditional term, which can be used for red, white, or rosato wines, is essentially the equivalent of *superiore* in other denominations. It indicates a higher minimum alcohol level, attained by using riper grapes.

Mount Vesuvius forms a backdrop for the archeological wonder of Pompeii, a Roman city buried by ash during an eruption of Vesuvius in A.D. 79.

Sicily

As mentioned in Unit 4, Sicily is the largest producer of wine in southern Italy and makes more white wine than red.

Its dominant grape variety by far, white or red, is Catarratto; however, Catarratto is considered a low-quality blending variety and is rarely produced as a varietal wine and labeled as such.

Sicily has several other indigenous white varieties that have a better reputation, including:

- Grillo, Sicily's most-planted quality white grape variety
- Ansonica—also known as Insolia or Inzolia—which is almost exclusive to Sicily except for a tiny amount in Tuscany
- Grecanico Dorato, which happens to be genetically identical with an important Venetian grape called Garganega (covered in Unit 6)
- Zibibbo, used primarily for sweet wines

These varieties may be seen by themselves or in various blends. In addition, there are large plantings of Chardonnay and Trebbiano.

Sicily has several DOCs for its white wine, but most are not familiar on the export market. The majority of white wine is labeled as either Sicilia DOC or IGP Terre Siciliane, which cover the entire region.

Temple of Concordia, Agrigento, Sicily

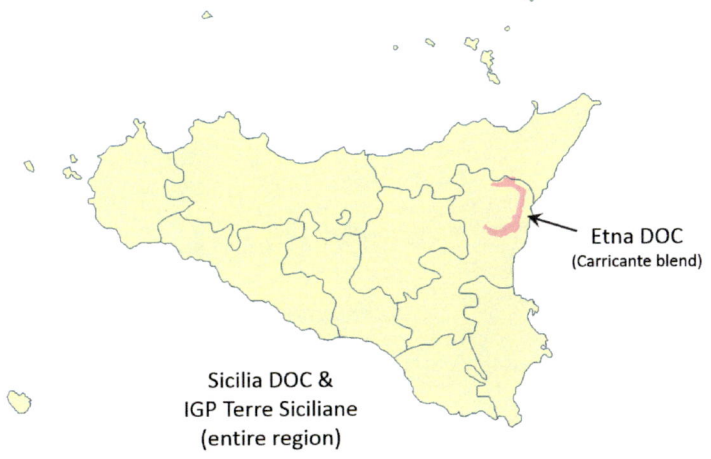

Above: *Mount Etna is a classic shield volcano near the town of Catania in north-eastern Sicily.*

One denomination that *is* well known internationally is Etna DOC, located around the base of Mount Etna, one of the most active volcanoes in the world, erupting frequently. The vineyards of Etna DOC are on the lower slopes of the 11,000-foot (3,300-meter) volcano, at elevations of 1,000–3,600 feet, which provides cooler temperatures than are typical for Sicily. In addition to red wines made from Nerello Mascalese, this denomination produces white wines from a blend based on a minor variety, Carricante.

Etna DOC
(Carricante blend)

Sicilia DOC &
IGP Terre Siciliane
(entire region)

Southeastern Italy

The bottom of the Italian boot, as noted earlier, is largely focused on red wine. The climate in this area is generally hot and dry in the summer, so it is not conducive to the high-acidity white wines that Italians generally prefer.

Molise, Basilicata, and Calabria collectively produce a minuscule amount of white wine. Probably the best-known white-wine denomination in southeastern Italy is Cirò DOC, which though known primarily for red wines made from Gaglioppo, also makes white wines based on Greco (80% minimum, like the red Cirò). For the record, Greco is another of those groups of grape varieties that share a name but are not in fact related; Cirò is made from Greco Bianco, which is different from the Greco of Campania.

Puglia, meanwhile, actually produces quite a bit of white wine, even if very little of it is at the DOP level. Trebbiano is the main white variety of Puglia, grown mostly in the northern section adjacent to Molise—the same area where Puglia's Montepulciano is grown.

Isola di Dino, Calabria

Marche and Verdicchio-Based DOPs

The last region for this unit is Le Marche. This region is home to one of Italy's finest white grape varieties, Verdicchio.

Marche's most famous white wine denominations, found near the towns of Jesi and Matelica, make varietal Verdicchio wines. Each area has a standard DOC version and a riserva DOCG. The ones near Jesi are Verdicchio dei Castelli di Jesi DOC and Castelli di Jesi Verdicchio Riserva DOCG (note the somewhat confusing reversal of the name). Jesi is not far from the coast, while Matelica lies on the east side of a mountain ridge in an interior valley. Its denominations are Verdicchio di Matelica DOC and Verdicchio di Matelica Riserva DOCG. The Matelica DOPs produce much less wine than their Jesi counterparts.

Another interesting white wine denomination in Marche is Offida DOCG, which was discussed earlier as a source of varietal Montepulciano red wines but also produces varietal white wines from either Passerina or Pecorino.

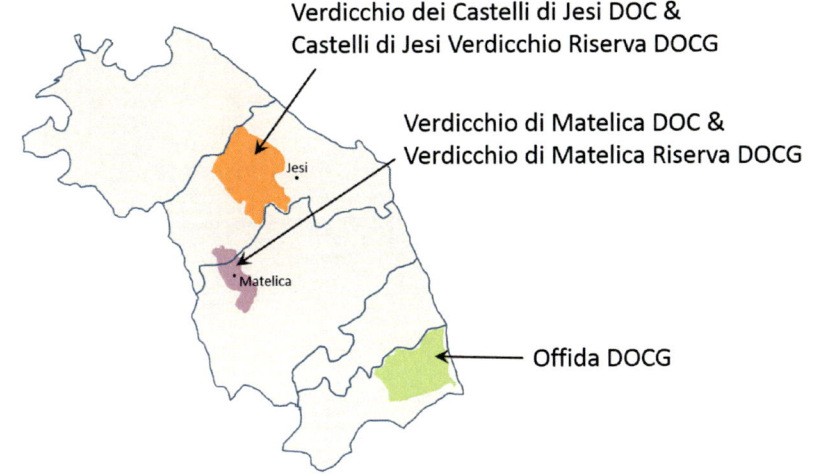

Verdicchio dei Castelli di Jesi DOC &
Castelli di Jesi Verdicchio Riserva DOCG

Verdicchio di Matelica DOC &
Verdicchio di Matelica Riserva DOCG

Offida DOCG

Abruzzo

Moving up the Adriatic coast, we come to Abruzzo. The dominant white grape variety here is unquestionably Trebbiano.

Abruzzo contains the largest denomination for Trebbiano, called simply Trebbiano d'Abruzzo DOC. It covers the same area as the Montepulciano d'Abruzzo and Cerasuolo d'Abruzzo DOCs—which is to say, all of the region except the mountains. Of course, since the grape variety name is in the denomination name, it must be a varietal wine with at least 85% Trebbiano.

The good news is that Abruzzo has cultivated one of the highest quality members of the Trebbiano family, known as Trebbiano Abruzzese.

Unfortunately, over the years, twice as much of the less exciting Trebbiano Toscano has been planted in the region, and the DOC rules allow either or both of the varieties to be used in Trebbiano d'Abruzzo. Thus, there is considerable variability in these wines.

Trebbiano d'Abruzzo DOC

Seafood-Based Italian Cuisine

Fish and shellfish play a large role in Italian cuisine in the areas that are close to the sea. The Mediterranean has provided a bounty of readily available food for millennia, and people in coastal areas and those who lived on the islands incorporated seafood into all sorts of dishes.

In these areas, shellfish may be served by themselves, with risotto, or with pasta. Freshly caught fish are featured in coastal regions as well, with or without pasta. And there are innumerable combinations.

With fish and shellfish making up a significant part of their diet, the people of the coastal and island regions naturally favored the production of wines that would complement these maritime ingredients—often crisp, light- to medium-bodied white wines or lighter, low-tannin reds.

Many of the white wines discussed in this unit are produced in these sea-facing areas. Remember that, in general, we're talking about wines that come from areas where seafood figures prominently in the local cuisine. That doesn't mean all of these wines should be paired *only* with seafood, or even that every one of them goes well with seafood at all. However, the majority of these wines are high in acid, unoaked, fresh rather than aged, and relatively simple and mild flavored, so that they will usually complement a seafood meal or a first course of fish or shellfish.

Pictured (top to bottom): *Frutti di mare misto (mixed seafood), shrimp scampi, black risotto with fried calamari, spaghetti con cozze (with mussels)*

Pictured (clockwise from top): *Gilthead bream (orado) stuffed with shrimp, whole gilthead bream awaiting preparation, baked Sicilian swordfish with linguine, fried sardines, whole roasted sea bass*

Pronunciation Practice: More Producers

Unit 3 included a list of producers and brand names from Tuscany as a pronunciation exercise. Below are other well-known producers and brands from Piedmont, Veneto, and other regions. Again, practice saying these names aloud.

Piedmont

1. Ceretto (cheh-*ret*-toh)
2. Coppo (*kohp*-po)
3. Gaja (*guy*-yah)
4. Giacosa (jah-*koh*-zah)
5. Marchesi di Gresy (mar-*kay*-zee dee *gray*-zee)
6. Michele Chiarlo (mee-*keh*-lay kee-*ahr*-lo)
7. Pio Cesare (*pee*-yo *chay*-zah-ray)
8. Principessa Gavia (prin-chee-*pess*-sa *gah*-viya)
9. Prunotto (proo-*noht*-toh)
10. Roberto Voerzio (roh-*bair*-toh *vwair*-tziyo)
11. Vietti (vee-*yet*-tee)

Trentino–Alto Adige

12. Alois Lageder (*al*-loyz lah-*gay*-da)
13. Cavit (cah-*veet*)
14. Mezzacorona (medza-koh-*roh*-na)
15. Santa Margherita (*san*-ta mar-gay-*ree*-ta)
16. Tiefenbrunner (*teef*-en-broo-ner)
17. Tramin (*trah*-meen)

Veneto

18. Allegrini (ahl-lay-*gree*-nee)
19. Anselmi (ahn-*sell*-me)
20. Masi (*mah*-zee)
21. Nicolis (nee-*koh*-leess)
22. Pieropan (pee-yeh-ro-*pan*)
23. Quintarelli (kwin-tah-*rell*-lee)
24. Sorelle Bronca (soh-*rell*-lay *brohn*-ka)
25. Speri (*spay*-ree)
26. Tedeschi (teh-*dess*-kee)
27. Tommasi (tohm-*mah*-zee)
28. Villa Sandi (*veel*-la *san*-dee)
29. Zardetto (dzar-*deht*-tow)
30. Zenato (dzeh-*nah*-tow)

Other Regions

31. Argiolas (ahr-*joh*-lahss)
32. Arnaldo Caprai (ahr-*nahl*-doh cah-*pry*)
33. Di Majo Norante (dee *my*-yo noh-*rahn*-tay)
34. Ecco Domani (*eh*-koh doh-*mah*-nee)
35. Feudo Maccari (*fyoo*-doh mahk-*kah*-ree)
36. Garofoli (gah-*roh*-foh-lee)
37. Mastroberardino (mass-stro-behr-ahr-*dee*-no)
38. Montevetrano (mohn-tay-veh-*trah*-no)
39. Regaleali (ray-gah-lee-*ah*-lay)
40. Umani Ronchi (oo-*mah*-nee *rohn*-kee)

Unit 5 Exercises

Note: Some of these exercises refer back to information discussed in previous units.

1. Name the most planted white and red grape varieties in Italy. Where are they mostly found?
2. Name the most prominent white grape variety of the following regions.
    - Tuscany
    - Sardinia
    - Abruzzo
    - Marche
3. When selecting a wine to serve with Sicilian seafood-based dish that calls for a white wine, what grape varieties would be obvious choices to consider? What denomination might be used for any of these?
4. Fill in the blanks in the following table. (There may be more than one correct answer in some spaces.)

Denomination	Level	Primary Grape Variety	Color	Region
	DOCG	Fiano		
		Negroamaro		
	DOCG		White	Tuscany
	DOC	Dolcetto		
			White	Abruzzo
		Greco		
	DOC		White	Sardinia

5. On an outline map of the regions of Italy (Fig. 2 on p. 22), write the following grape varieties in the region or regions where they are most commonly found.
    - Pecorino
    - Fiano
    - Zibibbo
    - Nuragus
    - Coda di Volpe
    - Grillo
    - Passerina
    - Vermentino
    - Greco
6. What difference(s) would you expect between two wines that are labeled identically except that only one is labeled "Superiore"?
7. For each of the following grape varieties, write down the name of a denomination whose wines are based on that variety.
    - Trebbiano
    - Negroamaro
    - Pecorino
    - Frappato
    - Vermentino
    - Montepulciano
    - Vernaccia
    - Barbera
    - Sangiovese
8. In which region is the second largest city in Italy, site of the 2015 World's Fair, located?

9. On the outline map at right (Fig. 6), draw the approximate boundaries of each of the following denominations. If necessary, review the maps in the handouts or presentations for units 3 through 5 first, then do the exercise. Check to see how close you came to the actual location and size.

- Aglianico del Taburno
- Chianti Classico
- Fiano di Avellino
- Cesanese del Piglio
- Falanghina del Sannio
- Verdicchio dei Castelli di Jesi
- Montepulciano d'Abruzzo
- Terre Siciliane
- Offida
- Maremma Toscana
- Vermentino di Gallura
- Etna
- Salice Salentino
- Taurasi

10. In the above list, what is the quality level for each denomination?
11. Which Italian region has the most DOPs? Which region is second?
12. Fill in the blanks in the following table. (There may be more than one correct answer in some spaces.)

Denomination	Level	Primary Grape Variety	Color	Region
Vesuvio			White	
_____ di Matelica				
Vino Nobile di Montepulciano				
Cirò			Red	
Valdadige				
_____ di Tufo				

13. Describe the difference between PGI, IGT, and IGP.
14. What is another name used on labels for Ansonica?
15. Name at least five DOPs that can make Nebbiolo-based wine.

Figure 6. Outline of the Italian Peninsula and Islands
Download a pdf of this image at http://italianwinecentral.com/exercise-maps

The Langhe hills of Piedmont with the Alps in the background

White Wines of Northern Italy

Unit 5 discussed the peninsula and islands of Italy, areas that are close to the Mediterranean Sea, where fish and shellfish are an everyday part of the cuisine and where many of the wines are made to go with this oceanic cuisine.

In this unit, we'll examine the northern tier of regions along the Alps, as well as the broad Po Valley— places where, historically, fresh seafood was unavailable and the cuisine was based on the crops farmers could grow, livestock they could raise, and game animals they could catch.

The wines that developed in the interior areas over the centuries were selected to go well with the meat and starch dishes here. In addition, the inland and upland regions are generally cooler and less sunny than the seaside regions in the fall and winter, calling for wines with a bit more substance. Reds and whites alike from the interior tend to be fuller bodied, more complex, and somewhat earthier than the average coastal wine. However, that

Regions covered in Unit 6

does not necessarily equate with lower acidity as might be the case in other countries, because most Italian grape varieties are naturally high in acid.

To begin, we'll examine the geographic range of the primary white grape varieties of the northern Italian wines.

Learning Objectives

Unit 6 completes the discussion of white wines. The learning objectives for this unit are:
- Major white grape varieties of the interior areas in Italy and where they are concentrated
- Commercially significant denominations
  - Which region are they located in?
  - White wines only, or other styles as well?
  - Primary grape variety or varieties
  - Single-variety, varietal, or blend?

White Grape Varieties of Northern Italy

We now turn to the white grape varieties grown in the plains, hills, and mountain valleys of northern Italy. Apart from international varieties, there is very little crossover of the northern grapes with those of points south.

To illustrate this, take Trebbiano, Italy's most prevalent white variety, which is widely planted in most regions of the peninsula and in Sicily. In the northern regions, Trebbiano is almost completely absent—except for an area in Lombardy and Veneto where one specific type of Trebbiano is grown. And, it turns out, that so-called Trebbiano isn't really a Trebbiano at all!

Some of the most abundant white varieties in the north are used mainly to make sparkling wine and not as often for still white wines. These include:

- Glera, grown mostly in Veneto
- Moscato in Piedmont
- Chardonnay, from Lombardy all the way over to Friuli–Venezia Giulia

Although these varieties will be mentioned in this unit, they will get more

of the focus when we cover sparkling wine in Unit 7.

The most important white variety in Italy for still wines is Pinot Grigio, 90% of which comes from the northern tier. This is a variety that is well known to most wine drinkers worldwide and is the top-selling category of Italian table wine in the United States. Although most widely recognized as Pinot Grigio today, this grape is an international variety that originated in France, where it is called Pinot Gris.

Another major white variety for still wines is Garganega, which is planted extensively in south-central Veneto. This ancient variety is an ancestor of many other Italian grapes. It has also been shown to be genetically the same as Sicily's Grecanico Dorato, which is now considered a biotype of Garganega.

Other white grape varieties of the Italian north are smaller in production than the ones listed above and tend to be localized to just one or two regions. In Piedmont, for example, well-known white grapes include Cortese, Arneis, and Erbaluce, but these are rare outside Piedmont.

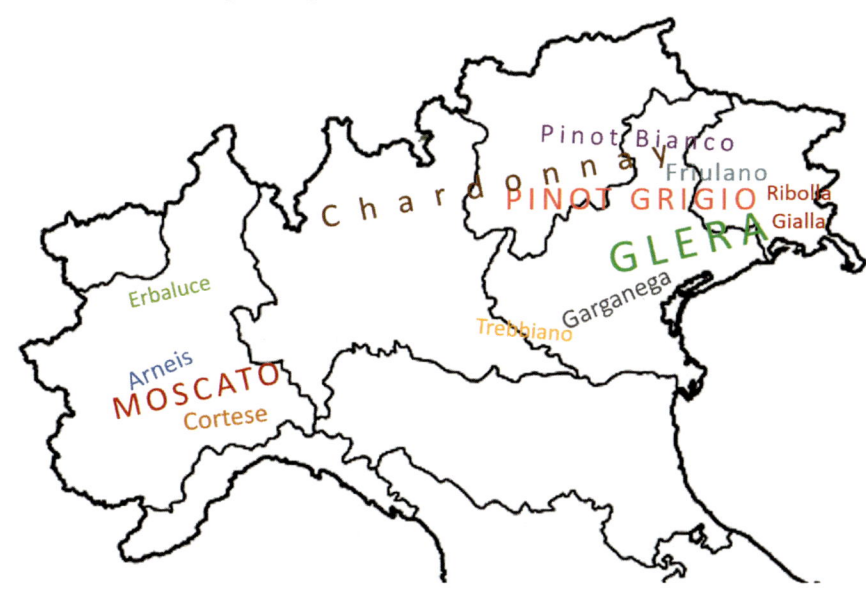

Glera

Friulano is a variety found in both Friuli–Venezia Giulia and Veneto. Until a few years ago, this grape was called Tocai Friulano. However, the Hungarian city of Tokaj, home of a famous type of sweet dessert wine, objected to the misappropriation of its name, and the European Union ruled in Tokaj's favor. The name of the grape variety was therefore changed to just Friulano—but in the Veneto, they prefer to call it Tai, a shortened form of Tocai.

A couple more varieties of note in Italy's north include Ribolla Gialla, a variety mainly grown in Friuli–Venezia Giulia, and Pinot Bianco, an international variety (aka Pinot Blanc) that is grown throughout the northeast for both still and sparkling wines.

The next segments will go over some of the better known denominations that use these white grape varieties of northern Italy.

Key indigenous white grape varieties of northern Italy

Ansonica: Aka Insolia, Inzolia. Naturally tannic white grape. Light to medium bodied in Sicily; fuller bodied in Tuscany. Golden color. *Aromas & flavors:* (Tuscany) Citrus; (Sicily) yellow apple, dried apricot. *Best DOP:* Elba.

Arneis: Sweet; low in acid. Straw green color. *Aromas & flavors:* White flowers, chamomile, peach, pear, apricot, citrus, almond. *Best DOP:* Roero.

Cortese: Very high in acidity; distinctive minerality. *Aromas & flavors:* Lemon, mineral, white flowers, herbs. *Best DOP:* Gavi, especially Rovereto frazione.

Erbaluce: High to very high acidity. *Aromas & flavors:* Floral, green apple, lemon, mineral, white flowers, apricot. *Best DOPs:* Erbaluce di Caluso, Colline Novaresi, Coste della Sesia.

Friulano: Pale straw green color. *Aromas & flavors:* White flowers, almond, green apple. Same as Sauvignon Vert (Sauvignonasse).

Garganega: One of Italy's greatest white varieties. Also one of its oldest, related to many other varieties. Many biotypes, including Grecanico Dorato. Steely, minerally, ageworthy. *Aromas & flavors:* White flowers, apricot, citrus, yellow apple, hay. *Best DOPs:* Soave, Gambellara, Bianco di Custoza, (as Grecanico Dorato) Alcamo.

Glera: Two distinct but related varieties: Glera Tondo (the most common Glera) and Glera Lunga—both interplanted in vineyards and blended into Prosecco. High in acidity. *Best DOP:* Conigliano Valdobbiadene Prosecco, especially the Cartizze subzone. *Aromas & flavors:* Buttercup, green apple, white peach.

Moscato Bianco: Most widespread member and probably progenitor of the Muscat family of varieties. Low acidity. *Aromas & flavors:* Grapefruit, floral. *Best DOP:* Moscato d'Asti.

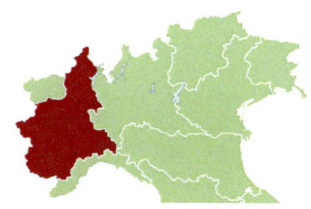

Piedmont

This survey of northern Italy will begin again in the west with Piedmont. Here, the primary white grape variety is Moscato. However, as mentioned, Moscato is used almost exclusively for sweet and effervescent wines—most notably from the Asti DOCG for sparkling and frizzante wines—so it will be covered in Unit 7.

For still (nonsparkling) wine, the important white grape varieties in Piedmont are Cortese, Arneis, and Erbaluce, each of which has one DOCG associated with it.

The most famous of Piedmont's white wine denominations is the DOCG for Cortese: Gavi DOCG, located in southeastern Piedmont. Remember from Unit 2 that Piedmont is unusual in that many of its premier wines are required to be 100% of a single variety. The wines of Gavi, as an example, are all 100% Cortese. In fact, it is sometimes labeled as Cortese di Gavi DOCG, just to make things clear. You may also see it labeled "Gavi di Gavi"—but only if it comes from the town of Gavi itself

Gavi is not exactly a coastal wine, but it is the closest thing Piedmont has

to one, because it is located near a pass in the Ligurian Alps that has always been the main route between Piedmont and the Mediterranean coast near Genoa.

The second most important of Piedmont's still-wine white grape varieties is Arneis. Its best examples come from the Roero DOCG. Although Roero was mentioned in Unit 2 as a producer of red wines from Nebbiolo, it is better known for its white wines made from Arneis. These wines are varietal wines, but do not have to reach the 100% level—Roero has set the minimum at 95% Arneis.

Erbaluce is probably the least familiar of Piedmont's DOCG white grape varieties, but it is the primary white grape of northern Piedmont. Its principal denomination is

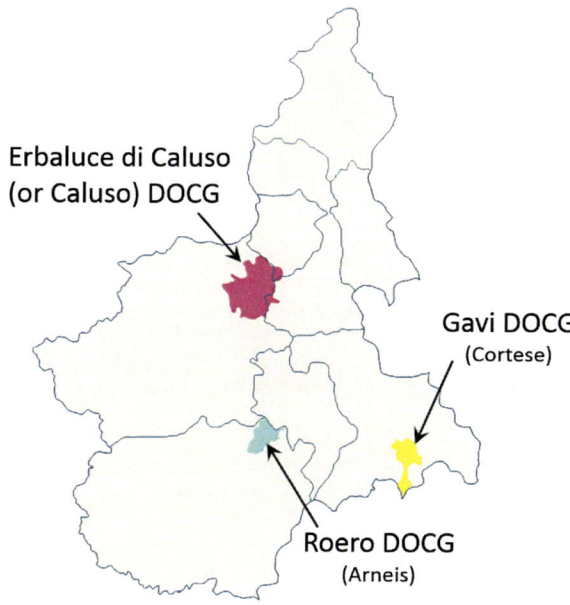

Erbaluce di Caluso (or Caluso) DOCG

Gavi DOCG (Cortese)

Roero DOCG (Arneis)

Cortese di Gavi is an alternative name for the Gavi denomination, as is Gavi di Gavi if the wine comes from the town of Gavi itself.

Erbaluce di Caluso DOCG, also called simply Caluso DOCG, made from 100% Erbaluce.

Unit 2 also introduced some large district- or regional-size DOCs that allow a wide range of styles and grape varieties—including white wines made from numerous indigenous and international varieties. These denominations include:

- Langhe DOC, which surrounds Roero and allows Arneis wines, among others
- Monferrato DOC, which is adjacent to Gavi and produces mainly blends
- Piemonte DOC, which encompasses all of these denominations

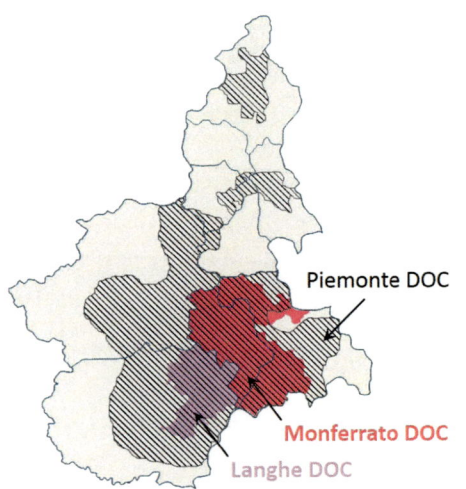

Valle d'Aosta

The region of Valle d'Aosta is the smallest producer of wine in Italy, and white wine makes up only a third of its output. All told, Valle d'Aosta produces only about 50,000 cases of white wine annually. Its leading white variety is a local grape called Prié Blanc. Nearly all of its wine is labeled as Valle d'Aosta or Vallée d'Aoste DOC.

Oltrepò Pavese

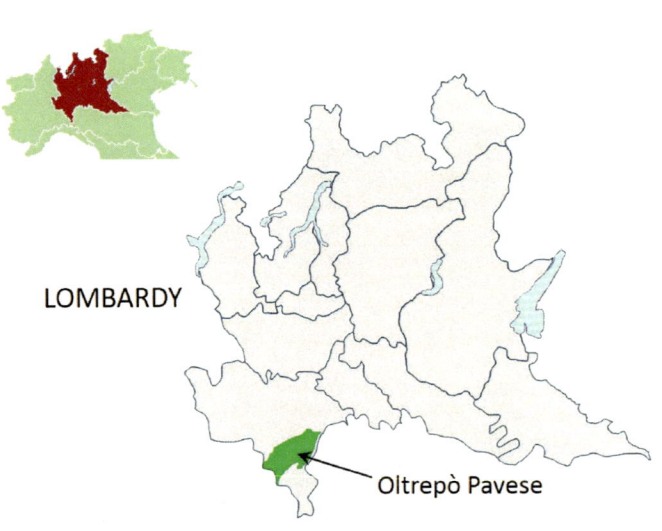

LOMBARDY

Oltrepò Pavese

Lombardy is well known for its sparkling wines, which will be covered in Unit 7. The largest source of still white wine in Lombardy is the fertile triangle formed by Piedmont on the west, Emilia Romagna on the east, and the Pò River on the north.

The Oltrepò Pavese DOC, introduced in Unit 2 for its red wines, produces a considerable amount of wine in all styles, including white wine made from mostly international varieties like Chardonnay and Riesling. There is also a separate Oltrepò Pavese denomination specifically for varietal Pinot Grigio—called, logically enough, Oltrepò Pavese Pinot Grigio DOC.

Lake Garda Area DOPs

Lake Garda, or Lago di Garda, lies on the border between Lombardy and Veneto, with a small portion in Trentino.

It is Italy's largest lake and creates significant moderating climatic effects in the neighboring vineyards, cooling them in the summer and preventing frost early and late in the season. Several DOPs crowd around the lake, including the Bardolino DOPs—for red wines only—which were discussed in Unit 2.

Another denomination mentioned in Unit 2 was the Garda DOC, which nearly surrounds the lake and is in both Lombardy and Veneto. Garda is a denomination for red, rosato (chiaretto), and white wines, mostly varietally labeled wines from any of a number of possible varieties.

The Lugana DOC also crosses the Lombardy-Veneto border. All of Lugana's wines are varietals made from Trebbiano—but not just any Trebbiano. The local variety, known as Trebbiano di Lugana or Trebbiano di Soave, has long been considered a cut above the other members of the Trebbiano family. Only recently has DNA testing shown that Trebbiano di Lugana is in fact Verdicchio, the great grape of Marche.

Just to the east, entirely within Veneto, is a denomination called Bianco di Custoza, or just Custoza, DOC. This DOC overlaps the southern half of the Bardolino denominations. Custoza makes only white wines, using a blend of typical Veneto grapes including Garganega, Trebbiano, and Friulano.

Lake Garda's western shoreline

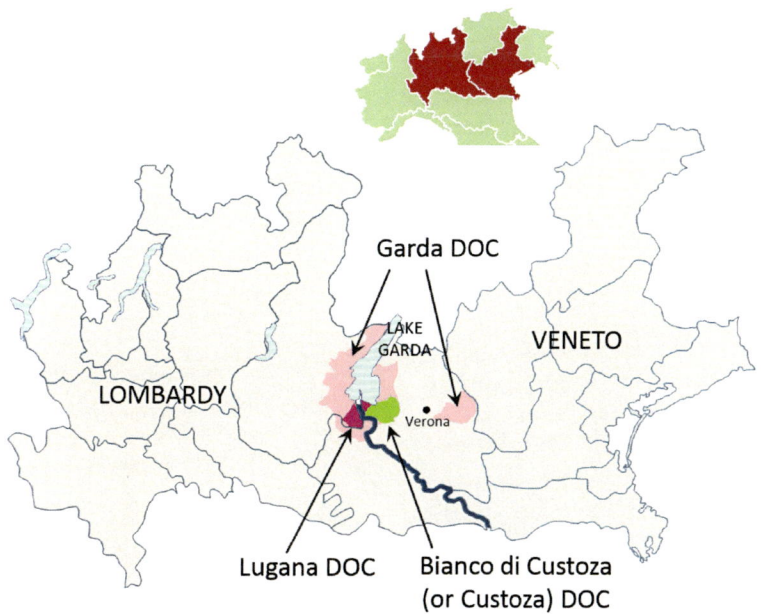

Garda DOC

LAKE GARDA

VENETO

LOMBARDY

Verona

Lugana DOC

Bianco di Custoza (or Custoza) DOC

109

More White Wines of Veneto

Veneto is the largest producer of wine in Italy overall, as well as being the largest producer of white wine.

The region's primary grape variety, white or otherwise, is Glera. However, Glera is used almost exclusively for sparkling wine, so it will be discussed in the next unit. Other abundant white varieties include:

- Garganega
- Pinot Grigio
- Chardonnay
- Pinot Bianco
- Friulano—or Tai as it is usually called in the Veneto

Veneto's most famous denomination for nonsparkling white wine is Soave. It is located a little farther to the east of Lake Garda, just east of the city of Verona and the Valpolicella red-wine denominations. It also happens to be within the eastern zone of the Garda DOC. Soave is the highest-volume production area for dry, still white wines in Italy.

There are actually two denominations around the town of Soave:

- Soave DOC
- Soave Superiore DOCG

Both cover the identical area and both are Garganega based; they just have different production standards.

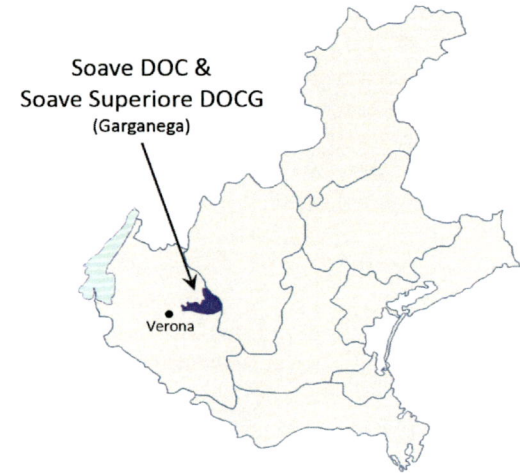

Soave DOC &
Soave Superiore DOCG
(Garganega)

Verona

As noted in Unit 2, the big IGPs of the area—including IGP Veneto, which encompasses the entire region of Veneto, and IGP delle Venezie, which includes most of northeast Italy—produce large quantities of all types of wines. White wines from these areas can be made with any of the local varieties—Garganega, Friulano, Glera, Pinot Grigio, and others—as well as international varieties such as Chardonnay or Pinot Bianco.

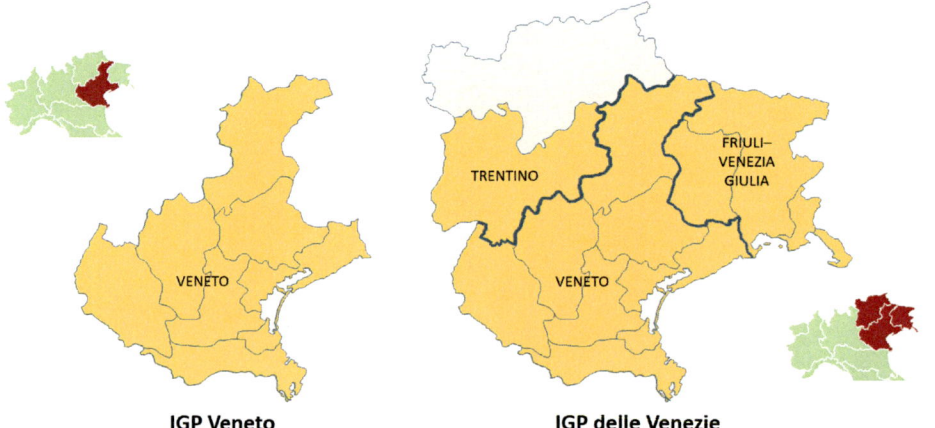

IGP Veneto   **IGP delle Venezie**

Trentino–Alto Adige

TRENTINO–ALTO ADIGE

The region of Trentino–Alto Adige makes three times as much white wine as red. The majority of its wines are varietally labeled, meaning that they contain at least 85% of a single grape variety.

Most of Trentino–Alto Adige's white grapes are familiar international varieties. The region's most prevalent ones are Chardonnay and Pinot Grigio. Others frequently seen include Pinot Bianco, Sauvignon Blanc—which the Italians often call simply Sauvignon or sometimes Sauvignon Bianco—and Traminer.

Traminer (or Traminer Aromatico) is more familiar to most people by the name Gewürztraminer. Although Gewürztraminer is better known as a grape of Alsace in France and a few New World locations, it actually originated in Alto Adige. The variety's home is a village called Tramin in Alto Adige or Südtirol. In Italy, the grape is called Traminer, meaning "From Tramin" or "Of Tramin" in German. However, it was long ago in Alsace that Traminer underwent a mutation into an aromatic variety and earned the *Gewürz* ("spicy") prefix.

Most of the production of still wines in Trentino–Alto Adige, whether red or white, is labeled as either Trentino DOC; Alto Adige DOC, known in German as Südtirol DOC; or Valdadige DOC, which more or less combines the other two and extends a short distance into Veneto in the south.

The town of Tramin in Südtirol (Alto Adige)

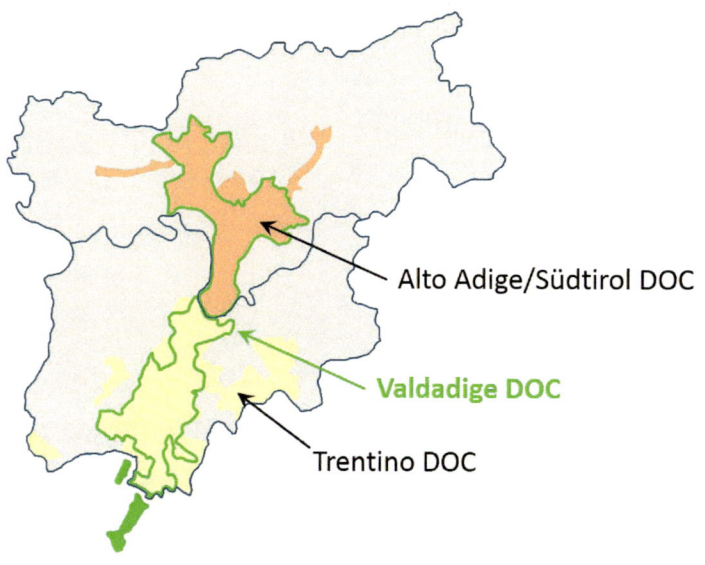

Alto Adige/Südtirol DOC

Valdadige DOC

Trentino DOC

Friuli–Venezia Giulia

Santa Maria di Barbana, Grado, Friuli

Friuli–Venezia Giulia has the highest proportion of white wine of any Italian region. The primary grape variety in this region is Pinot Grigio. Other white varieties that are prevalent in Friuli include the international varieties Chardonnay and Sauvignon Blanc and the native grapes Friulano and Ribolla Gialla.

The largest denomination for both white and red wine in Friuli is Friuli Grave DOC, which lies mostly in the flatlands of the coastal plain. Some of Friuli's most interesting wines, though, come from the hilly area along the border with Slovenia. In this area are Collio Goriziano DOC—often shortened to Collio—and, to its north, Friuli Colli Orientali DOC. These two denominations produce a wide range of wines, red and white, blends and varietals, from any of a dozen varieties, including Friulano and Ribolla Gialla along with several international varieties.

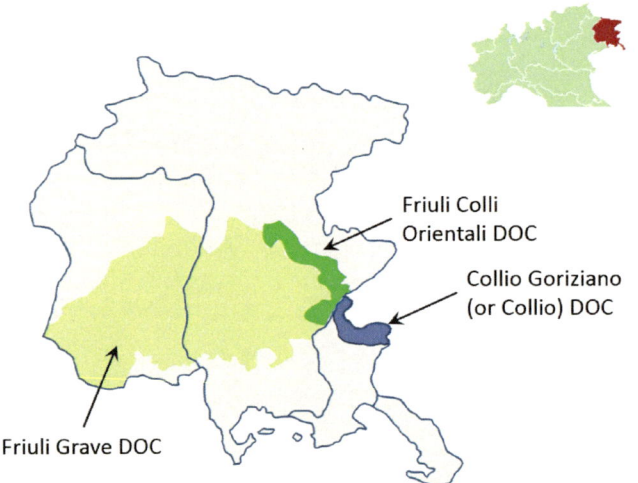

Friuli Colli Orientali DOC

Collio Goriziano (or Collio) DOC

Friuli Grave DOC

Pronunciation Practice: White Grape Varieties

Below are phonetic pronunciations of the names of the white Italian grape varieties mentioned in Units 5 and 6. Practice saying them while reviewing the denominations in which they are used and where these grapes are found.

1. Ansonica (ahn-*soh*-nee-kah)
2. Arneis (ahr-*naiss*)
3. Catarratto (kah-tah-*raht*-toh)
4. Coda di Volpe (*koh*-dah dee *vohl*-pay)
5. Cortese (kor-*tay*-zay)
6. Erbaluce (air-bah-*loo*-chay)
7. Falanghina (fah-lahn-*ghee*-na)
8. Favorita (fah-voh-*ree*-tah)
9. Fiano (fee-*yah*-no)
10. Friulano (free-yoo-*lah*-no)
11. Garganega (gar-*gah*-nay-gah)
12. Glera (*glay*-ra)
13. Grecanico Dorato (gray-*kah*-nee-koh doh-*rah*-to)
14. Grechetto (gray-*ket*-toh)
15. Greco (*gray*-koh)
16. Grillo (*greel*-lo)
17. Malvasia (mahl-vah-*zee*-ya)
18. Moscato (mohss-*kah*-toh)
19. Nuragus (noo-*rah*-guss)
20. Passerina (pahss-sehr-*ee*-na)
21. Pecorino (pay-koh-*ree*-no)
22. Pigato (pee-*gah*-toh)
23. Pinot Bianco (*pee*-no *byahn*-koh)
24. Pinot Grigio (*pee*-no *gree*-jo)
25. Ribolla Gialla (ree-*boll*-la *jahl*-la)
26. Trebbiano (trayb-*byah*-no)
27. Verdicchio (vair-*deek*-kyo)
28. Vermentino (vair-men-*tee*-no)
29. Vernaccia (vair-*notch*-chah)
30. Zibibbo (zee-*bee*-bo)

Unit 6 Exercises

1. Name the two mountain ranges and the valley between them that define the geography of northern Italy.
2. Name the most important grape variety for nonsparkling white wines in the following regions:
    *   Veneto
    *   Marche
    *   Piedmont
    *   Sardinia
    *   Friuli–Venezia Giulia
    *   Umbria
3. How did the Roman Empire affect the development of the global wine industry?
4. Fill in the blanks in the following table. (There may be more than one correct answer in some spaces.)

Denomination	Level	Primary Grape Variety	Color	Region
		Grechetto		_____ and _____
		Various	Red	Friuli–Venezia Giulia
	DOCG	Vernaccia		
		Coda di Volpe		
	DOCG			Sicily
	DOC	Various	White	Southern province of Trentino–Alto Adige
	DOCG	Malvasia		

5. What is another name used for the variety Friulano? Where is that name most often used?
6. Name at least one Italian region that has no IGPs.
7. On an outline map of the regions of Italy (Fig. 2 on p. 22), write the following grape varieties in the region or regions where they are most commonly found.
    *   Arneis
    *   Ribolla Gialla
    *   Falanghina
    *   Grecanico Dorato
    *   Cortese
    *   Teroldego
    *   Erbaluce
    *   Catarratto
    *   Garganega
    *   Gaglioppo
    *   Vermentino
    *   Greco
8. What difference(s) would you expect between two wines that are labeled identically except that only one is labeled "Riserva"?
9. When selecting a wine to serve with seafood-based dish that is typical of Naples, what grape varieties would be obvious choices to consider?
10. In which two regions is most of Italy's Grechetto grown? Name a denomination in each region that uses Grechetto.

11. Name at least four white grape varieties that might be used to make a varietal wine in the Valdadige DOC.

12. On the outline map of northern Italy below (Fig. 7), draw the approximate boundaries of each of the following denominations. If necessary, review the maps in the handouts or presentations for units 2 and 6 first, then do the exercise. Check to see how close you came to the actual location and size.

- Oltrepò Pavese
- Barbaresco
- Delle Venezie
- Barbera d'Asti

- Valpolicella
- Gavi
- Barolo
- Collio

- Custoza
- Soave
- Südtirol
- Dolcetto d'Alba

13. In the above list, what is the quality level for each denomination?

14. What is Italy's largest city, and in which region is it located?

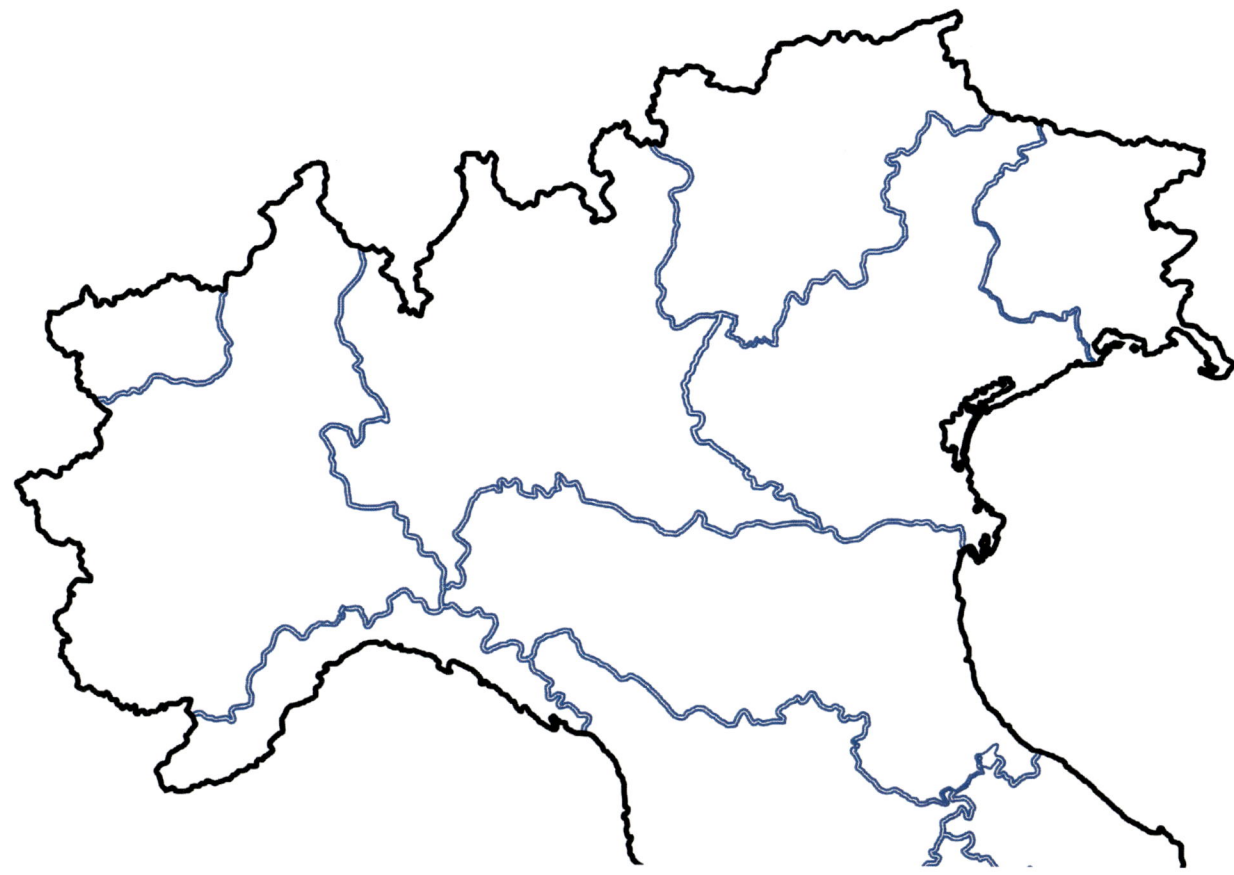

Figure 7. Outline of the Regions of Northern Italy

Download a pdf of this image at http://italianwinecentral.com/exercise-maps

15. In the wine whose label is shown above, based on EU and Italian varietal labeling laws, what is the minimum percentage of Pinot Grigio it could contain?

16. Which wine would you expect to sell for a higher price, Cònero or Rosso Cònero? Why?

17. Name at least five DOPs that can make Montepulciano-based wine.

18. Fill in the blanks in the following table. (There may be more than one correct answer in some spaces.)

Denomination	Level	Primary Grape Variety	Color	Region
_____ di Caluso				
Soave Superiore				
_____ di Montalcino	DOC			
Lugana				
Roero			White	
_____ del Vulture				

Unit 7

Sparkling Wines, Dessert Wines, & Spirits

SPARKLING WINE

The first segment of this unit examines Italian sparkling wine. "Sparkling" in Italian is *spumante*, and that's the word for sparkling wine as well. Italy is not the world's largest producer of sparkling wine, but it is the largest exporter of sparkling wine by volume.

Italy undoubtedly makes more styles of sparkling and effervescent wines than any other country:

- Slightly fizzy to fully sparkling
- White, pink, and red
- Dry to sweet
- Low alcohol to high alcohol
- Fresh and fruity to aged and yeasty
- Dozens of different grape varieties

We'll begin by highlighting some of the key features of how sparkling wine is made. Then we'll list the grape varieties most often used to make sparkling wine in Italy and the main denominations devoted specifically to sparkling wine.

Learning Objectives

Unit 7 moves beyond table wines to examine the sparkling wines and dessert wines of Italy, as well as a few other Italian specialties such as grappa. The learning objectives for this unit are:

- Grapegrowing and winemaking techniques for sparkling and dessert wines in Italy
- Commercially significant sparkling and dessert wine denominations
  - Which region are they located in?
  - Sparkling/dessert wines only, or other styles as well?
  - Primary grape variety or varieties
  - Single-variety, varietal, or blend?
- Procedures for making vermouth and grappa

Making Sparkling Wine

The winemaking process for sparkling wine begins about the same as that for white table wine. One of the main differences at this stage is the selection of grapes.

High acidity is more important than rich flavors or high sugar levels when it comes to sparkling wine; that's why sparkling wine is usually made in cool regions where the grapes naturally retain high acidity. In addition, the grapes are handled and pressed with greater care for sparkling wine, to avoid transferring tannin or other harsh flavors from the skins to the juice. Nevertheless, the winemaking process is basically the same for both, and the result is a still—that is, non-sparkling—white wine.

Where the job is essentially complete for a white wine, however, the work is just beginning for a sparkling wine, because a second fermentation is required to put the bubbles into the wine. A small amount of yeast and sugar is usually added to the base wine to initiate this second fermentation, but this time the fermentation takes place in a closed container so that the carbon dioxide created by the fermentation is trapped and dissolves into the wine.

There are two main choices for the closed containers:

- Wine bottles
- Tanks

There are significant differences in the wine that results, depending on which of these containers is used—most importantly in terms of flavor and price. The two processes will be discussed in turn.

Whole clusters of grapes for sparkling wine being loaded into a press in Franciacorta

The Classic Method

The most famous way of making sparkling wine carries out the second fermentation *in the same wine bottle in which it will be sold.* This is the method used for Champagne, which has been emulated in every winemaking country, including Italy. In English, this is known as the classic method or the traditional method. In Italian, it's called metodo classico.

In this procedure, a small measure of yeast and sugar is added to a full bottle of wine, and the bottle is sealed. As the yeast ferments the sugar, carbon dioxide is released, but it can't escape the bottle. When the process is complete, the wine has built up about six atmospheres of pressure due to the trapped gas, which will erupt as bubbles when the bottle is opened.

The yeast from fermentation, however, becomes a sediment in the bottle and must be removed before sending the bottle to market. In the meantime, the longer the yeast stays in the bottle, the more it affects the flavor of the wine. The yeasty, toasty flavors that develop are the primary characteristic of this type of sparkling wine, and some wines may age for years on the lees (yeast sediment) to maximize these flavors.

The yeast is eventually removed by causing it to settle in the neck of the bottle, freezing just the neck, and opening the bottle so the pressure pushes the frozen plug out. The wine is then topped up with more wine and usually a small amount of sugar—for sweetness this time, not for fermentation.

In the classic method of sparkling winemaking, the yeast that performs the second fermentation in the bottles eventually settles and must be removed by getting it to collect in the bottle's neck, freezing just the neck to solidify the yeast in ice, and then opening the bottle long enough to let the trapped gas push the yeast out.

The Tank Method

The classic method of making sparkling wine produces excellent wine, but is quite labor intensive and therefore expensive. In addition, it is not always the best way of making sparkling wines from aromatic grapes that don't benefit from the yeasty flavors that come with the classic method.

In the late 19th century, an Italian named Federico Martinotti realized this and developed a process for making sparkling wine in tanks; his process was refined and marketed by a Frenchman named Eugène Charmat. That procedure is usually called either the tank method or the Charmat method in English. In Italy, it may be referred to as metodo Charmat or, especially in Piedmont, as metodo Martinotti.

This method is often portrayed as a cheap, inferior alternative to the classic method, but it is in fact the best way to make fruity or aromatic sparkling wines—an Italian specialty. Wines made by the tank method in Italy include:

- Prosecco
- Asti
- Lambrusco
- Brachetto d'Acqui

For the tank method, the second fermentation takes place *in a temperature-controlled pressure tank,* also known as an autoclave. The basic idea is the same as the bottle method, with a new fermentation induced in wine in a sealed, pressurized vessel—in this case, a tank. This new fermentation may be started using yeast and sugar in a finished wine, just like in the classic method. As in the classic method, the yeast from fermentation becomes a sediment that must be removed, but in a tank, the wine can easily be drained off and filtered, always under pressure. After filtration, wine can

be sweetened if desired, then bottled ready for sale.

Another option that is common in Asti and also frequently seen in Prosecco is really just a single fermentation in an autoclave: The winery holds the freshly pressed juice at near-freezing temperatures so that no fermentation can take place. Later, small batches of the juice are transferred into a pressurized tank, warmed up, and allowed to begin fermenting. Partway through the process, the tank is sealed airtight, and fermentation continues until the desired levels of pressure and residual sugar are reached.

The duration of the yeast contact depends on the style of wine. For sparkling wines in which yeastiness is not desirable, such as those made with aromatic grape varieties, the tank method allows yeast removal by filtration much sooner than with the bottle method, which requires waiting for all the yeast to collect at the neck of the bottle. For other sparkling wines, yeast contact can be extended as long as necessary.

The tank method also makes it easier for the winemaker to control the amount of effervescence by allowing excess pressure to escape through a relief valve.

Sparkling wine made by the tank or Martinotti method undergoes its second fermentation in tanks rather than in bottles.

Grape Varieties for Sparkling Wine

There are only a few grape varieties used in the majority of the world's sparkling wines, even though it's possible to make sparkling wine with any grapes.

Most sparkling wines use mainly white grapes that are relatively neutral in flavor—in order to allow the yeast flavors to dominate—and that are either naturally high in acidity or are picked early before the grapes' acidity starts to decline with ripeness.

Red grapes may be used for additional complexity and a bit of color, as well. Pinot Noir is overwhelmingly the choice for this role because it is fairly low in tannin and coloration and ripens early.

Looking first at sparkling wines made by the classic method, the world standard for this style of sparkling wine is Champagne in France, where the grapes used are Chardonnay, Pinot Noir, and/or Pinot Meunier. Italian metodo classico wines—like the majority of classic-method sparkling wines worldwide—usually follow this formula up to a point. Chardonnay and Pinot Nero (Pinot Noir) are typically allowed for metodo classico wines, but in Italy, Pinot Meunier is rare, so Pinot Bianco (Pinot Blanc) is

Right: *Pinot Bianco grapes on the vine*

often substituted. Some denominations may authorize Pinot Grigio or other local grapes for the blend.

It is Italy that sets the world standard for sparkling wine made by the tank method. The primary grape varieties used for this style of wine include:

- Glera
- Moscato
- Lambrusco

Italian tank-method sparkling wines are often single-varietals.

Some denominations in Italy allow production of sparkling wine by either the tank or classic method, but if that is the case, the wines made by the classic method will usually state "Metodo Classico" on the label.

The great majority of Italian sparkling wine is made in the northern regions. Those made by the classic method are most associated with the northeast, from Lombardy to Veneto. The foremost white varieties for tank-method wines are Glera in the northeast and Moscato in Piedmont. The red varieties most known for tank-method sparkling wines are Lambrusco in Emilia Romagna and Brachetto in Piedmont.

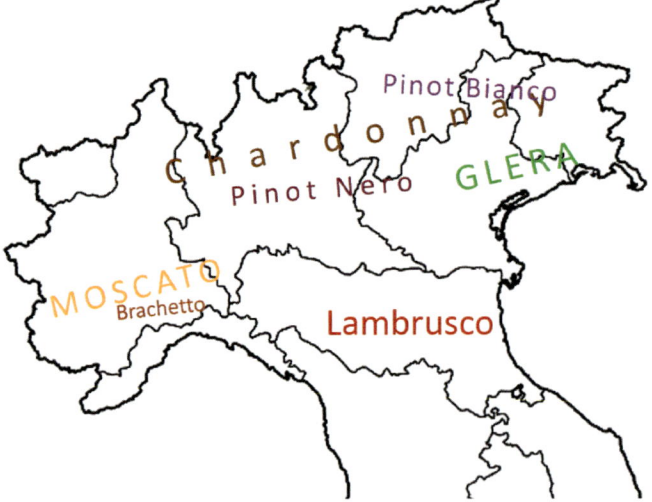

Sparkling Wine Styles

There are many different styles of sparkling wine, all of which are represented in Italy.

One variation in style is in the wine's color. Most sparkling wines are white wines, even if made with some red grapes. If a brief period of skin contact is allowed for red grapes, though, the wine becomes rosato or rosé (the Italians often use the French terminology when referring to sparkling wines, especially classic-method ones). Some Italian sparkling wines are made with enough skin contact with red grapes that the wine is sparkling red.

Another variation is how effervescent the wine is. True sparkling wine—*spumante* in Italian—is under significant pressure (5 to 6 atmospheres). Spumante wines are recognized by the bottle being sealed with a mushroom cork and cage to hold in the pressure *(below left),* the energetic froth of bubbles when the bottle is opened, and the bubbles that continue to stream upward continuously when poured in a glass.

Wines with about half that pressure (typically 1½ to 2½ atmospheres) are called *frizzante*. By comparison, these have minimal froth when poured. Bubbles form on the glass but don't make continuous streams, although they can be felt in the mouth. A bottle of frizzante wine *(below right),* is usually sealed with a standard cork.

A third variation among sparkling wines is how sweet they are. Sparkling wines in the EU use standard terms to describe their sweetness levels. In Italy, from driest to sweetest, they are:

- Brut nature or Dosaggio zero = Bone dry (no dosage added)
- Extra brut = Very dry
- Brut = Dry to just perceptibly sweet
- Extra dry = Slightly sweet
- Secco = Sweeter than extra dry
- Abboccato or Demisec = Semi-sweet
- Dolce = Sweetest

The sweeter styles may be lower in alcohol, but not necessarily.

Metodo Classico Sparkling Wine DOPs

More than a third of the Italian DOPs permit the making of sparkling wine, but for most of them, it is essentially a novelty that is made for local consumption.

For example, Aglianico del Vulture—a full-bodied red wine from Basilicata—can be made as a sparkling wine from 100% Aglianico, but don't expect to find it at your neighborhood wine shop. Similarly, Gavi and Roero Arneis in Piedmont can be sparkling, but very little of it is.

The next few segments will look at the denominations in Italy that are most famous for producing sparkling wine, starting with wines made by the classic method.

Nearly all the classic-method sparkling wine in Italy is made in the northern regions. There are three DOCGs that produce nothing but classic-method sparkling wine:

• Alta Langa DOCG in Piedmont

• Oltrepò Pavese Metodo Classico DOCG in Lombardy
• Franciacorta DOCG in Lombardy

At the DOC level, perhaps the denomination best known for classic-method sparkling wine is Trento DOC, which covers the same territory as the separate Trentino DOC for nonsparkling wines.

All four of these metodo classico denominations use primarily Pinot Nero and/or Chardonnay, and all except Alta Langa also allow Pinot Bianco. Varietals are allowed, but most of the production is nonvarietal blends. In addition, all four make both white and rosato sparkling wines.

While Italy is very proud of its classic-method sparkling wines, its reputation and tradition are more closely tied to the Martinotti-Charmat method wines. The next segments describe the leading tank-method Italian sparkling wine DOPs.

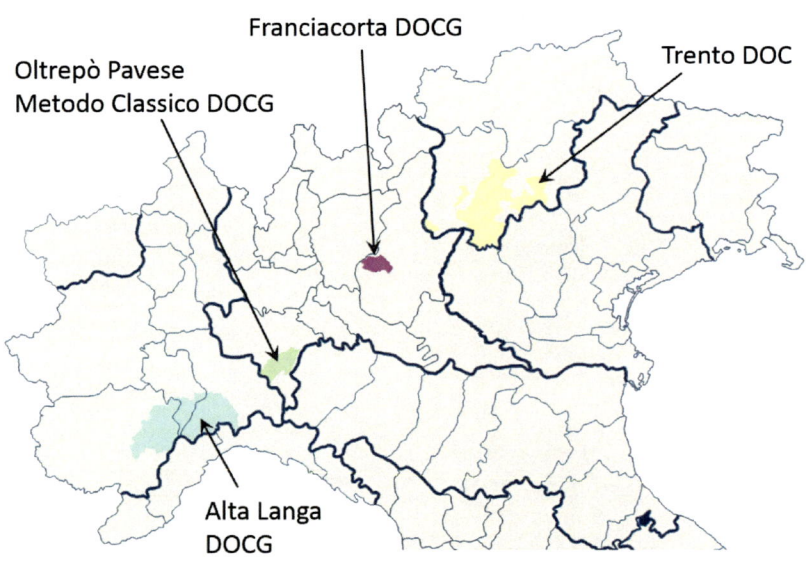

Oltrepò Pavese
Metodo Classico DOCG

Franciacorta DOCG

Trento DOC

Alta Langa
DOCG

Prosecco

Italy's single biggest wine category is Prosecco, the tank-method sparkling wine that may be the most well-known Italian wine globally. Prosecco is:

- A sparkling wine typically made by the tank method
- Made mostly in Veneto, with a small percentage in Friuli–Venezia Giulia
- Always a white wine
- Usually extra dry in style (meaning slightly sweet), but also available as brut or demisec

One thing Prosecco is *not* is a grape variety. Until a few years ago, the variety used to make this wine was in fact called Prosecco, but that changed when European Union laws decreed that only place-names are eligible for trade protection, not grape names. That meant that anyone who made wine from the Prosecco grape anywhere in the world could legally call it Prosecco. To avoid having their reputation squandered, Prosecco producers chose to rename the grape variety Glera and to protect Prosecco as the name of the region where this wine is made. All Prosecco wines are varietal Glera.

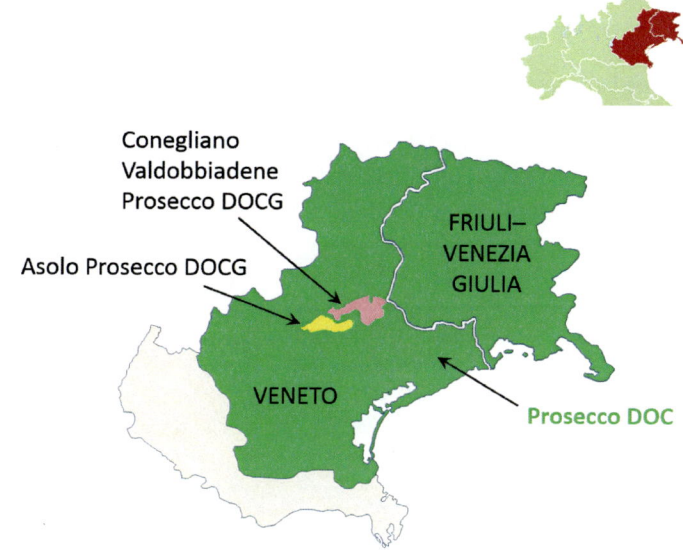

Prosecco can be made in three different denominations. The largest of these is the Prosecco DOC, which produces the highest volume of any Italian DOP. It is also one of the largest denominations geographically, covering most of the Veneto and all of Friuli–Venezia Giulia. Prosecco DOC is required by law to be made by the tank method.

There are two much smaller DOCGs inside the Prosecco DOC, both named after towns in the area. Of these, the key one—and one of the most difficult names of any major denomination—is Conegliano Valdobbiadene Prosecco DOCG, named for the towns of Conegliano and Valdobbiadene. This area is more prestigious than the sprawling Prosecco DOC, covering a relatively small area in the center of the Prosecco zone, and yet it is still one of the highest-volume DOPs in all of Italy. The other DOCG for Prosecco is Asolo Prosecco, around the town of Asolo, which produces only a tiny amount of wine compared to the other two denominations.

The DOCG versions of Prosecco are usually made by the tank method but can be metodo classico.

Remember that, like Champagne, Prosecco is a protected place-name, not a style of wine. True Prosecco can be made only in the Prosecco DOC, the Conegliano Valdobbiadene Prosecco DOCG, or the Asolo Prosecco DOCG. No other wines can legally be called Prosecco in most countries.

Asti and Moscato d'Asti

The Asti DOCG in Piedmont is another of Italy's largest-volume DOPs.

Despite the simple name, Asti DOCG can be confusing because it actually produces two similar but distinct types of wine:

- Asti—aka Asti Spumante—which is a fully sparkling wine
- Moscato d'Asti, which is always frizzante

Thus, all Asti is Asti DOCG, but not all Asti DOCG is Asti. "Moscato d'Asti DOCG" doesn't technically exist, although you will still sometimes see it on labels. And, of course, Barbera d'Asti DOCG and five other "d'Asti" DOCs are entirely separate, if overlapping, denominations.

Both Asti and Moscato d'Asti are produced in the same part of Piedmont south of the city of Asti. Both are 100% Moscato, and therefore they are always white (that is, no rosato version). Nearly all of this wine is made by the tank method. Asti can be bottle fermented, but if it is, it will be labeled as metodo classico.

Both types of Asti DOCG are made in a low-alcohol (4.5–9.5%), sweet style that has reduced their popularity in the U.S., where drier sparkling wines are usually preferred, but they are well suited for many sweet and/or spicy dishes. Producers generally consider Moscato d'Asti the more important of the two types and use their best grapes in its production.

Red Sparkling Wines

There is no shortage of red sparkling wine made in Italy, but not a lot of it is exported. The most famous and largest-production wine from Italy in this category is Lambrusco from Emilia Romagna.

Lambrusco DOCs

Lambrusco was mentioned earlier in Unit 3 when talking about red wines. Recall that Lambrusco is a red grape variety that is grown primarily in Emilia Romagna, where there are three DOCs solely for Lambrusco wines: Lambrusco Salamino di Santa Croce, Lambrusco di Sorbara, and Lambrusco Grasparossa di Castelvetro. (For the record, there is another one, Lambrusco Mantovano DOC, with much smaller production volume directly across the border in Lombardy.) Lambrusco from these denominations is never a still wine; the majority is frizzante, and spumante versions are also widely made. Most exported Lambrusco is sweet, but dry versions are more popular in Italy and are gaining popularity in the U.S.

One of the few other red sparkling wines from Italy known in export markets is a sweet wine from Piedmont. Brachetto d'Acqui (or just Acqui) DOCG from Piedmont is made from the Brachetto grape. It is usually very low in alcohol (as little as 6%), usually 100% Brachetto (technically it can be 97%, but close enough), and usually fully sparkling (although it can be a still wine). Brachetto d'Acqui is typically served with desserts, especially those featuring chocolate or red fruits such as raspberries.

The Brachetto d'Acqui DOCG is yet another overlapping denomination in the crowded Asti area. It is located within both the Asti and Alta Langa DOCGs. In fact, this is one of the densest areas for DOPs in Italy, and most wineries in the Brachetto d'Acqui DOCG—if they have the right grape varieties planted—can also produce wines under the Barbera d'Asti, Barbera del Monferrato Superiore, Dolcetto d'Acqui, Monferrato, and Piemonte denominations, among others.

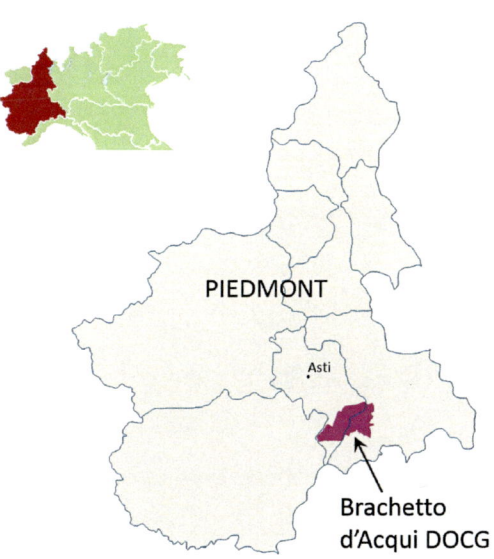

PIEDMONT

Asti

Brachetto d'Acqui DOCG

Brachetto d'Acqui makes a fitting transition from the discussion of sparkling wines to the next segment of this unit: dessert wines.

DESSERT WINES

The term "dessert wine" has various definitions to different people or in different situations.

It can mean any wine served after a meal, any sweet wine, or (to the U.S. Tax and Trade Bureau, anyway) any high-alcohol wine. Taking a middle ground, for this curriculum, "dessert wine" is loosely defined as any sweet and/or high-alcohol wine that would be appropriate to serve after a meal or with a dessert course.

Italy produces a diverse range of dessert wines throughout the country. Italian dessert wines can be slightly sweet to very sweet. They usually have normal to high alcohol levels, but some have low alcohol and are extremely sweet. Italian dessert wines also include fortified or *liquoroso* wines that have extra alcohol added to raise the alcohol content above the level natural fermentation can achieve.

Making Dessert Wines

Any wine will be sweet if the winemaker stops the fermentation early, while there is still a lot of unfermented sugar in the juice. However, making a sweet wine of normal- or even higher-alcohol level requires starting with unusually sweet grapes.

The three most common ways of increasing the sugar-to-water ratio in grapes are:

- Letting the grapes continue to ripen on the vine after most other grapes are picked
- Allowing botrytis to affect them
- Drying the grapes after harvest, before pressing them

With a high sugar-to-water ratio, there will still be sweetness left in the wine even after the yeast are unable to ferment the juice any further.

Late Harvest

Letting the grapes continue to ripen on the vine longer than normal is known as a late harvest, or in Italian, *vendemmia tardiva*. Sugars continue to accumulate in grapes as long as the vine is still active. However, at the same time, the acidity continues to decrease. After the vines shut down with the approach of winter, the grapes begin to shrivel and lose water, resulting in a higher sugar-to-water ratio.

Shriveled grapes await harvest for vendemmia tardiva wine.

Botrytis

Botrytis cinerea is a fungus that attacks grapes in a beneficial way under certain climatic circumstances. In English, botrytis is sometimes called "noble rot." In Italian, it's the equivalent: *muffa nobile.*

Botrytis draws water out of grapes and concentrates the sugars. It also adds distinctive flavor components. Botrytis sometimes occurs in conjunction with late-harvested or dried grapes.

Dried Grapes

The third method of increasing the sugar-to-water ratio in grapes is by drying them. Most Italian sweet wines—as well as some dry wines—are made using dried grapes. Drying grapes after they have been harvested increases the sugar concentration as the water inside the grapes evaporates.

Usually, grapes intended for drying are harvested in whole bunches when they are at their optimum ripeness, not late-harvested. They are brought inside a well-ventilated drying room, where they are often laid on shelves, in layers only one bunch thick to avoid crushing the grapes on the bottom. Alternatively, they may be hung to dry. In some places in southern Italy where rain is not a concern,

grapes may be laid outside to dry in the sun. In cooler areas such as the Veneto, grapes may dry for several months before pressing.

In Italian, the process of drying grapes is called *appassimento.* Wines made from dried grapes are called *passito* wines. Passito wines can be either sweet with low to normal alcohol levels or dry with higher alcohol levels.

Left: *Grapes covered by botrytis mold or* muffa nobile.
Below: *Traditional drying rooms in Valpolicella allow grapes to raisinate slowly either on shallow racks or tied in long strands hung from the rafters.*

Grape Varieties for Dessert Wine

Moscato Bianco

Over a hundred DOPs and most IGPs make dessert wines, so clearly there are a lot of variations.

Grape varieties commonly used to make dessert wine include Trebbiano and Sangiovese—the two most planted varieties in Italy overall—and aromatic varieties such as Malvasia, Moscato, and the red Aleatico. However, dessert wines are made with almost every grape variety grown in Italy. Usually, the grape varieties used for dessert wines are the same ones used for dry wines in that denomination.

Dessert wines made from white grapes are most prevalent, although their actual color is usually yellow to gold to brown. Red and rosato dessert wines made from red grapes are also common, with colors ranging from pink to ruby to garnet to black.

Vin Santo

Above: *A glass of vin santo accompanied by biscotti.* Right: *The color of Sangiovese-based vin santo is reminiscent of the Red-Legged Partridge's eyes, as shown here, leading to the wine's name Occhio di Pernice (Eye of the Partridge).*

The most famous dessert wine of Italy is Vin Santo. Vin Santo, sometimes spelled Vino Santo, is a passito wine made by fermenting juice from dried grapes very slowly for a period of years in small, sealed wooden barrels. It is usually sweet, but if it ferments long enough, it can be dry. Vin Santo is classically served with hard *biscotti* biscuits.

Vin Santo wines are typically blends of an assortment of local varieties. Trebbiano is the variety most often called for in Vin Santo, but other varieties such as Malvasia are blended in. Made with white varieties, Vin Santos are normally gold in color. A rosato version called Occhio di Pernice, meaning "Eye of the Partridge," is made with red grapes, usually Sangiovese.

Many different areas make Vin Santo wines, but they are most prevalent in central Italy, especially Tuscany. Twenty-six of Tuscany's 41 DOCs make a Vin Santo, as do a few DOCs in other regions. There are no DOCGs

or IGPs whose regulations include a wine called Vin Santo—although there are certainly passito wines at both levels.

In Tuscany, there are four DOCs that make *only* Vin Santo. Each of these corresponds to a major red-wine-only DOCG zone, which do not themselves allow Vin Santo production. The largest of these DOCs are Vin Santo del Chianti and Vin Santo del Chianti Classico. The other two are Vin Santo di Carmignano and Vin Santo di Montepulciano. Vin Santo from Montalcino is produced under the banner of Sant'Antimo DOC.

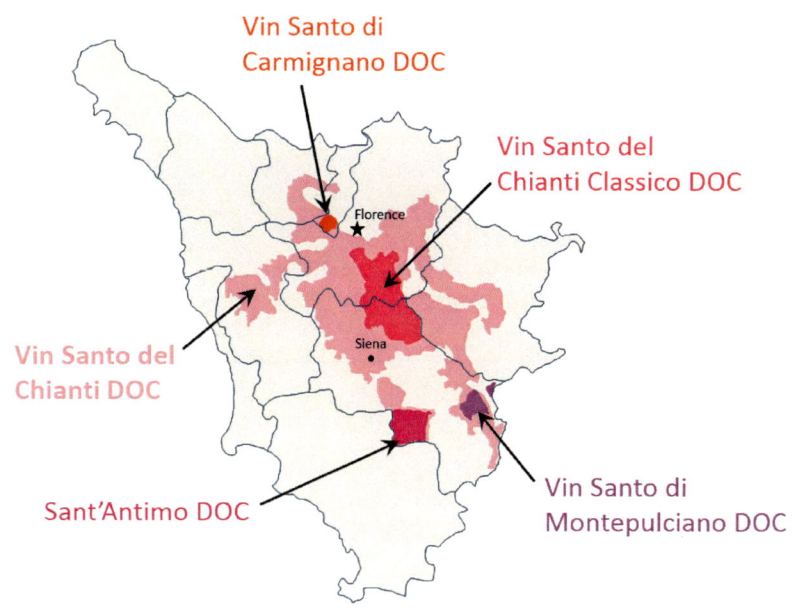

Recioto

Another well-known category of passito dessert wines is Recioto from the Veneto.

There are three DOCGs in the Valpolicella-Soave area for dried-grape wines called Recioto. Two—Recioto di Soave and Recioto di Gambellara—are white wines, based on Garganega. The other, Recioto della Valpolicella, is red and based on Corvina, like all the Valpolicella wines. All three Reciotos are sweet wines, although there was a time when Recioto della Valpolicella was sometimes fermented into a dry, high-alcohol red wine. That style was eventually recognized for its excellence and became known as Amarone della Valpolicella. More about that in the next unit.

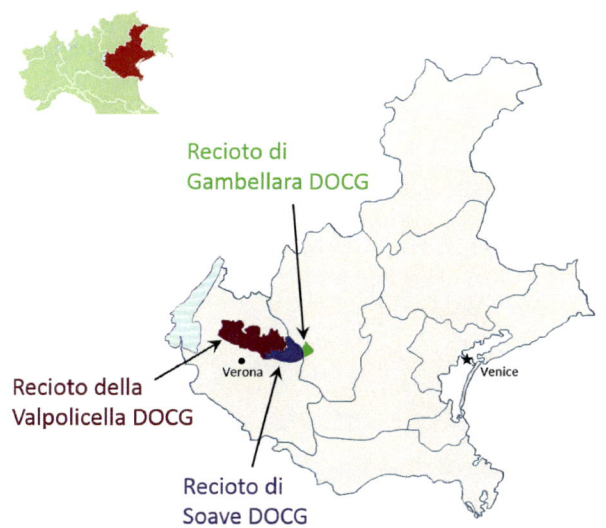

Dessert Wines of Southern Italy

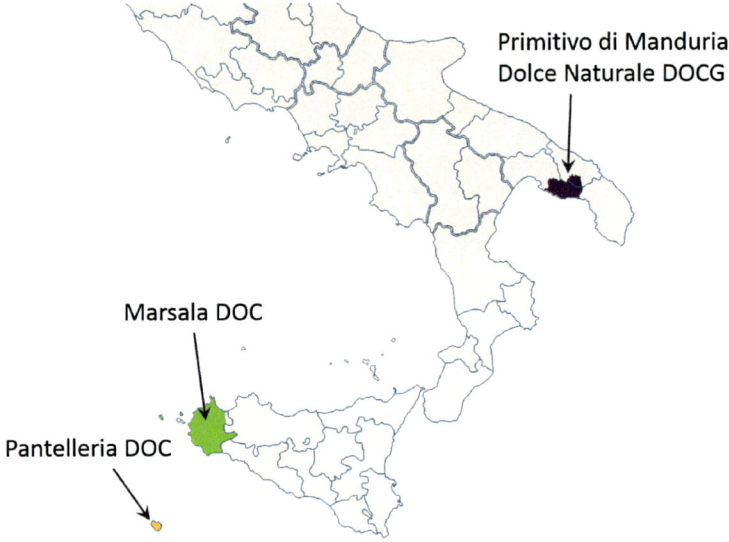

Primitivo di Manduria
Dolce Naturale DOCG

Marsala DOC

Pantelleria DOC

In the south of Italy, hot and dry conditions make it easy to grow grapes with very high sugar levels and to dry grapes. Consequently, dessert wines are numerous in the southern regions.

One of the best examples is the Pantelleria DOC. Winemakers on the small Sicilian island of Pantelleria—closer to Tunisia than mainland Sicily—produce several styles of wines, all from Zibibbo. The island is best known for its sweet passito, made from 100% Zibibbo.

Not far away on the western tip of Sicily is Marsala. Marsala was once perhaps Italy's most renowned wine worldwide, back in the days of sailing ships when table wines did not travel well but fortified wines could remain intact through long voyages. Its fame led to the name being used for sweet wines made in other countries, but true Marsala is made only in the Marsala DOC in western Sicily.

Marsala is a sweet fortified wine that is produced in several styles, including both white and rosato. It is made from a blend of Sicilian grape varieties, notably Ansonica, Catarratto, and Grillo. The rosato style—known as *rubino* (ruby) here—uses red grapes such as Nerello Mascalese and Nero d'Avola.

Another example of southern Italy's dessert wines from the peninsula is Primitivo di Manduria Dolce Naturale, a DOCG in Puglia—covering the same territory as the Primitivo di Manduria DOC—that produces a sweet red wine from Primitivo grapes.

That basically completes the discussion of Italian wine styles, but before finishing, there are a couple more specialized beverages that should be mentioned.

VERMOUTH, AMARO, AND GRAPPA

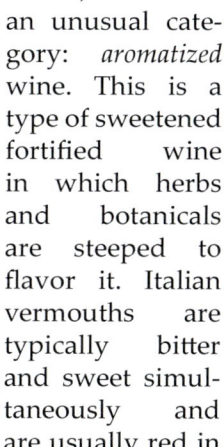

Although a bit beyond the scope of this course, it's hard to end the discussion without saying something about three Italian beverage specialties: vermouth, amaro, and grappa.

Of the three, vermouth is the only one that is actually a wine, and it is in an unusual category: *aromatized* wine. This is a type of sweetened fortified wine in which herbs and botanicals are steeped to flavor it. Italian vermouths are typically bitter and sweet simultaneously and are usually red in color, as opposed to the drier, white French vermouths. Vermouth is often served as an aperitif before a meal and is an ingredient in many cocktails.

An amaro is an aromatized *liqueur*. Amaros, or amari, are similar to vermouth or any aromatized wine, but the herbs and botanicals, rather than having wine as a base, are ordinarily steeped in distilled spirits. For this reason, their alcohol level is much higher (up to 40%), and consequently they are usually served as a digestif after a meal. Like the Italian vermouths, amaros are both bitter and sweet at the same time. They can also be used as an ingredient in a mixed drink such as the ever-popular Spritz.

Other Italian liqueurs are also popular as digestifs, including:

- Limoncello, flavored with lemons
- Amaretto, nocello, and nocino, flavored with nuts
- Sambuca, flavored with anise

Grappa is a *distilled spirit,* not a fortified wine or a liqueur. Nor is it technically a distilled wine (brandy). Grappa is made by distilling the alcohol out of pomace—the solids left over after wine has been pressed, consisting primarily of grape skins. With an alcohol level typically in the 40–60% range, grappa is initially clear, but becomes golden if aged in barrels. It is sometimes aromatized after distillation, but not sweetened. Grappa is the quintessential digestif.

Pomace (below) *is the mass of grape skins, seeds, and other solids that remains after wine is pressed. Though it appears dry, there is enough liquid alcohol left in the skins to allow distillation into grappa.*

ITALIAN DESSERTS

Pictured (clockwise from top left): *Cassata cake, cantucci, mostaccioli with walnuts, pandoro, apfelstrudel, Sicilian almond cookies*

Since the subject of this unit was dessert wines, it's appropriate to take a quick look at some of the desserts they might be paired with.

A dessert item that was already mentioned is biscotti. These are literally "twice-baked" hard cookies like the almond-flavored cantucci that are often served in Tuscany with Vin Santo. Other cookies include fregolate in Veneto and, in the south, mostaccioli, an unleavened biscuit of Arabic origin made with flour, caramelized honey, anise liqueur, and other flavorings, sometimes covered with chocolate.

Italian cakes include Verona's pandoro, a tall, sweet yeast bread, often coated with powdered sugar and sometimes filled with cream, and Milan's panettone, a sweet bread containing candied orange, citron, lemon zest, and raisins. Both are served around Christmas and New Year's in Italy and are popular in the U.S. as well.

In Friuli, gubana is made from sweet dough leavened with a filling of nuts, raisins, pine nuts, sugar, brandy, and lemon rind, baked in a spiral, snail shape. At the other end of the country, Palermo, Sicily, is the home of cassata, a round sponge cake moistened with fruit juices or liqueur, layered with ricotta cheese and a chocolate or vanilla filling, and covered with a shell of marzipan.

Among the Italian pastries and fried-dough desserts, cannoli—a Sicilian specialty consisting of tube-shaped shells of fried pastry dough filled with a sweet, creamy filling usually containing ricotta—are perhaps the most famous. Others include:

- Apfelküchel (Alto Adige): Fried apple rings (donuts)
- Apfelstrudel (Alto Adige): Fried flattened pastry containing a sugary apple filling

- Bocconotti (Calabria to Puglia): Filled pastry containing honey, custard, pear or quince jam, or chocolate
- Castagnoli (central and northern regions): Fried dough, sometimes with a custard filling, usually made for Carnevale
- Sfogliatelle (Campania): Rolled pastry filled with such things as orange-flavored ricotta, almond paste, or candied peel of citron
- Struffoli (Campania): Deep-fried balls of dough about the size of grapes, crunchy on the outside and light inside, mixed with honey and other sweet ingredients
- Zeppole (Campania): Deep-fried fritters, usually topped with powdered sugar and possibly filled with custard, jelly, pastry cream, or a butter-and-honey mixture

Deep-fried thin twisted ribbons of dough, sprinkled with powdered sugar, are ubiquitous—especially around Carnevale—and go by many names, including sfrappole, chiacchiere, and bugie, as well as angel wings and other names in other countries.

Tiramisù is among the most familiar desserts in Italian restaurants in the U.S. This specialty of Veneto is a layered confection of ladyfingers dipped in coffee and a whipped mixture of eggs, sugar, and mascarpone cheese, flavored with cocoa.

Pictured (clockwise from top left): *Castagnole decorated for Carnevale, sfogliatelle, zeppole, cannoli, sfrappole di carnevale bolognesi*

Other well-known puddings include panna cotta, a thick combination of cream, milk, egg white, and sugar or honey, baked in a low oven and then served chilled; semifreddo, made from equal parts of ice cream and whipped cream mixed together and served partially frozen; and zabaione or zabaglione, a light whipped custard of egg yolks, sugar, and sweet wine (usually Marsala).

And finally, there's gelato, the Italian frozen dessert with a lower milk fat content than ice cream.

Pictured (clockwise from top left): *Tiramisù, panna cotta, a range of choices at the gelato counter, zabaione*

Italian Language: Effervescence & Sweetness Terms

1. Spumante (spoo-*mahn*-tay) = Sparkling

2. Frizzante (freet-*zahn*-tay) = Fizzy

3. Spuma (*spoo*-ma) = Foam

4. Millesimato (meel-lay-zee-*mah*-toh) = Vintage dated

5. Bollicine (bowl-lee-*chee*-nay) = Bubbles

6. Brut (*broot*) = Very dry

7. Secco (*sek*-ko) = Dry

8. Abboccato (ahb-bo-*kah*-toh) = Off-dry; slightly sweet

9. Amabile (ah-*mah*-bee-lay) = Semisweet (term used only for still and frizzante wines, not sparkling wines)

10. Dolce (*dohl*-chay) = Sweet

11. Appassimento (ahp-pahss-see-*men*-toh) = The process of drying grapes

12. Passito (pahss-*see*-toh) = Dried-grape wine

Bottled sparkling wine aging in a winery's cellar

Unit 7 Exercises

1. In which Italian region are you most likely to hear German spoken? What are some of the primary grape varieties of that region (both red and white)?
2. Describe how Vin Santo differs from other dried-grape wines.
3. What is a quality pyramid? Describe its elements and how the top of the pyramid relates to the bottom.
4. Define/translate the following terms:
   - Vendemmia tardiva
   - Liquoroso
   - Spumante
   - Muffa nobile
   - Passito
   - Occhio di pernice
5. Fill in the blanks in the following table. (There may be more than one correct answer in some spaces.) *For "Primary Style," choose from Still, Classic Method, or Tank Method.*

Denomination	Level	Primary Grape Variety or Varieties	Primary Style	Color	Region(s)
	DOCG		Classic Method	White, rosato	Piedmont
		Nebbiolo for reds & Arneis for whites	Still	Red & white	
		Brachetto			
			Classic Method	White, rosato	Trentino–Alto Adige
		Uva di Troia			
	DOCG		Classic Method	White, rosato	Lombardy
	DOCG	Glera			

6. How do vermouth, amaro, and grappa differ? Which of them is technically wine?
7. Describe how the Classic Method and Tank Method differ in making sparkling wine. What are the advantages of each? Name four grape varieties that are commonly used to make Tank Method sparkling wine in Italy.
8. Name at least three ways to increase the concentration of sugar in grape juice/must. Which of those is most often used in Italy for making dessert wines?
9. What is the difference between a frizzante wine and a spumante?
10. What is the most commercially important sparkling wine from Italy?
11. What difference(s) would you expect between a wine labeled Asti DOCG and one labeled Moscato d'Asti DOCG? How could you tell them apart before opening and without looking at the label?

12. Fill in the blanks in the following table. (There may be more than one correct answer in some spaces.) *For "Primary Style," choose from Still, Classic Method, or Tank Method.*

Denomination	Level	Primary Grape Variety or Varieties	Primary Style	Color	Region(s)
Diano d'Alba					
Oltrepò Pavese Metodo Classico				White, rosato	
Asti					
Barbaresco					
Prosecco					
Lambrusco di Sorbara					

13. Name as many sweetness levels of sparkling wine as you can, from driest to sweetest. Check your work.

14. Fill in the blanks in the following table. (There may be more than one correct answer in some spaces.) *For "Primary Style," choose from Dry Still, Dry Sparkling, Sweet Still, or Sweet Sparkling.*

Denomination	Level	Primary Grape Variety or Varieties	Primary Style	Color	Region(s)
	DOCG	Prugnolo Gentile (aka _____)			
Recioto della Valpolicella					
Primitivo di Manduria					
Primitivo di Manduria Dolce Naturale					
		Fiano			
Marsala					

15. Name at least two subzones of Chianti DOCG. How many are there?
16. What is the gas that forms the bubbles in sparkling wine?

17. In the wine whose label is shown above, from what grape variety is the wine made? What is the minimum percentage of grapes that must have been grown within the boundaries of the denomination?

18. Can rosato or rosé sparkling wine be made without using red grapes? Why or why not? What red grape variety is typically used to make classic-method sparkling wine in Italy?

Unit 8
Luxury Wines

This final unit is about luxury wines, an elite group that includes the most famous and most expensive of Italian wines.

By definition, a luxury is something that is a bit too expensive for everyday consumption—something that might be purchased as a gift or for a special occasion. Consequently, when someone decides to buy a luxury wine, they are more likely to choose among a small number of top wines from all over Italy and beyond, rather than focusing on a specific geographical region or even a particular grape variety or flavor profile. For that reason, this unit examines a set of Italian luxury wines together as a group.

All of the denominations in this unit have been discussed already, but here we go into additional detail. Given the renown of these wines, Italian Wine Professionals should have a little more information about them committed to memory, including the rules on grape varieties used, aging requirements, and zones of production.

Of course, the distinction between a luxury wine and a non-luxury wine varies. Certainly price is a key factor, but there is no agreement on a specific cutoff point. Wine trade publications often start the "luxury" category at prices as low as $20 retail. On the other hand, some people wouldn't consider anything under $100 to be worthy of being called a luxury wine.

Apart from price, what are some of the features that make a wine a *luxury* wine? Before moving on, think of a few things that luxury wines have in common in your experience.

Brolio Castle, home of the noble Ricasoli family

Learning Objectives

The final unit of this course takes a closer look at some of Italy's most renowned and iconic wines. For the key red wine denominations covered, the learning objectives are:

- Why are they so famous?
- Location
- Primary grape variety or varieties and percentages allowed
- Subregions and primary communes
- Aging requirements
- Premier types or classifications

Luxury Wine Characteristics

In general, luxury wines benefit from many if not all of the following features:

- Ideal vineyard locations
- Top-quality fruit harvested at optimum ripeness
- Careful, talented winemaking
- Complex aromas and depth of flavors
- Usually, extended barrel aging in the cellar
- An ability—and often a necessity—to age for years before their reaching peak of flavor
- A perception of scarcity (even if production is in reality greater than people might think)
- High scores from reviewers
- Successful marketing

The more of these features a wine has, the higher a price it ought to be able to command.

Another thing the majority of luxury wines have in common is that they are red. Why? The answer lies in the fact that red wines can take better advantage of some of the luxury wine characteristics listed above. For example, the flavor and aroma components in grape skins—which are used in red winemaking but normally discarded in white winemaking—add to the wine's complexity. Similarly, tannin

from the skins and seeds increases the wine's ageability. Furthermore, red wines have a greater affinity with wood than most white wines, again increasing complexity and ageability for barrel-aged reds.

In Italy, all the luxury wine categories are red wines. That does not mean that there aren't excellent white wines, sparkling wines, and dessert wines—some of which command high prices—but in those categories, the luxury wines are highly producer dependent. On the other hand, Italy has several denominations for red wines that are highly regarded from almost *all* of their producers. This unit delves into several of those denominations in the top tier of Italian wines.

Above: *Wine library at Castello di Bossi in Chianti Classico*
Below: *Bottles of Barolo for sale at the regional enoteca*

Luxury Wines in Italy

As in any country, the most sought-after wines in Italy are producer driven.

In a few cases, these producers who make exalted wines are anomalies, singularly elevating an otherwise obscure denomination or grape variety to lofty heights. More often, though, these producers are simply the first among many who make great wines from respected varieties in legendary winemaking regions. It is on these regions and their predominant grape varieties that this unit focuses.

As already noted, the Italian denominations that routinely cross into the luxury category are all red-wine areas. Italy's most respected red grape varieties overall are Nebbiolo and Sangiovese. Other premier red grape varieties used in luxury wines include the less-familiar Corvina and Aglianico, as well as the ubiquitous international star Cabernet Sauvignon.

This unit details six denominations in three regions. Starting in Piedmont, Barolo and Barbaresco are obviously among Italy's great wines. Tuscany's Brunello di Montalcino is another clear choice, as is Bolgheri and the Super Tuscans it represents.

Chianti Classico is perhaps too broad a category to include in its entirety, but that is why the producers there have introduced a new classification called Gran Selezione to showcase their very best wines. It's too soon to know whether this new designation will be embraced by consumers as a player in the luxury market, but early indications are positive.

The unit will finish with Veneto's great "meditation wine," Amarone della Valpolicella.

Certainly, the list could have been made longer, with the inclusion of such stars as Taurasi, Franciacorta, Nizza, perhaps a dessert wine or two, and others—but six is a good number.

Brunello di Montalcino is one of Italy's most celebrated wines.

Piedmont
- Barbaresco DOCG
- Barolo DOCG

Veneto
- Amarone della Valpolicella DOCG

Tuscany
- Brunello di Montalcino DOCG
- Bolgheri DOC
- Chianti Classico DOCG Gran Selezione

Twin Giants of Piedmont

The red grape varieties of Piedmont have a definite hierarchy, with Nebbiolo on the top pedestal, given the best vineyard sites. Nebbiolo wines are held in high esteem, and two legendary wines—Barolo and Barbaresco—are considered the best of Nebbiolo, producing the greatest, longest-lived wines from this grape variety.

The Barolo and Barbaresco denominations are located just 4 miles apart in southern Piedmont, on opposite sides of the town of Alba in the province of Cuneo. This part of Piedmont is very picturesque. In fact, the area of Barolo and Barbaresco was recently named a UNESCO World Heritage site for their beauty as well as their wine tradition.

The two DOCGs both make wines from 100% Nebbiolo. Their styles are similar, but Barolo tends to be the more powerful of the two, Barbaresco the more elegant. Barolo's geographic area and wine production are both approximately three times that of Barbaresco. Both regions are part of the area known as the Langhe, and the

Langhe DOC *(see map, below right)* is an alternative denomination for producers of either Barolo or Barbaresco. What that means is that sometimes—such as during difficult vintages or when vineyards are replanted—excellent values can be found in Langhe Nebbiolos that are nearly up to the standards of the more famous denominations but sell at a much lower price.

The next sections will describe the specifics of these two wines.

La Morra, in the Barolo denomination, Piedmont

Barolo

Barolo village, the namesake of the Barolo denomination

The Barolo DOCG covers an area of about 25 square miles in the Langhe hills, of which 1,977 hectares (4,883 acres) are Barolo DOCG vineyards. The denomination takes its name from the village of Barolo, which is one of 11 communes (i.e., villages or towns) within the Barolo appellation. Other communes include La Morra, Castiglione Falletto, Serralunga d'Alba, Monforte d'Alba, Novello, Verduno, and Grinzane Cavour (*see map, below*).

In addition to the various communes, the Barolo DOCG has been further divided into named parcels called *menzioni geografiche aggiuntive* ("additional geographical definitions")—often

Barolo, as a category, is one of the most expensive and highly sought-after Italian wines. Perhaps more than any other Italian wine, Barolo has the capability to age and develop profound complexity over many years, typically reaching its peak of flavor no less than 10 years after the vintage.

Due to its renown, Barolo was one of the first DOCs established in 1966 and was among the first elevated to DOCG status in 1980.

There are two designations for wine labeled as Barolo DOCG. All Barolos are dry red wines made from 100% Nebbiolo. The standard or *normale* Barolo must be aged in the cellar for a minimum of three years, including at least a year and a half in wood, before being released to the market. The higher-quality Barolo Riserva has to age for an additional two years before release, for a total of five years (still with at least 18 months in wood). Riserva wines are considered the best of the best and are not made every year if the conditions don't warrant that status.

Barolo DOCG

Verduno

Grinzane Cavour

La Morra

Castiglione Falletto

Barolo

Serralunga d'Alba

Novello

Monforte d'Alba

0   1   2   3
miles

called *crus* in comparison with Burgundy, although the comparison is inexact. The menzioni are defined primarily by historical use and terroir (topography, soil, climate). There are 181 menzioni, including the 11 communes.

At right is a section of the official map of the Barolo denomination, showing the various crus around the village of Barolo. The name of a menzione—Cerequio, Cannubi, or Bussia, for example—can appear on the label if the grapes all come from that parcel, but one is not required. The crus do not overlap. They are larger than single vineyards, but too small and numerous to be considered subzones. The expectation is that the truly great crus will show themselves and become famous, and the others will fall into disuse and possibly be discarded.

There are 170 producer-bottlers of Barolo DOCG in the local *consorzio* (the vintners group that administers the denomination's rules), with an annual production of about 100,000 hectoliters of Barolo (the equivalent of 1.1 million cases).

The menzioni geografiche or "crus" of the Barolo denomination around the village of Barolo are shown in different colors on this official map from the consorzio. Download the complete map at www.langhevini.it/pdf/mappe/mappa-del-barolo.pdf.

CONSORZIO DI TUTELA
BAROLO BARBARESCO
ALBA LANGHE E ROERO

Barolo Denomination Regulations

	Barolo	Barolo Riserva
Composition	100% Nebbiolo	100% Nebbiolo
Minimum alcohol	13.0%	13.0%
Minimum aging	3 years, including 18 months in barrel	5 years, including 18 months in barrel

Barbaresco

Barolo
DOCG

Top: Barbaresco's vineyards lie at the feet of the village of Barbaresco itself.

Barolo's counterpart is Barbaresco, with Nebbiolos of equal quality but a different style.

Barbaresco wines are similar in many ways to those of Barolo, but less tannic and softer—some say more elegant and "fresher." Barbaresco sells for less than Barolo and often represents good value by comparison.

The Barbaresco DOCG is located near Barolo, just on the other side of Alba. As noted earlier, the denomination is about a third the size of Barolo. It contains just three communes: Barbaresco, Neive, and Treiso. As in Barolo, vineyard areas within the denomination have been designated as menzioni geografiche aggiuntive or crus. Being smaller, Barbaresco has only 66 crus designated *(see map next page)*.

Like Barolo, Barbaresco was one of the first wine areas to receive DOC status in 1966 and became a DOCG in 1980. There are 684 hectares (1,689 acres) of vineyard area.

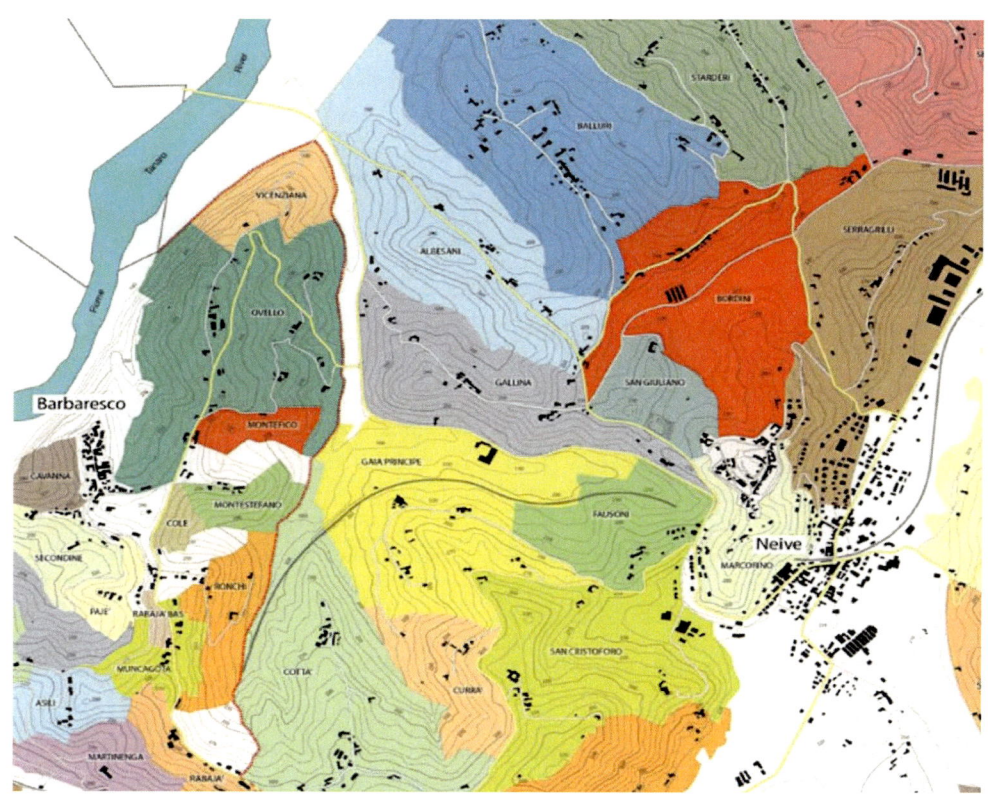

Like Barolo, the Barbaresco denomination has been subdivided into menzioni geografiche. This map detail shows the area between the towns of Barbaresco and Neive. The complete map is available from the consorzio at www.langhevini.it.

The Barbaresco DOCG has an annual production of approximately 33,000 hectoliters (360,000 cases).

Again, there are just two styles of Barbaresco DOCG wine: Barbaresco and Barbaresco Riserva. All Barbarescos are 100% Nebbiolo, like Barolo, although here the minimum alcohol level is 12.5%, compared to 13% in Barolo. Barbaresco tends to be ready to drink earlier than Barolo and requires less aging prior to release. Standard Barbaresco must age for two years, including at least 9 months of wood aging. The riserva designation for Barbaresco's best wines requires two additional years of aging.

We now move from Piedmont to Tuscany, where Sangiovese is king.

Barbaresco Denomination Regulations

	Barbaresco	Barbaresco Riserva
Composition	100% Nebbiolo	100% Nebbiolo
Minimum alcohol	12.5%	12.5%
Minimum aging	2 years, including 9 months in barrel	4 years, including 9 months in barrel

CONSORZIO DI TUTELA
BAROLO BARBARESCO
ALBA LANGHE E ROERO

Chianti Classico Gran Selezione

One of the most recognizable names in Tuscany is Chianti, the Sangiovese-based wine that is Italy's largest red export. Chianti has a long history as a winemaking region recognized by name far and wide. Its boundaries were first defined in 1716, making it one of the first-ever appellations in the world, celebrating its 300th birthday this year.

from the rest of Chianti to distance itself from the declining quality of Chianti wines in general. Chianti Classico now exists as an island with the Chianti denomination.

Chianti Classico's nine communes include the original 18th-century zone made up of Castellina, Gaiole, Greve, and Radda—all of which added "in Chianti" to their names due to the fame of the wine made there. The denomination also includes parts of Barberino Val d'Elsa, Castelnuovo Berardenga, Poggibonsi, San Casciano Val di Pesa, and Tavarnelle Val di Pesa. The northern half of the denomination is in the province of Firenze, or Florence, and the southern half is in the province of Siena, but neither of those cities is inside the denomination.

Chianti Classico is a relatively large denomination, about 30 miles long, and as might be expected in an area that size, the terroir varies considerably and its wines range from excellent to ordinary. As a result, the reputation of the excellent wines suffered.

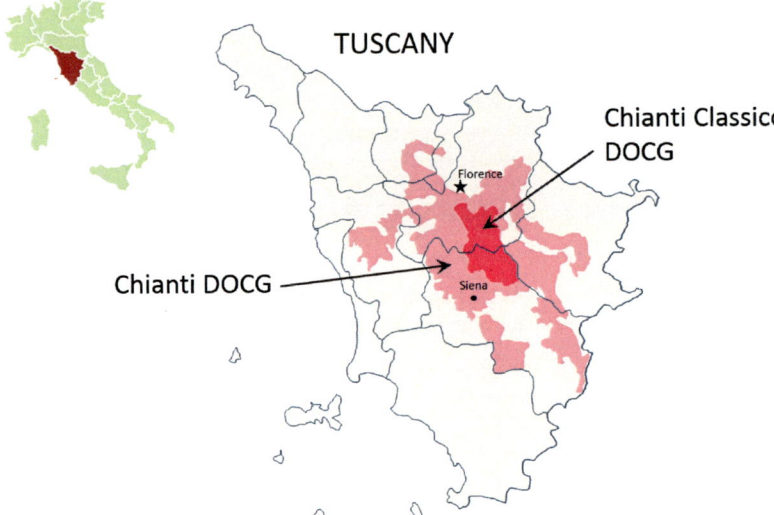

TUSCANY

Chianti Classico DOCG

Chianti DOCG

The original Chianti area was about half the size of today's Chianti Classico denomination. Chianti expanded over the centuries, reaching the territory of what is today incorporated in the Chianti DOCG. The traditional heart of the area became known as Chianti Classico.

Chianti Classico was designated a DOC in 1967 as a subzone of Chianti, and together they were elevated to DOCG status in 1984. In 1996, Chianti Classico DOCG split off

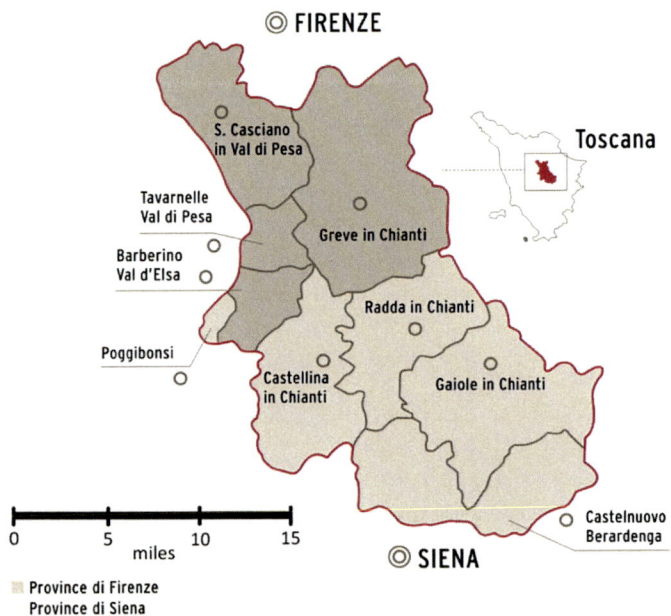

◎ FIRENZE

Toscana

S. Casciano in Val di Pesa

Tavarnelle Val di Pesa

Greve in Chianti

Barberino Val d'Elsa

Radda in Chianti

Poggibonsi

Castellina in Chianti

Gaiole in Chianti

Castelnuovo Berardenga

◎ SIENA

0   5   10   15
miles

▨ Province di Firenze
   Province di Siena

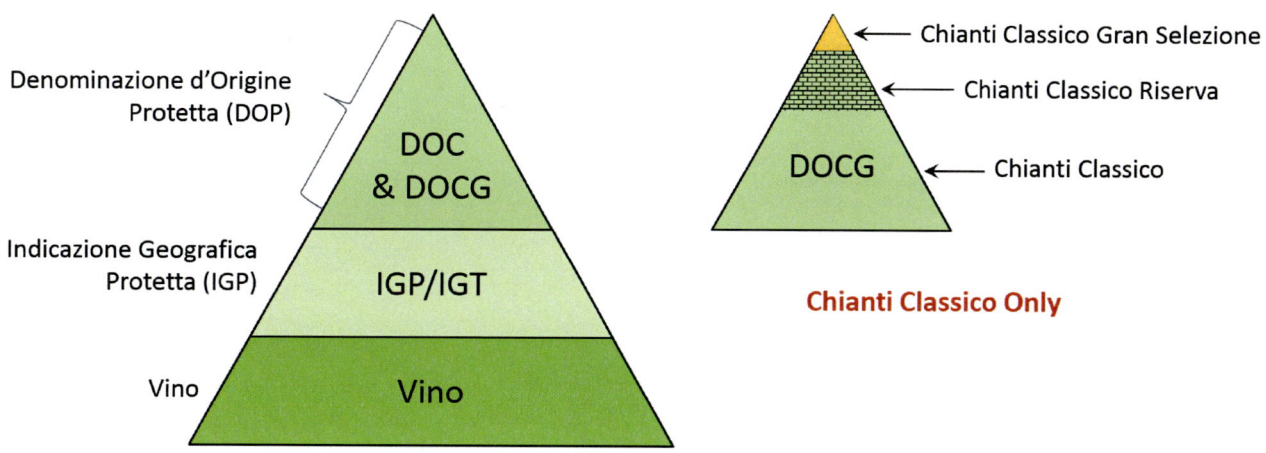

Denominazione d'Origine Protetta (DOP)

DOC & DOCG

Indicazione Geografica Protetta (IGP)

IGP/IGT

Vino

Vino

Chianti Classico Gran Selezione
Chianti Classico Riserva
Chianti Classico

DOCG

Chianti Classico Only

As in many denominations, Chianti Classico established a riserva classification to help identify its best wines from the average ones. However, it still wasn't able to raise the bar high enough that Chianti Classico Riserva was seen as a peer of Barolo, Barbaresco, and Brunello. Therefore, it decided to create a new classification with even higher standards than riserva. In 2014, Chianti Classico approved the new level called Gran Selezione (Great Selection). It is the first and only region to have such a classification.

With this new category, Chianti Classico DOCG now produces three kinds of wine:

- Chianti Classico (the standard version, also called *annata*)
- Chianti Classico Riserva, with extra aging and higher production requirements
- Chianti Classico Gran Selezione, a designation for only the very best Chianti Classico wines, which, like some of the other top-tier wines, will be made only in good years

All three levels of Chianti Classico have the same rules for grape composition and are required to contain a minimum of 80% Sangiovese. The other 20% can include a number of red varieties such as Canaiolo Nero or Cabernet Sauvignon, or the wine can be 100% Sangiovese. White varieties, which were once a required element of the blend, are no longer allowed in Chianti Classico.

Chianti Classico Denomination Regulations

	Chianti Classico	Chianti Classico Riserva	Chianti Classico Gran Selezione
Composition	Min. 80% Sangiovese	Min. 80% Sangiovese	Min. 80% Sangiovese (estate grown)
Minimum alcohol	12.0%	12.5%	13.0%
Minimum aging	1 year	2 years	2½ years

How does Gran Selezione differ from the other Chianti Classicos? Naturally, the higher designation involves some tighter restrictions on production, such as lower vineyard yields and higher grape ripeness. A significant twist is that for Gran Selezione all the fruit must be estate grown. In other words, the winery must own or lease the vineyards that are the source of the grapes and cannot buy additional fruit from other growers.

The minimum alcohol level for Gran Selezione is higher at 13%, reflecting the requirement for riper grapes. The aging requirement is longer as well: Gran Selezione must be aged for at least two and a half years before it can be sold, compared to one year and two years for normale and riserva, respectively. There is no requirement for wood aging, although most producers do age their wines in barrels or casks.

The entire Chianti Classico denomination produces an average of 270,000 hectoliters (3 million cases) annually from 6,518 hectares (16,100 acres) of vineyards. Of this, the Chianti Classico consorzio estimates that about 11,000 hectoliters (125,000 cases) is at the Gran Selezione level. The denomination is famous for its iconic black rooster (*gallo nero*) symbol.

It is important to realize that there is no other DOP underlying Chianti Classico. Chianti Classico and Chianti are totally separate denominations, so there is no option to fall back to Chianti or a DOC. Thus, anything that does not qualify for Chianti Classico DOCG (by not meeting the minimum standards or usings a nonstandard blend) would most likely be labeled IGP Toscana.

Above: *The Black Rooster logo as it currently appears on every bottle of Chianti Classico*
Below and opposite: *Views of the Chianti Classico countryside*

Montalcino is the principal town in the commune of Montalcino, source of one of Italy's most prized wines.

Brunello di Montalcino

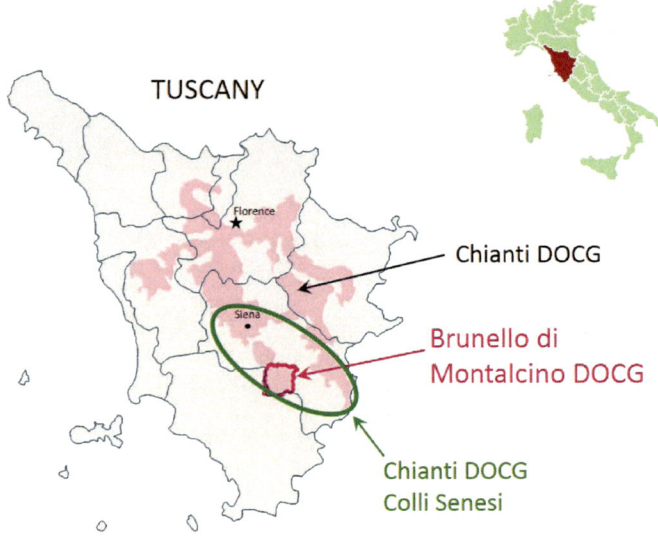

TUSCANY

Florence ★

Chianti DOCG

Siena

Brunello di
Montalcino DOCG

Chianti DOCG
Colli Senesi

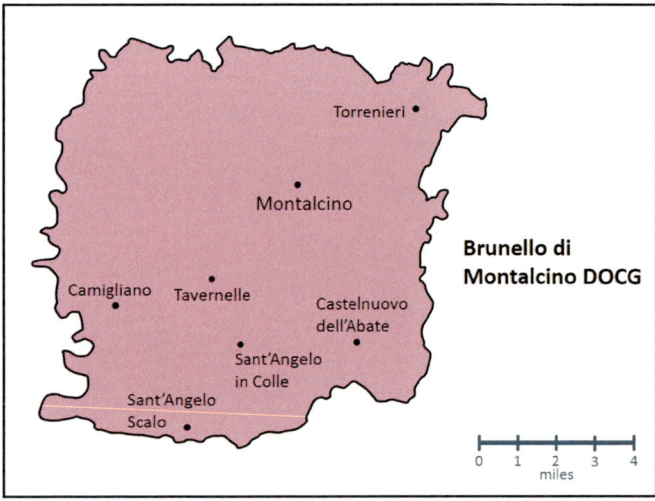

Torrenieri

Montalcino

**Brunello di
Montalcino DOCG**

Camigliano   Tavernelle

Castelnuovo
dell'Abate

Sant'Angelo
in Colle

Sant'Angelo
Scalo

0 1 2 3 4
miles

The area around the hill town of Montalcino is renowned for the superior quality of its Sangiovese, which locally goes by the name Brunello. Brunello di Montalcino DOCG is one of the most esteemed and expensive denominations for wine in Italy.

Montalcino is located south of Siena in Tuscany. It is within the boundaries of Chianti—more specifically within the Chianti subzone of Colli Senesi. But the Montalcino area set itself apart from the wider Chianti region largely due to the efforts of Ferruccio Biondi-Santi, who in the late 1800s took an avant-garde scientific approach to viticulture, isolating the very best Sangiovese vines in his vineyards and propagating them. It is the descendants of these Biondi-Santi vines that were called Brunello and that are used to make the wines of Montalcino today.

The boundaries of the commune of Montalcino coincide with those of the Montalcino denomination, although there are several smaller villages or hamlets (*frazioni*) within the commune (*see the expanded map at left*) including Camigliano, Castelnuovo dell'Abate, Sant'Angelo in Colle, Sant'Angelo Scalo, Tavernelle, and Torrenieri.

Brunello di Montalcino was another of the first DOCs in 1966 and first DOCGs in 1980, along with Barolo and Barbaresco. Like those two Piedmont regions, the Brunello di Montalcino DOCG produces two kinds of wine, a normale and a riserva. Both are made from 100% Brunello, aka Sangiovese, and both have a minimum alcohol level of 12.5%. The standard Brunello di Montalcino is aged for a minimum of four years before being released, including two years or more in barrels. The riserva requires one additional year of total aging.

There are 1,932 hectares (4,772 acres) of vineyards in the Brunello denomination and 208 producers in the Brunello consorzio. They produce 66,000 hectoliters (730,000 cases) of wine—less than Barolo, but twice as much as Barbaresco. These producers have the option of "declassifying" from Brunello di Montalcino DOCG to the Rosso di Montalcino DOC, another denomination with the same boundaries and producing only 100% Sangiovese wines. Or, if they want to blend in something other than Sangiovese, they can opt for the Sant'Antimo DOC. And of course, there's always IGP Toscana, which is available to any producer in Tuscany.

Brunello di Montalcino Denomination Regulations

	Brunello	Brunello Riserva
Composition	100% Sangiovese	100% Sangiovese
Minimum alcohol	12.5%	12.5%
Minimum aging	4 years, including 2 years in barrel	5 years, including 2 years in barrel

Bolgheri

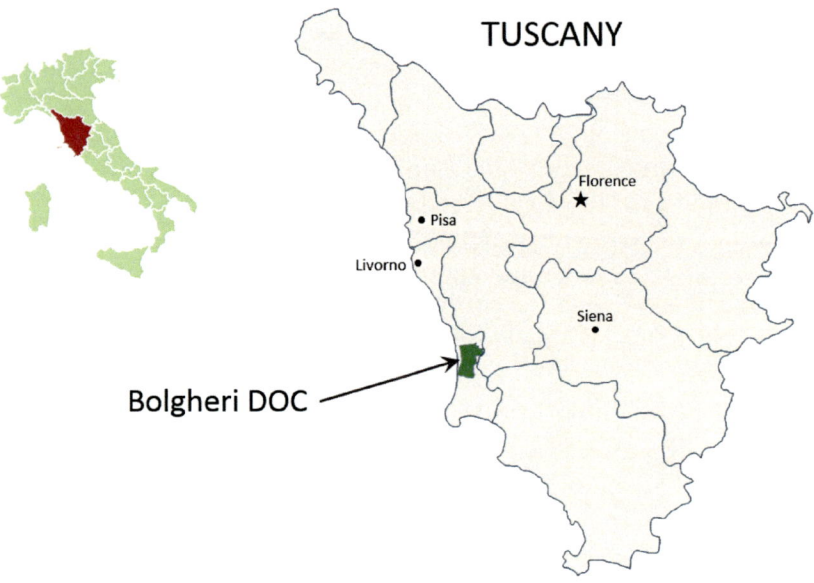

TUSCANY

Bolgheri DOC

As discussed in Unit 3, the Super Tuscan category evolved from world-class winemakers deciding to experiment with formulas and grape varieties that were modern and international rather than traditional. When they created some of the most sought-after wines in Italy, it became apparent that the wine laws needed to be rewritten to find a place to acknowledge high-quality, nontraditional wines such as these. Consequently, the IGT category was added to the existing denomination system in Italy in 1992. Since then, a few DOCs have been established for areas that have achieved acclaim for international varieties. Bolgheri is the most recognizable of these DOCs.

Many of the wines that rival Barolo and Brunello di Montalcino in fame and price are Super Tuscans located in the Bolgheri area of Tuscany. Bolgheri DOC is one of a handful of denominations created to give official status to Super Tuscan wines.

Bolgheri is located in coastal Tuscany, west of Siena and south of Livorno and Pisa. The denomination comprises most of the commune of Castagneto Carducci. The actual town of Bolgheri is near the top of the denomination, near some of the estates that originally created the Super Tuscan category, such as Tenuta dell'Ornellaia and Tenuta San Guido, maker of Sassicaia. In fact, Sassicaia is so famous that its vineyards were given the status of a subzone of the Bolgheri DOC in 1994 and then became a separate denomination called Bolgheri Sassicaia DOC in 2013.

Bolgheri achieved DOC status in 1983. Unlike the other denominations in this unit, Bolgheri is a denomination for not only red wines but also rosato and white wines. Whites can be varietals made from Sauvignon Blanc or Vermentino, or blends of Vermentino, Sauvignon Blanc, and/or Trebbiano.

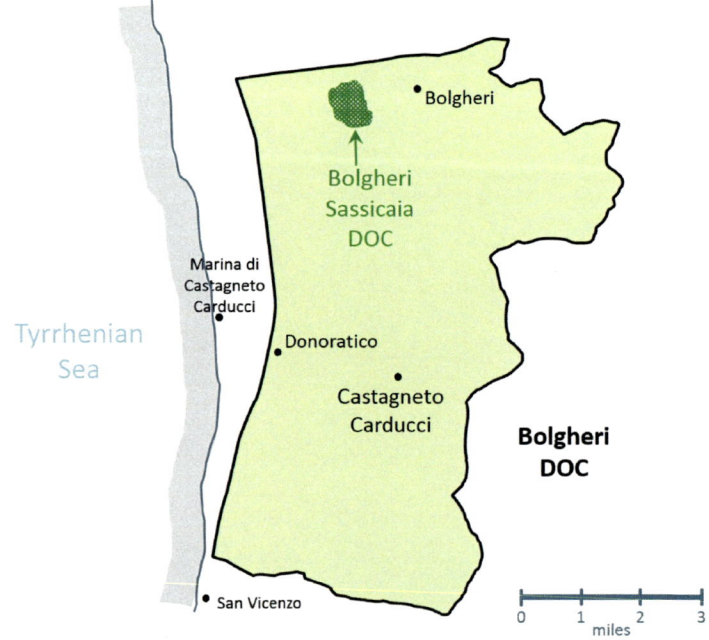

This famous alley of cypresses (left) *is the symbol of the Bolgheri DOC, as reflected in the denomination's logo* (below).

The red and rosato wines of Bolgheri can contain any proportions of the Bordeaux varieties Cabernet Sauvignon, Cabernet Franc, or Merlot—meaning they can be a blend or can be 100% of any of those. In addition, the wines can include Sangiovese and/or Syrah in the blend, but not more than 50% of either one. The standard Bolgheri red must be aged for a minimum of a year before being released. There is also a superiore (not riserva) version, which requires at least 12.5% alcohol and two years or more of aging, with at least a year in barrel.

The denomination has 1,050 hectares (2,594 acres) planted and produces 34,000 hectoliters (375,000 cases) per year. The Bolgheri consorzio has 40 producer-members.

Bolgheri Denomination Regulations (White Wines)

	Bianco	Sauvignon	Vermentino
Composition	0–70% Vermentino, 0–40% Sauvignon, 0–40% Trebbiano	85–100% Sauvignon Blanc	85–100% Vermentino
Minimum alcohol	11.0%	10.5%	11.0%
Minimum aging	No minimum	No minimum	No minimum

Bolgheri Denomination Regulations (Red Wines)

	Rosato	Rosso	Superiore
Composition	0–100% Cabernet Sauvignon, Cabernet Franc, or Merlot; 0–50% Sangiovese; 0–50% Syrah		
Minimum alcohol	11.5%	11.5%	12.5%
Minimum aging	No minimum	1 year	2 years, including 1 year in barrel

Amarone della Valpolicella

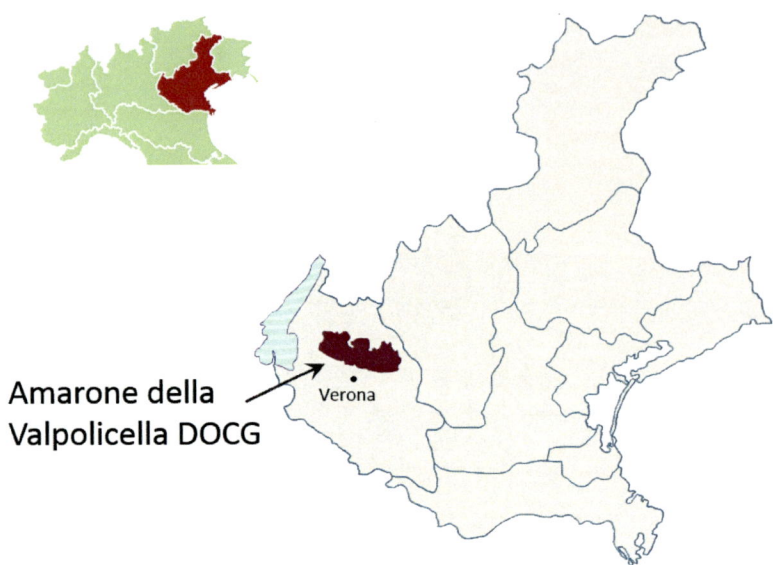

Amarone della
Valpolicella DOCG

Verona

grapes, but produce different styles of wine:

- Valpolicella DOC
- Valpolicella Ripasso DOC
- Recioto della Valpolicella DOCG
- Amarone della Valpolicella DOCG

All of these were originally part of the Valpolicella DOC when it was established in 1968, but they have been distinguished individually since then. Amarone, which has been lauded as a great wine for decades, officially remained just a style of Valpolicella DOC until finally becoming a separate DOCG in 2010.

The Valpolicella zone is just north of the city of Verona and contains several villages. The five villages of Fumane, Marano, Negrar, San Pietro in Cariano, and Sant'Ambrogio are the historical center of Valpolicella wines and make up the Classico subzone for all four denominations. Just to the east is another valley called Valpantena that also has subzone status.

Amarone della Valpolicella is probably the most famous example of a dry wine made from dried grapes. As

The last denomination to be covered in this unit is Amarone della Valpolicella.

The Valpolicella area has already been discussed in Unit 2 in the context of red wines and again in Unit 7 with regard to the sweet wine Recioto della Valpolicella. There are in fact four denominations that have the same boundaries and use the same blend of

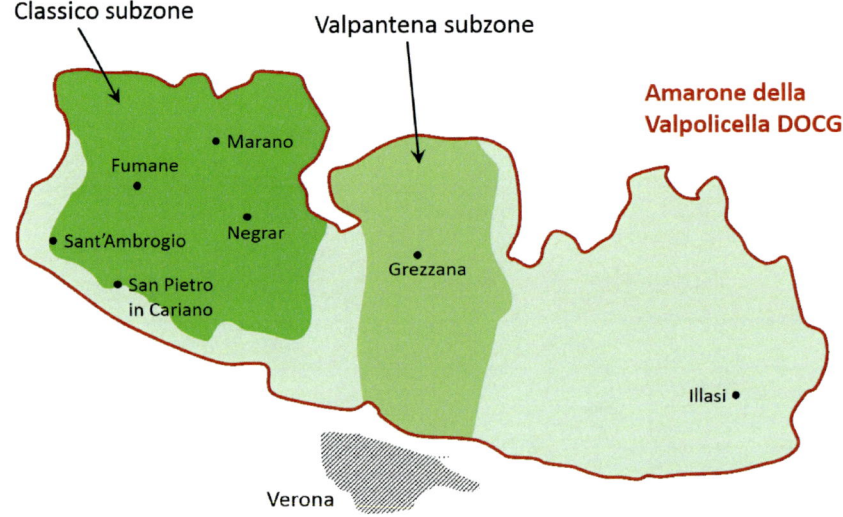

Classico subzone

Valpantena subzone

Amarone della
Valpolicella DOCG

Marano

Fumane

Sant'Ambrogio   Negrar

San Pietro
in Cariano

Grezzana

Illasi

Verona

noted in the discussion of sweet dried-grape wines, producers in Valpolicella harvest their best grapes at peak ripeness and then bring them into a drying room to undergo the appassimento process as they slowly lose their water and the sugar-to-water ratio increases. Top producers of Amarone will dry the grapes in the *fruttaio* or drying room until February or March of the year after the harvest before starting fermentation.

If these grapes are fermented such that there is residual sugar remaining at the end of the process, they will become Recioto della Valpolicella. Amarone della Valpolicella is made using essentially the same grapes but fermenting the must completely to produce a dry wine.

The fruttaio *or drying room in many Valpolicella wineries is in the attic of the winery itself or an outbuilding, where it gets hot but can be opened to the outside air for circulation and to promote drying. Over a period of months, the grapes slowly lose moisture and concentrate their sugars and flavors.*

Amarone della Valpolicella Denomination Regulations

	Amarone	Amarone Riserva
Composition	45–95% Corvina, 5–30% Rondinella	45–95% Corvina, 5–30% Rondinella
Minimum alcohol	14.0%	14.0%
Minimum aging	2 years	4 years

Amarone della Valpolicella is always a blended wine, using primarily Corvina grapes with a small to moderate percentage of Rondinella. The Rondinella component can range from 5% to 30%, while the Corvina content is nominally 45–95%. Other grape varieties may be included in the blend as well. One is Corvinone, a grape that is traditionally planted in and among the Corvina vines and can substitute for up to half the Corvina component. Molinara is another variety that is traditional in the blend; it was once required, but is now optional.

The minimum alcohol level, given that Amarone is made with sugar-laden dried grapes, is a hefty 14%, and many go much higher. Wines with 16% alcohol are common. All Amarone della Valpolicella is aged for at least two years, and if it is aged for four years, it can be designated as Riserva. Wood aging is not required.

The nearly 200 Amarone della Valpolicella DOCG producers make a bit less than 100,000 hectoliters (1.1 million cases) of Amarone annually.

That completes the discussion of Italian luxury wines for this lesson. In the remainder of this unit, we'll turn to two areas of Italian cuisine that are important in everyday life and a few terms that can come in handy if traveling to Italy.

Vineyards in the Valpolicella in Veneto

Italian Cheeses

Many well-known cheeses are Italian in origin. Chances are, you've tasted several of them.

Those cheeses that are traditional to specific areas are, like wine, eligible for place-name protection under EU law. Some Italian cheeses with DOP status include:

- Fontina, a semisoft cow's milk cheese of Valle d'Aosta
- Gorgonzola *(right),* a semisoft cow's milk blue cheese of Piedmont and Lombardy
- Taleggio, a semisoft cow's milk cheese of Piedmont, Lombardy, and Veneto
- Asiago, a hard cow's milk cheese of Veneto and Trentino
- Grana Padano, a hard cow's milk cheese made throughout most of northern Italy
- Provolone Valpadana, a firm cow's milk cheese of northern Italy
- Parmigiano Reggiano, a hard cow's milk cheese of Emilia Romagna and Lombardy
- Mozzarella di Bufala Campana *(right),* a soft to firm buffalo's milk cheese of Campania and neighboring regions
- Pecorino, a hard sheep's milk cheese with five DOPs from Tuscany to Basilicata and the islands

Other familiar Italian cheeses include ricotta, a whey cheese made from the milk solids left over from making of other types of cheeses, and mascarpone, a soft cheese from Lombardy made from curdled cream and often used for desserts such as tiramisù.

Top: *Gorgonzola for sale at an open-air market*
Bottom: *Balls of fresh mozzarella*

Coffee

Coffee is serious business in Italy, consumed morning, noon, and night. The word is *caffè*, with two *f*'s. In Italy, it's always espresso—unless it's powdered instant, as is normal for decaf.

Coffee is served everywhere, from the innumerable caffè bars to gas stations and movie theaters.

In most establishments, to get a cup of coffee, you can either stand at the bar or sit at a table. Prices are generally a little higher if you sit. If you choose to stand, the procedure is to pay first at the cash register, and then to take your receipt to the bar and order from the barista. Seated customers order from the waiter. In either case, tips are not expected, although leaving some small change for the waiter is common.

If you ask for *un caffè,* you will receive an espresso in what by American standards is a very small cup. There are many coffee drinks available besides a straight espresso, though. A short list includes:

- **Cappuccino:** espresso with steamed milk and milk foam
- **Caffè latte:** espresso with steamed milk (don't order just "latte" or you'll get only milk)
- **Macchiato:** espresso with a spot of steamed milk, unstirred
- **Doppio:** double shot of espresso
- **Caffè americano:** watered-down espresso (which tastes different than American brewed coffee)
- **Caffè corretto:** espresso "corrected" with grappa or other liquor

Italian Language: Dining, Drinking, & Travel Terms

Some basic dining terms and phrases

1. Lunch = **Pranzo** (*prahn*-zoh)
2. Dinner = **Cena** (*chay*-nah)
3. Restaurant = **Ristorante** (riss-sto-*rahn*-tay) or **Trattoria** (tra-*toh*-rya)
4. Tavern = **Osteria** (oh-stay-*ree*-ya) or **Enoteca** (eh-no-*tay*-kah)
5. Appetizer = **Antipasto** (ahn-tee-*pah*-sto) or **spuntino** (spoon-*tee*-no)
6. First/second course = **Primo/secondo piatto** (*pree*-mo/say-*kohn*-do *pyaht*-toh)
7. Fish = **Pesce** (*pay*-shay)
8. Meat = **Carne** (*kar*-nay)
9. Side dish = **Contorno** (kohn-*tor*-no), plural **contorni** (kohn-*tor*-nee)
10. Dessert = **Dolce** (*dohl*-chay), plural **dolci** (*dohl*-chee)
11. I/We would like . . . = **Vorrei** (vohr-*ray*)/**Vorremmo** (vohr-*ray*-mo)
12. May I/we have . . . ? = **Posso/Possiamo avere** (*pohss*-soh/poh-see-*ah*-mo ah-*vay*-ray)**?**
13. Do you have a table for two? = **C'e un tavolo per due?** (Chay oon *tah*-vo-lo pair *doo*-ay?)
14. Where is the restroom? = **Dov'è il bagno?** (Doh-*vay* eel *bah*-nyo?)
15. The check, please = **Il conto, per favore** (Eel *kohn*-toh, pair fah-*voh*-ray)

Ordering wine

1. Wine = **Vino** (*vee*-no), plural **vini** (*vee*-nee)
2. Glass = **Bicchiere** (beek-*kyay*-ray), plural **bicchieri** (beek-*kyay*-ree)
3. Bottle = **Bottiglia** (boat-*tee*-lyah), plural **bottiglie** (boat-*tee*-lyay)
4. Carafe = **Caraffa** (kah-*rahf*-fah)
5. Tasting = **Degustazione** (day-goo-stah-tzee-*oh*-nay)
6. I would like a glass of red wine = **Vorrei** (vohr-*ray*) **un bicchiere di vino rosso**
7. May we have a bottle of white wine? = **Possiamo avere una bottiglia di vino bianco?**

Traveling and shopping

1. **Uscita** (oo-*shee*-ta) = Exit
2. **Spingere** (*speen*-jay-ray) = Push
3. **Tirare** (tee-*rah*-ray) = Pull
4. P = **Parcheggio** (par-*kay*-jo) = Parking
5. **Stazione** (staht-*zyoh*-nay) **(ferroviaria)** = (Train) station
6. **Biglietto** (bee-*lyet*-toh) = Ticket
7. **Andata** (ahn-*dah*-ta) = One-way
8. **Andata e ritorno** (ree-*tor*-no) = Round-trip
9. Price = **Prezzo** (*pret*-tzoh)
10. Discount = **Sconto** (*skohn*-toh)
11. Size = **Misura** (mee-*zoo*-ra) or **Numero** (*noo*-may-roh)
12. Receipt = **Ricevuta** (ree-chay-*voo*-tah)
13. How much does this cost? = **Quanto costa?** (*kwan*-toh *koh*-stah)

Unit 8 Exercises

These last exercises focus on the six denominations discussed in Unit 8: Barolo, Barbaresco, Chianti Classico, Brunello di Montalcino, Bolgheri, and Amarone della Valpolicella.

1. Which three Italian regions are represented by the luxury wines highlighted in this unit? Why do you think luxury wines are concentrated in these three regions rather than being more widely dispersed? How would you rank the following factors in the success of these wines relative to other Italian wines? (There is no one correct answer, but think about how you would explain to another wine professional why these denominations have reached luxury status.)
    *   Local climatic conditions
    *   History and cultural influences
    *   Individual winemakers
    *   Grape varieties used
    *   Proximity to export channels/markets
    *   Other factors
2. Based on your own experiences with these luxury wines, if any, how would you rank them in terms of quality and personal enjoyment? Why? Are there other Italian wines you would add to this list based on personal experience?
3. Of the six denominations of Unit 8, which ones have a Riserva designation? Which one has a designation higher than Riserva? Which one has a Superiore wine?
4. Fill in the blanks in the following table listing the aging requirements for Unit 8 wines.

Minimum Aging Required Before Release		Denomination
Total	In wood	
1 year		Bolgheri Rosso and _____
2 years	Not required	_____ and Chianti Classico Riserva
	9 months	Barbaresco
	1 year	
2½ years	Not required	
3 years		Barolo
4 years		Amarone Riserva
4 years	9 months	
4 years	2 years	
	18 months	Barolo Riserva
5 years		Brunello di Montalcino Riserva

5. Which of the six denominations *require* 100% of a single grape variety in their red wines? Name the denomination(s) and variety(ies). Which additional ones *allow* 100% varietal wines? Name the denomination(s) and variety(ies).
6. Of the six denominations, how many produce white and/or rosato wines? Which two white grape varieties can make up a majority component in the white wines?
7. Match the following communes with the denomination in which they are located:

- Barbaresco
- Barolo
- Castagneto Carducci
- Castellina
- Castelnuovo Berardenga
- Castiglione Falletto

- Fumane
- Gaiole
- Greve
- La Morra
- Monforte d'Alba
- Montalcino
- Negrar
- Neive

- Radda
- San Casciano in Val di Pesa
- San Pietro in Cariano
- Sant'Ambrogio
- Serralunga d'Alba
- Treiso

8. What are menzioni geografiche aggiuntive? Which of the six denominations have them?
9. Only one of the six denominations requires at least two grape varieties in the wine. What are the required varieties and percentages for this denomination?
10. What differences, if any, are there in the requirements for the three levels of Chianti Classico with regard to the grapes used?
11. Only one of the six denominations currently has subzones. Which one is it, and what are the two subzones? Which one had a small but very famous subzone until it became a separate DOC in 2013?
12. Which of the six denominations has the highest minimum alcohol requirement? Why is it so high?
13. Which of the six denominations have another denomination with the same boundaries that producers can use for similar but simpler wines?
14. Fill in the blanks in the following table.

Denomination	Level	Region	Primary Grape Variety	Min. Alcohol	Minimum Aging
Amarone della Valpolicella	DOCG				
Barbaresco Riserva				12.5%	
Barolo					3 years, incl. 18 mo. in wood
Bolgheri Rosso		Tuscany			
Brunello di Montalcino Riserva					
Chianti Classico Gran Selezione			Sangiovese		

Sunset in Piedmont

Synopsis of Rules for Selected Denominations

This section lists the key facts and wine production rules of the DOCs and DOCGs discussed in the Italian Wine Professional course, including region, wine styles produced, grape varieties used, and minimum aging requirements for the denomination's primary wines. The information is accurate as of the print date. For updates and additional information on these and all of the Italian denominations, see the Italian Wine Central website at ItalianWineCentral.com.

Affile DOC *see* Cesanese di Affile DOC

Aglianico del Taburno DOCG

REGION: CAMPANIA

Red and rosato wines
- Min. 85% Aglianico
- *Aging:* Min. 2 years for Rosso (min. 3 years for Rosso Riserva with 1 year in wood)

Aglianico del Vulture DOC

REGION: BASILICATA
- Same boundaries as Aglianico del Vulture Superiore DOCG

Red wines
- 100% Aglianico
- *Aging:* Min. 1 year

Aglianico del Vulture Superiore DOCG

REGION: BASILICATA
- Same boundaries as Aglianico del Vulture DOC

Red wines
- 100% Aglianico
- *Aging:* Min. 1 year

OTHER WINES: Sparkling red wines (Aglianico)

Alta Langa DOCG

REGION: PIEDMONT

White or rosato metodo classico sparkling wines
- Min. 90% Chardonnay and/or Pinot Nero
- *Aging:* Min. 2½ years (min. 3 years for Riserva)

Alto Adige (Südtirol) DOC

REGION: TRENTINO–ALTO ADIGE
- Subzones: Colli di Bolzano (Bozner Leiten), Meranese di Collina (Meraner Hügel), Santa Maddalena (St. Magdalener), Terlano (Terlaner), Valle Isarco (Eisacktal), and Valle Venosta (Vinschgau)

White wines
- Nonvarietal Bianco: Min. 75% Chardonnay, Pinot Bianco, and/or Pinot Grigio
- Numerous varietals allowed (min. 85% of stated variety)
- *Aging:* For Riserva, min. 2 years

Red and rosato wines
- Numerous varietals allowed (min. 85% of stated variety)
- *Aging:* For Riserva, min. 2 years

White or rosato metodo classico sparkling wines
- Blend of Chardonnay, Pinot Bianco, and/or Pinot Nero (min. 20% Pinot Nero for Rosato or Rosé)

- *Aging:* Min. 20 months, incl. 15 months on the lees (min. 42 months for Riserva with 3 years on the lees)

OTHER WINES: Klausner Laitacher (red blend); vendemmia tardiva; passito

Amarone della Valpolicella DOCG

REGION: VENETO

- Same boundaries as three other Valpolicella denominations
- Subzones: Classico and Valpantena

Red wines

- 45–95% Corvina and/or Corvinone; 5–30% Rondinella
- Dried-grape wine, fermented dry
- *Aging:* Min. 2 years (min. 4 years for Riserva)

Asolo Prosecco DOCG

REGION: VENETO

Sparkling wines

- Min. 85% Glera
- Usually made by tank method but can be metodo classico

OTHER WINES: Still wines (min. 85% Glera)

Asti DOCG

REGION: PIEDMONT

Moscato d'Asti: White, sweet frizzante wines

- 100% Moscato
- Always made by tank method

Asti: White, sweet sparkling wines

- 100% Moscato
- Usually made by tank method but can be metodo classico

OTHER WINES: Vendemmia tardiva; subzones Canelli, Santa Vittoria d'Alba, and Strevi

Barbaresco DOCG

REGION: PIEDMONT

Red wines

- 100% Nebbiolo
- 66 menzioni geografiche aggiuntive (crus)
- *Aging:* Min. 2 years, incl. 9 months in wood (min. 4 years for Riserva with 9 months in wood)

Barbera d'Alba DOC

REGION: PIEDMONT

Red wines

- Min. 85% Barbera
- *Aging:* For Superiore, min. 1 year, incl. 4 months in wood

Barbera d'Asti DOCG

REGION: PIEDMONT

Red wines

- Min. 90% Barbera
- *Aging:* For Superiore, min. 1 year, incl. 6 months in wood (more for subzones)

OTHER WINES: Subzones Colli Astiani and Tinella (and before 2014, Nizza)

Bardolino DOC

REGION: VENETO

- Same boundaries as Bardolino Superiore DOCG

Rosato wines

- Chiaretto: 35–80% Corvina and/or Corvinone; 10–40% Rondinella

Red wines

- 35–80% Corvina and/or Corvinone; 10–40% Rondinella

OTHER WINES: Novello; sparkling Chiaretto; subzone Classico

Bardolino Superiore DOCG

REGION: VENETO

- Same boundaries as Bardolino DOC

Red wines

- 35–80% Corvina and/or Corvinone; 10–40% Rondinella
- *Aging:* Min. 1 year

OTHER WINES: Subzone Classico

Barolo DOCG

REGION: PIEDMONT

Red wines

- 100% Nebbiolo
- 181 menzioni geografiche aggiuntive (crus)
- *Aging:* Min. 3 years, incl. 18 months in wood (min. 5 years for Riserva with 18 months in wood)

Bianco di Custoza (Custoza) DOC

REGION: VENETO

White wines

- Blend of Friulano, Garganega, and Trebbiano, possibly with other white grapes

OTHER WINES: Sparkling wines; passito

Bolgheri DOC

REGION: TUSCANY

White wines

- Nonvarietal Bianco: Blend of primarily Vermentino (max. 70%) with Sauvignon Blanc and/or Trebbiano
- Varietals: Min. 85% Sauvignon Blanc or Vermentino

Red and rosato wines

- Any proportions of Cabernet Franc, Cabernet Sauvignon, and/or Merlot; max. 50% Sangiovese; max. 50% Syrah
- *Aging:* Min. 1 year (min. 2 years for Superiore, incl. 1 year in wood)

Bolgheri Sassicaia DOC

REGION: TUSCANY

Red wines

- Min. 80% Cabernet Sauvignon
- *Aging:* Min. 2 years, incl. 18 months in wood

Bonarda dell'Oltrepò Pavese DOC

REGION: LOMBARDY

- Same boundaries as Oltrepò Pavese DOC

Red wines

- Min. 85% Croatina

Brachetto d'Acqui DOCG

REGION: PIEDMONT

Red, sweet sparkling wines

- Min. 97% Brachetto
- Usually made by tank method but can be metodo classico

OTHER WINES: Red sweet still wines (Brachetto); passito

Brunello di Montalcino DOCG

REGION: TUSCANY

- Same boundaries as Rosso di Montalcino DOC and Sant'Antimo DOC

Red wines

- 100% Sangiovese (aka Brunello)
- *Aging:* Min. 4 years, incl. 2 years in wood (min. 5 years for Riserva with 2 years in wood)

Caluso DOCG *see* Erbaluce di Caluso DOCG

Cannonau di Sardegna DOC

REGION: SARDINIA

Red and rosato wines

- Min. 85% Cannonau (min. 90% for Classico)
- *Aging:* For Classico, min. 2 years, incl. 1 year in wood

OTHER WINES: Passito; liquoroso wines; subzones Capo Ferrato, Jerzu, and (Nepente di) Oliena

Carmignano DOCG

REGION: TUSCANY

Red wines

- Min. 50% Sangiovese; 10–20% Cabernet Franc and/or Cabernet Sauvignon
- *Aging:* Min. 20 months, incl. 8 months in wood (min. 3 years for Riserva with 1 year in wood)

Castel del Monte DOC

REGION: PUGLIA

- Same boundaries as three Castel del Monte DOCGs

White wines

- Nonvarietal Bianco: Blend of Bombino Bianco, Chardonnay, and/or Pampanuto
- Varietals: Min. 90% Bombino Bianco, Chardonnay, or Sauvignon Blanc

Rosato wines

- Blend of Aglianico, Bombino Nero, and/or Uva di Troia

Red wines

- Nonvarietal Rosso: Blend of Aglianico, Montepulciano, and/or Uva di Troia
- Varietals: Min. 90% Aglianico, Cabernet (Franc and/or Sauvignon), or Uva di Troia
- *Aging:* For Riserva, min. 2 years, incl. 1 year in wood

OTHER WINES: Novello; sparkling wines

Castel del Monte Bombino Nero DOCG

REGION: PUGLIA

- Same boundaries as three other Castel del Monte denominations

Rosato wines

- Min. 90% Bombino Nero

Castel del Monte Nero di Troia Riserva DOCG

REGION: PUGLIA

- Same boundaries as three other Castel del Monte denominations

Red wines

- Min. 90% Uva di Troia
- *Aging:* Min. 2 years, incl. 1 year in wood

Castel del Monte Rosso Riserva DOCG

REGION: PUGLIA

- Same boundaries as three other Castel del Monte denominations

Red wines

- Min. 65% Uva di Troia
- *Aging:* Min. 2 years, incl. 1 year in wood

Castelli di Jesi Verdicchio Riserva DOCG

REGION: MARCHE

- Same boundaries as Verdicchio dei Castelli di Jesi DOC

White wines

- Min. 85% Verdicchio
- *Aging:* Min. 1½ years

OTHER WINES: Classico subzone and 99 *menzioni geografiche aggiuntive* (crus)

Cerasuolo d'Abruzzo DOC

REGION: ABRUZZO

- Same boundaries as Montepulciano d'Abruzzo DOC and Trebbiano d'Abruzzo DOC

Rosato wines

- Min. 85% Montepulciano

Cerasuolo di Vittoria DOCG

REGION: SICILY

Red wines

- 50–70% Nero d'Avola; 30–50% Frappato
- *Aging:* For Rosso from the Classico subzone, min. 1½ years

Cesanese del Piglio (Piglio) DOCG

REGION: LAZIO

Red wines

- Min. 90% Cesanese
- *Aging:* For Superiore, min. 18 months; for Superiore Riserva, min. 20 months

Cesanese di Affile (Affile) DOC

REGION: LAZIO

Red wines

- Min. 90% Cesanese
- *Aging:* For Riserva, min. 18 months

Cesanese di Olevano Romano (Olevano Romano) DOC

REGION: LAZIO

Red wines

- Min. 85% Cesanese
- *Aging:* For Riserva, min. 2 years

Chianti DOCG

REGION: TUSCANY

- Subzones: Colli Aretini, Colli Fiorentini, Colline Pisane, Colli Senesi, Montalbano, Montespertoli, and Rufina

Red wines

- Min. 70% Sangiovese (min. 75% Sangiovese for subzone Colli Senesi)
- *Aging:* For Superiore, min. 1 year; for Riserva, min. 2 years (requirements differ in some subzones)

Chianti Classico DOCG

REGION: TUSCANY

Red wines

- Min. 80% Sangiovese (aka Sangioveto)
- Grapes for Gran Selezione level must be estate grown

- *Aging:* Min. 1 year (min. 2 years for Riserva; min. 2½ years for Gran Selezione)

Cirò DOC

REGION: CALABRIA

White wines
- Min. 80% Greco Bianco

Red and rosato wines
- Min. 80% Gaglioppo
- *Aging:* For Rosso Riserva, min. 2 years

OTHER WINES: Subzone Classico; Rosso Superiore

Colli Bolognesi Pignoletto DOCG

REGION: EMILIA ROMAGNA
- Same boundaries as Pignoletto DOC

White wines
- Min. 85% Grechetto (min. 95% for Classico Superiore)
- *Aging:* For Classico Superiore, min. 1 year

White sparkling wines
- Min. 85% Grechetto

Collio Goriziano (Collio) DOC

REGION: FRIULI–VENEZIA GIULIA

White wines
- Blend of (or varietal) Chardonnay, Friulano, Pinot Bianco, Pinot Grigio, Ribolla Gialla, Sauvignon Blanc, and/or several other white grapes
- *Aging:* For Riserva, min. 1½ years

Red wines
- Blend of (or varietal) Cabernet Franc, Cabernet Sauvignon, Merlot, and/or Pinot Nero
- *Aging:* For Riserva, min. 1½ years, incl. 6 months in wood

Conegliano Valdobbiadene Prosecco DOCG

REGION: VENETO

Sparkling wines
- Min. 85% Glera
- Usually made by tank method but can be metodo classico
- Subzone: Cartizze

OTHER WINES: Still wines (Glera); Rive (from specific communes, hand harvested, and vintage dated)

Cònero DOCG

REGION: MARCHE
- Same boundaries as Rosso Cònero DOC

Red wines
- Min. 85% Montepulciano
- *Aging:* Min. 2 years

Cortese di Gavi DOCG *see* Gavi DOCG

Custoza DOC *see* Bianco di Custoza DOC

Diano d'Alba (Dolcetto di Diano d'Alba) DOCG

REGION: PIEDMONT

Red wines
- 100% Dolcetto
- *Aging:* For Superiore, min. 1 year

OTHER WINES: 75 *menzioni geografiche aggiuntive* (sori)

Dogliani DOCG

REGION: PIEDMONT

Red wines
- 100% Dolcetto
- *Aging:* Min. 1 year

Dolcetto d'Acqui DOC

REGION: PIEDMONT

Red wines
- 100% Dolcetto
- *Aging:* Min. 1 year for Superiore

Dolcetto d'Alba DOC

REGION: PIEDMONT

Red wines
- 100% Dolcetto
- *Aging:* Min. 1 year for Superiore

Dolcetto d'Asti DOC

REGION: PIEDMONT

Red wines
- 100% Dolcetto
- *Aging:* Min. 1 year for Superiore

Dolcetto di Diano d'Alba *see* Diano d'Alba DOCG

Dolcetto di Ovada DOC

REGION: PIEDMONT

- Same boundaries as Dolcetto di Ovada Superiore DOCG

Red wines

- Min. 97% Dolcetto

Dolcetto di Ovada Superiore DOCG *see* Ovada DOCG

Erbaluce di Caluso (Caluso) DOCG

REGION: PIEDMONT

White wines

- 100% Erbaluce

OTHER WINES: Metodo classico sparkling wines; passito

Est! Est!! Est!!! di Montefiascone DOC

REGION: LAZIO

White wines

- Min. 75% Trebbiano (Toscano and Giallo/Rossetto) with 10–20% Malvasia

OTHER WINES: Subzone Classico; sparkling wines

Etna DOC

REGION: SICILY

White wines

- Min. 60% Carricante

Red and rosato wines

- Min. 80% Nerello Mascalese
- *Aging:* For Rosso Riserva, min. 4 years, incl. 1 year in wood

OTHER WINES: Bianco Superiore (min. 80% Carricante); white and rosato metodo classico sparkling wines (min. 60% Nerello Mascalese)

Etschtaler DOC *see* Valdadige DOC

Falanghina del Sannio DOC

REGION: CAMPANIA

White wines

- Min. 85% Falanghina
- *Aging:* Min. 1 year on the lees for metodo

classico sparkling wines

OTHER WINES: Sparkling wine; vendemmia tardiva; passito; subzones Guardia Sanframondi, Sant'Agata dei Goti, Solopaca, and Taburno

Fiano di Avellino DOCG

REGION: CAMPANIA

White wines

- Min. 85% Fiano

Franciacorta DOCG

REGION: LOMBARDY

White or rosato metodo classico sparkling wines

- Min. 50% Chardonnay and/or Pinot Nero; max. 50% Pinot Bianco
- For Rosato (Rosé), min. 25% Pinot Nero
- For Satén, no Pinot Nero
- *Aging:* Min. 1½ years on the lees (min. 2 years for Rosato and Satén; min. 2½ years for vintage-dated [Millesimato] wines; min. 5 years for Riserva)

Frascati DOC

REGION: LAZIO

- Same boundaries as Frascati Superiore DOCG

White wines

- Min. 70% Malvasia

OTHER WINES: Sparkling wines

Frascati Superiore DOCG

REGION: LAZIO

- Same boundaries as Frascati DOC

White wines

- Min. 70% Malvasia
- *Aging:* For Riserva, min. 1 year

Friuli Colli Orientali DOC

REGION: FRIULI–VENEZIA GIULIA

White wines

- Blend of (or varietal) Chardonnay, Friulano, Pinot Bianco, Pinot Grigio, Ribolla Gialla, Sauvignon Blanc, and/or several other white grapes
- *Aging:* For Riserva, min. 2 years

Red wines

- Blend of (or varietal) Cabernet (Franc and/or Sauvignon), Merlot, Pinot Nero, Refosco, and/or a few other red grapes
- *Aging:* For Riserva, min. 2 years (min. 3 years for varietal Pignolo)

OTHER WINES: Dolce dessert wine; subzones Cialla, Faedis, Prepotto, and Rosazzo with some variations in rules

Friuli Grave DOC

REGION: FRIULI–VENEZIA GIULIA

White wines

- Blend of (or varietal) Chardonnay, Friulano, Gewürztraminer (Traminer Aromatico), Pinot Bianco, Pinot Grigio, Riesling, Sauvignon Blanc, and/or Verduzzo
- *Aging:* For Riserva, min. 2 years

Red and rosato wines

- Blend of (or varietal red) Cabernet Franc, Cabernet Sauvignon, Carmenère, Merlot, Pinot Nero, and/or Refosco
- *Aging:* For Riserva, min. 2 years

White or rosato sparkling wines

- Blend of (or varietal) Chardonnay, Pinot Bianco, and/or Pinot Nero

OTHER WINES: Novello; Superiore

Garda DOC

REGIONS: LOMBARDY AND VENETO

White wines

- Nonvarietal Bianco: Min. 70% Riesling and/or Welschriesling (Riesling Italico)
- Numerous varietals allowed (min. 85% of stated variety)

Red and rosato wines

- Nonvarietal Rosso and Chiaretto (rosato): Blend of Groppello, Barbera, Marzemino, and/or Sangiovese
- Numerous red varietals allowed (min. 85% of stated variety)
- *Aging:* For Rosso Superiore, min. 1½ years; for Rosso Riserva, min. 2 years

OTHER WINES: Novello; sparkling wines; subzone Classico

Gattinara DOCG

REGION: PIEDMONT

Red wines

- Min. 90% Nebbiolo (aka Spanna)
- *Aging:* Min. 3 years, incl. 2 years in wood (min. 4 years for Riserva with 3 years in wood)

Gavi (Cortese di Gavi) DOCG

REGION: PIEDMONT

White wines

- 100% Cortese
- *Aging:* For Riserva, min. 1 year

OTHER WINES: Sparkling wines

Ghemme DOCG

REGION: PIEDMONT

Red wines

- Min. 85% Nebbiolo (aka Spanna)
- *Aging:* Min. 3 years, incl. 18 months in wood (min. 4 years for Riserva with 2 years in wood)

Greco di Tufo DOCG

REGION: CAMPANIA

White wines

- Min. 85% Greco

OTHER WINES: Metodo classico sparkling wines

Lambrusco di Sorbara DOC

REGION: EMILIA ROMAGNA

Red and rosato frizzante wines

- 100% Lambrusco (min. 60% of the Lambrusco di Sorbara subtype)

OTHER WINES: Sparkling wine

Lambrusco Grasparossa di Castelvetro DOC

REGION: EMILIA ROMAGNA

Red and rosato frizzante wines

- Min. 85% Lambrusco Grasparossa

OTHER WINES: Sparkling wine

Lambrusco Salamino di Santa Croce DOC

REGION: EMILIA ROMAGNA

Red and rosato frizzante wines

- Min. 85% Lambrusco Salamino

OTHER WINES: Sparkling wine

Langhe DOC

REGION: PIEDMONT

White wines

- Nonvarietal Bianco: Blend of any locally authorized white grapes
- Varietals: Min. 85% Arneis, Chardonnay, Favorita, Nascetta, Riesling, Rossese Bianco, or Sauvignon Blanc

Rosato wines

- Min. 60% Barbera, Dolcetto, and/or Nebbiolo

Red wines

- Nonvarietal Rosso: Blend of any locally authorized red grapes
- Varietals: Min. 85% Barbera, Cabernet Sauvignon, Dolcetto, Freisa, Merlot, Nebbiolo, or Pinot Nero

OTHER WINES: Novello; 100% Nascetta from subzone Nascetta; Passito wines

Lugana DOC

REGIONS: LOMBARDY AND VENETO

White wines

- Min. 90% Trebbiano di Soave (aka Trebbiano di Lugana or Turbiana)
- *Aging:* For Superiore, min. 1 year; for Riserva, min. 2 years

Sparkling wines

- Min. 90% Trebbiano di Soave

OTHER WINES: Vendemmia tardiva

Maremma Toscana DOC

REGION: TUSCANY

White wines

- Nonvarietal Bianco: Min. 40% Trebbiano and/or Vermentino
- Varietals: Min. 85% Ansonica, Chardonnay, Sauvignon Blanc, Trebbiano, Vermentino, or Viognier

Rosato wines

- Min. 40% Ciliegiolo and/or Sangiovese

Red wines

- Nonvarietal Rosso: Min. 40% Sangiovese
- Varietals: Min. 85% Alicante, Cabernet (Franc and/or Sauvignon), Canaiolo, Ciliegiolo, Merlot, Sangiovese, or Syrah

OTHER WINES: Novello; sparkling wines; vendemmia tardiva; passito; Vin Santo

Marsala DOC

REGION: SICILY

Sweet fortified dessert wines

- Ambra (amber-colored) and Oro (golden): Blend of Ansonica (aka Inzolia), Catarratto, Damaschino, and/or Grillo
- Rubino (ruby-colored): Min. 70% Nerello Mascalese, Nero d'Avola, and/or Perricone
- *Aging:* for Fine, min. 1 year; for Superiore, min. 2 years; for Superiore Riserva, min. 4 years; for Vergine, min. 5 years; for Vergine Stravecchio, min. 10 years (in each case, all but 4 months in wood)

Monferrato DOC

REGION: PIEDMONT

White wines

- Blend of any locally authorized white grapes

Rosato wines

- Chiaretto: Blend of locally authorized red grapes

Red wines

- Nonvarietal Rosso: Blend of any locally authorized red grapes
- Varietals: Min. 85% Dolcetto or Freisa

OTHER WINES: Novello; varietal Cortese from subzone Casalese

Montefalco Sagrantino DOCG

REGION: UMBRIA

Red wines

- 100% Sagrantino
- *Aging:* Min. 3 years, incl. 1 year in wood

OTHER WINES: Passito

Montepulciano d'Abruzzo DOC

REGION: ABRUZZO

- Same boundaries as Cerasuolo d'Abruzzo

DOC and Trebbiano d'Abruzzo DOC

Red wines

- Min. 85% Montepulciano
- *Aging:* For Riserva, min. 2 years

OTHER WINES: Subzones Alto Tirino, (Terre di) Casauria, Teate, Terre dei Peligni, and Terre dei Vestini (subzones have higher percentages of Montepulciano and different, longer aging requirements)

Montepulciano d'Abruzzo Colline Teramane DOCG

REGION: ABRUZZO

Red wines

- Min. 90% Montepulciano
- *Aging:* Min. 1 year (min. 3 years for Riserva with 1 year in wood)

Morellino di Scansano DOCG

REGION: TUSCANY

Red wines

- Min. 85% Sangiovese (aka Morellino)
- *Aging:* For Riserva, min. 2 years, incl. 1 year in wood

Nizza DOCG

REGION: PIEDMONT

Red wines

- 100% Barbera
- *Aging:* Min. 1½ years, incl. 6 months in wood (min. 2½ years for Riserva with 1 year in wood)

Nuragus di Cagliari DOC

REGION: SARDINIA

White still and frizzante wines

- Min. 85% Nuragus

Offida DOCG

REGION: MARCHE

White wines

- Varietals: Min. 85% Passerina or Pecorino

Red wines

- Varietal: Min. 85% Montepulciano
- *Aging:* Min. 2 years, incl. 1 year in wood

Olevano Romano DOC *see* Cesanese di Olevano Romano DOC

Oltrepò Pavese DOC

REGION: LOMBARDY

- Same boundaries as four other Oltrepò Pavese denominations (Bonarda, Metodo Classico, Pinot Grigio, Pinot Nero)

White wines

- Nonvarietal Bianco: Min. 60% Riesling and/or Welschriesling (Riesling Italico)
- Varietals: Min. 85% Chardonnay, Cortese, Malvasia, Moscato, Pinot Nero (as a white wine), Riesling, or Sauvignon Blanc

Red and rosato wines

- Nonvarietal Rosso and Rosato: Blend primarily of Barbera and Croatina
- Varietals: Min. 85% Barbera, Cabernet Sauvignon, or Pinot Nero
- *Aging:* For Riserva, min. 2 years

OTHER WINES: Tank-method sparkling wines; passito; liquoroso wines

Oltrepò Pavese Metodo Classico DOCG

REGION: LOMBARDY

- Same boundaries as Oltrepò Pavese DOC

White or rosato metodo classico sparkling wines

- Min. 70% Pinot Nero; remainder Chardonnay, Pinot Bianco, and/or Pinot Grigio
- *Aging:* Min. 15 months on the lees (min. 2 years for vintage-dated [Millesimato] wines)

Oltrepò Pavese Pinot Grigio DOC

REGION: LOMBARDY

- Same boundaries as Oltrepò Pavese DOC

White wines

- Min. 85% Pinot Grigio

Orvieto DOC

REGIONS: LAZIO AND UMBRIA

White wines

- Blend primarily of Grechetto and/or Trebbiano

OTHER WINES: Muffa nobile; vendemmia tardiva; subzone Classico

Ovada (Dolcetto di Ovada Superiore) DOCG

REGION: PIEDMONT
- Same boundaries as Dolcetto di Ovada DOC

Red wines
- 100% Dolcetto
- *Aging:* Min. 1 year (min. 20 months if single-vineyard, min. 2 years for Riserva)

Pantelleria DOC

REGION: SICILY

Sweet dessert wines
- 100% Zibibbo
- Passito (dried-grape) and/or liquoroso (fortified) wine

OTHER WINES: Dry or sweet, still or frizzante table wine (85–100% Zibibbo); sweet sparkling wine (100% Zibibbo)

Piemonte DOC

REGION: PIEDMONT

White wines
- Nonvarietal Bianco: Min. 60% Chardonnay, Cortese, Erbaluce, and/or Favorita
- Varietals: Min. 85% Chardonnay, Cortese, or Sauvignon Blanc; 100% Moscato

Red and rosato wines
- Nonvarietal Rosso and Rosato: Min. 60% Barbera, Croatina, Dolcetto, Freisa, and/or Nebbiolo
- Numerous varietals allowed (min. 85% of stated variety)

OTHER WINES: Novello; sparkling wines; passito wines; subzone Vigneti di Montagna for higher-elevation vineyards

Piglio DOCG *see* Cesanese di Piglio DOCG

Pignoletto DOC

REGION: EMILIA ROMAGNA
- Same boundaries as Colli Bolognesi Pignoletto DOCG

White wines
- Min. 85% Grechetto

White sparkling wines
- Min. 85% Grechetto

OTHER WINES: Vendemmia tardiva; passito; subzones Colli d'Imola, Modena, and Reno

Primitivo di Manduria DOC

REGION: PUGLIA
- Same boundaries as Primitivo di Manduria Dolce Naturale DOCG

Red wines
- Min. 85% Primitivo
- *Aging:* For Riserva, min. 2 years, incl. 9 months in wood

Primitivo di Manduria Dolce Naturale DOCG

REGION: PUGLIA
- Same boundaries as Primitivo di Manduria DOC

Sweet red dessert wines
- 100% Primitivo

Prosecco DOC

REGIONS: VENETO AND FRIULI–VENEZIA GIULIA

Tank-method sparkling wines
- Min. 85% Glera

OTHER WINES: Still wines (Glera)

Recioto della Valpolicella DOCG

REGION: VENETO
- Same boundaries as three other Valpolicella denominations

Sweet red dessert wines
- 45–95% Corvina and/or Corvinone; 5–30% Rondinella
- Passito (dried-grape) wine

OTHER WINES: Sweet red sparkling wine; subzones Classico and Valpantena

Recioto di Gambellara DOCG

REGION: VENETO

Sweet dessert wines
- 100% Garganega
- Passito (dried-grape) wine

OTHER WINES: Sweet sparkling wine

Recioto di Soave DOCG

REGION: VENETO

- Same boundaries as Soave Superiore DOCG and Soave DOC

Sweet dessert wines

- Min. 70% Garganega
- Passito (dried-grape) wine

OTHER WINES: Sweet sparkling wine; subzone Classico

Roero DOCG

REGION: PIEDMONT

White wines

- Min. 95% Arneis

Red wines

- Min. 95% Nebbiolo
- *Aging:* Min. 1½ years, incl. 6 months in wood (min. 2½ years for Riserva with 6 months in wood)

OTHER WINES: Sparkling Arneis

Rosso Cònero DOC

REGION: MARCHE

- Same boundaries as Cònero DOCG

Red wines

- Min. 85% Montepulciano

Rosso di Montalcino DOC

REGION: TUSCANY

- Same boundaries as Brunello di Montalcino DOCG and Sant'Antimo DOC

Red wines

- 100% Sangiovese (aka Brunello)
- *Aging:* Min. 1 year

Rosso di Valtellina DOC *see* Valtellina Rosso DOC

Rosso Piceno DOC

REGION: MARCHE

Red wines

- Blend of (or varietal) Montepulciano and Sangiovese
- *Aging:* For Superiore, min. 1 year

OTHER WINES: Novello

Salice Salentino DOC

REGION: PUGLIA

White wines

- Nonvarietal Bianco: Min. 70% Chardonnay
- Varietals: Min. 85% Chardonnay, Fiano, or Pinot Bianco

Red and rosato wines

- Nonvarietal Rosso and Rosato: Min. 75% Negroamaro
- Varietals: Min. 85% Negroamaro rosato; min. 90% Negroamaro red; min. 85% Aleatico red
- *Aging:* For Riserva, min. 2 years, incl. 6 months in wood (no wood for Aleatico)

OTHER WINES: Sparkling white wines; liquoroso and dolce dessert wines

Sant'Antimo DOC

REGION: TUSCANY

- Same boundaries as Brunello di Montalcino DOCG and Rosso di Montalcino DOC

White wines

- Nonvarietal Bianco: Blend of any authorized white grapes
- Varietals: Min. 85% Chardonnay, Pinot Grigio, or Sauvignon Blanc

Red wines

- Nonvarietal Rosso: Blend of any authorized red grapes
- Varietals: Min. 85% Cabernet Sauvignon, Merlot, or Pinot Nero

Sweet dessert wines

- Vin Santo: Min. 70% Malvasia and/or Trebbiano

OTHER WINES: Novello; Vin Santo Occhio di Pernice

Sforzato di Valtellina (Sfursat di Valtellina) DOCG

REGION: LOMBARDY

- Same boundaries as Valtellina Superiore DOCG and Valtellina Rosso DOC

Red wines

- Min. 90% Nebbiolo (aka Chiavennasca)
- Dried-grape wine, fermented dry
- *Aging:* Min. 1½ years, incl. 1 year in wood

Sicilia DOC

REGION: SICILY

White wines

- Nonvarietal Bianco: Blend of Ansonica (aka Insolia), Catarratto, Grecanico Dorato, and/or Grillo
- Numerous varietals allowed (min. 85% of stated variety)

Red and rosato wines

- Nonvarietal Rosso and Rosato: Blend of Frappato, Nerello Mascalese, Nero d'Avola, and/or Perricone
- Numerous red varietals allowed (min. 85% of stated variety)
- *Aging:* For Rosso Riserva, min. 2 years

OTHER WINES: Sparkling wines; vendemmia tardiva

Soave DOC

REGION: VENETO

- Same boundaries as Recioto di Soave DOCG and Soave Superiore DOCG

White wines

- Min. 70% Garganega

OTHER WINES: Sparkling wine; subzones Classico and Colli Scaligeri

Soave Superiore DOCG

REGION: VENETO

- Same boundaries as Recioto di Soave DOCG and Soave DOC

White wines

- Min. 70% Garganega
- *Aging:* For Riserva, min. 1 year

OTHER WINES: Subzone Classico

Südtirol DOC *see* Alto Adige DOC

Taurasi DOCG

REGION: CAMPANIA

Red wines

- Min. 85% Aglianico
- *Aging:* Min. 3 years, incl. 1 year in wood (min. 4 years for Riserva with 1½ years in wood)

Trebbiano d'Abruzzo DOC

REGION: ABRUZZO

- Same boundaries as Cerasuolo d'Abruzzo DOC and Montepulciano d'Abruzzo DOC

White wines

- Min. 85% Trebbiano
- *Aging:* For Riserva, min. 1½ years

OTHER WINES: Superiore

Trentino DOC

REGION: TRENTINO–ALTO ADIGE

White wines

- Nonvarietal Bianco: Min. 80% Chardonnay and/or Pinot Bianco; for Superiore, min. 85% Chardonnay, Pinot Bianco, and/or Pinot Grigio
- Numerous varietals allowed (min. 85% of stated variety)
- *Aging:* For white Riserva and most white Superiore, min. 1 year

Rosato wines

- Nonvarietal Rosato: Blend of Lagrein, Lambrusco, Schiava, and/or Teroldego
- Varietals: Min. 85% Lagrein

Red wines

- Nonvarietal Rosso: Blend of Cabernet Franc, Cabernet Sauvignon, Carmenère, and/or Merlot
- Numerous varietals allowed (min. 85% of stated variety)
- *Aging:* For red Riserva and most red Superiore, min. 2 years

OTHER WINES: Vendemmia tardiva; passito; liquoroso wines; Vino Santo (min. 85% Nosiola); subzones Castel Beseno, Isera, Sorni, and Ziresi

Trento DOC

REGION: TRENTINO–ALTO ADIGE

- Same boundaries as Trentino DOC

White or rosato metodo classico sparkling wines

- Blend of (or varietal) Chardonnay, Pinot Bianco, Pinot Meunier, and/or Pinot Nero
- *Aging:* Min. 15 months on the lees (min. 2 years for vintage-dated [Millesimato] wines; min. 3 years for Riserva)

Valdadige (Etschtaler) DOC

REGIONS: TRENTINO–ALTO ADIGE AND VENETO

White wines

- Nonvarietal Bianco: Blend of Chardonnay, Müller-Thurgau, Pinot Bianco, Pinot Grigio, and/or several other white grapes
- Varietals: Min. 85% Chardonnay, Pinot Bianco, or Pinot Grigio

Red and rosato wines

- Nonvarietal Rosso and Rosato: Min. 50% Lambrusco and/or Schiava
- Varietal reds: Min. 85% Schiava

Valle d'Aosta (Vallée d'Aoste) DOC

REGION: VALLE D'AOSTA

- Subzones: Arnad-Montjovet, Chambave, Donnas, Enfer d'Arvier, Morgex e La Salle, Nus, and Torrette

White wines

- Nonvarietal Bianco: Any proportions of allowed varieties
- Numerous varietals allowed (min. 85% of stated variety; 100% for subzones)

Rosato wines

- Nonvarietal Rosato: Any proportions of allowed varieties

Red wines

- Nonvarietal Rosso: Any proportions of allowed varieties (subzones have minimum requirements)
- Numerous varietals allowed (min. 85% of stated variety)
- *Aging:* For Superiore (Supérieur) from subzones, min. 8–30 months

OTHER WINES: Novello; sparkling wine from subzone Morgex e La Salle only; vendemmia tardiva; passito

Valpolicella DOC

REGION: VENETO

- Same boundaries as three other Valpolicella denominations
- Subzones: Classico and Valpantena

Red wines

- 45–95% Corvina and/or Corvinone; 5–30% Rondinella
- *Aging:* For Superiore, min. 1 year

Valpolicella Ripasso DOC

REGION: VENETO

- Same boundaries as three other Valpolicella denominations

Red wines

- 45–95% Corvina and/or Corvinone; 5–30% Rondinella
- Refermentation of fresh wine with Amarone lees, fermented dry
- *Aging:* Min. 1 year

OTHER WINES: Subzones Classico and Valpantena

Valtellina Rosso (Rosso di Valtellina) DOC

REGION: LOMBARDY

- Same boundaries as Sforzato di Valtellina DOCG and Valtellina Superiore DOCG

Red wines

- Min. 90% Nebbiolo (aka Chiavennasca)

Valtellina Superiore DOCG

REGION: LOMBARDY

- Same boundaries as Sforzato di Valtellina DOCG and Valtellina Rosso DOC

Red wines

- Min. 90% Nebbiolo (aka Chiavennasca)
- *Aging:* Min. 2 years, incl. 1 year in wood (min. 3 years for Riserva)

OTHER WINES: Subzones Grumello, Inferno, Maroggia, Sassella, and Valgella

Verdicchio dei Castelli di Jesi DOC

REGION: MARCHE

- Same boundaries as Castelli di Jesi Verdicchio Riserva DOCG

White wines

- Min. 85% Verdicchio

OTHER WINES: Superiore; sparkling wines; passito; Classico subzone and 99 *menzioni geografiche aggiuntive* (crus)

Verdicchio di Matelica DOC

REGION: MARCHE

- Same boundaries as Verdicchio di Matelica Riserva DOCG

White wines

- Min. 85% Verdicchio

OTHER WINES: Sparkling wines; passito; 13 *menzioni geografiche aggiuntive* (crus) and 3 communes

Verdicchio di Matelica Riserva DOCG

REGION: MARCHE

- Same boundaries as Verdicchio di Matelica DOC

White wines

- Min. 85% Verdicchio
- *Aging:* Min. 1½ years

OTHER WINES: 13 *menzioni geografiche aggiuntive* (crus) and 3 communes

Vermentino di Gallura DOCG

REGION: SARDINIA

White dry and sweet wines

- Min. 95% Vermentino

OTHER WINES: Superiore; sparkling Vermentino; passito; vendemmia tardiva

Vermentino di Sardegna DOC

REGION: SARDINIA

White wines

- Min. 85% Vermentino

OTHER WINES: Sparkling Vermentino

Vernaccia di San Gimignano DOCG

REGION: TUSCANY

White wines

- Min. 85% Vernaccia
- *Aging:* For Riserva, min. 1 year

Vesuvio DOC

REGION: CAMPANIA

White wines

- Blend of Coda di Volpe (min. 35%), Falanghina, Greco, and/or Verdeca

Red and rosato wines

- Min. 50% Piedirosso

OTHER WINES: Sparkling white wines; liquoroso wines; Lacryma (or Lacrima) Christi versions are like Superiore

Vin Santo del Chianti DOC

REGION: TUSCANY

- Same boundaries and subzones as Chianti DOCG

Sweet dessert wines

- Vin Santo: Min. 70% Malvasia and/or Trebbiano

- Occhio di Pernice: Min. 50% Sangiovese
- *Aging:* Min. 3 years in wood (min. 4 years for Riserva)

Vin Santo del Chianti Classico DOC

REGION: TUSCANY

- Same boundaries as Chianti Classico DOCG

Sweet dessert wines

- Vin Santo: Min. 60% Malvasia and/or Trebbiano
- Occhio di Pernice: Min. 80% Sangiovese
- *Aging:* Min. 3 years, incl. 2 years in wood

Vin Santo di Carmignano DOC

REGION: TUSCANY

- Same boundaries as Carmignano DOCG

Sweet dessert wines

- Vin Santo: Min. 75% Malvasia and/or Trebbiano
- Occhio di Pernice: Min. 50% Sangiovese
- *Aging:* Min. 3 years in wood (min. 4 years for Riserva)

Vin Santo di Montepulciano DOC

REGION: TUSCANY

- Same boundaries as Vino Nobile di Montepulciano DOCG and Rosso di Montepulciano DOC

Sweet dessert wines

- Vin Santo: Min. 70% Grechetto, Malvasia, and/or Trebbiano
- Occhio di Pernice: Min. 50% Sangiovese (aka Prugnolo Gentile)
- *Aging:* Min. 3 years in wood for Vin Santo (min. 5 years for Riserva); min. 6 years in wood for Occhio di Pernice

Vino Nobile di Montepulciano DOCG

REGION: TUSCANY

- Same boundaries as Rosso di Montepulciano DOC and Vin Santo di Montepulciano DOC

Red wines

- Min. 70% Sangiovese (aka Prugnolo Gentile)
- *Aging:* Min. 2 years, incl. 1–1½ years in wood (min. 3 years for Riserva with 1 year in wood)

Complete List of Denominations

The following is a complete list of Italian quality-wine denominations as of 2016, consisting of:

74 Denominazioni di Origine Controllata e Garantita (DOCG) and

333 Denominazioni di Origine Controllata (DOC)

= 407 Denominazioni di Origine Protetta (DOP)

The list is organized by region, with DOCGs appearing first (in **bold**) followed by the region's DOCs, both in alphabetical order. Denominations that are partly in two regions are shown with an asterisk (*).

Abruzzo (1 DOCG, 8 DOC)

Montepulciano d'Abruzzo Colline Teramane DOCG
Abruzzo DOC
Cerasuolo d'Abruzzo DOC
Controguerra DOC
Montepulciano d'Abruzzo DOC
Ortona DOC
Terre Tollesi (Tullum) DOC
Trebbiano d'Abruzzo DOC
Villamagna DOC

Basilicata (1 DOCG, 4 DOC)

Aglianico del Vulture Superiore DOCG
Aglianico del Vulture DOC
Grottino di Roccanova DOC
Matera DOC
Terre dell'Alta Val d'Agri DOC

Calabria (9 DOC)

Bivongi DOC
Cirò DOC
Greco di Bianco DOC
Lamezia DOC
Melissa DOC
S. Anna di Isola Capo Rizzuto DOC
Savuto DOC
Scavigna DOC
Terre di Cosenza DOC

Campania (4 DOCG, 15 DOC)

Aglianico del Taburno DOCG
Fiano di Avellino DOCG
Greco di Tufo DOCG
Taurasi DOCG
Aversa DOC
Campi Flegrei DOC
Capri DOC
Casavecchia di Pontelatone DOC
Castel San Lorenzo DOC
Cilento DOC
Costa d'Amalfi DOC
Falanghina del Sannio DOC
Falerno del Massico DOC
Galluccio DOC
Irpinia DOC
Ischia DOC
Penisola Sorrentina DOC
Sannio DOC
Vesuvio DOC

Emilia Romagna (2 DOCG, 19 DOC)

Colli Bolognesi Pignoletto DOCG
Romagna Albana DOCG
Bosco Eliceo DOC
Colli Bolognesi DOC
Colli di Faenza DOC
Colli d'Imola DOC
Colli di Parma DOC

Colli di Rimini DOC
Colli di Scandiano e di Canossa DOC
Colli Piacentini DOC
Colli Romagna Centrale DOC
Gutturnio DOC
Lambrusco di Sorbara DOC
Lambrusco Grasparossa di Castelvetro DOC
Lambrusco Salamino di Santa Croce DOC
Modena DOC
Ortrugo DOC
Pignoletto DOC
Reggiano DOC
Reno DOC
Romagna DOC

Friuli–Venezia Giulia (4 DOCG, 10 DOC)

Colli Orientali del Friuli Picolit DOCG
Lison* DOCG
Ramandolo DOCG
Rosazzo DOCG
Carso (Carso-Kras) DOC
Collio Goriziano (Collio) DOC
Friuli Annia DOC
Friuli Aquileia DOC
Friuli Colli Orientali DOC
Friuli Grave DOC
Friuli Isonzo (Isonzo del Friuli) DOC
Friuli Latisana DOC
Lison-Pramaggiore* DOC
Prosecco* DOC

Lazio (3 DOCG, 27 DOC)

Cannellino di Frascati DOCG
Cesanese del Piglio (Piglio) DOCG
Frascati Superiore DOCG
Aleatico di Gradoli DOC
Aprilia DOC
Atina DOC
Bianco Capena DOC
Castelli Romani DOC
Cerveteri DOC
Cesanese di Affile (Affile) DOC
Cesanese di Olevano Romano (Olevano Romano) DOC
Circeo DOC
Colli Albani DOC
Colli della Sabina DOC

Colli Etruschi Viterbesi (Tuscia) DOC
Colli Lanuvini DOC
Cori DOC
Est! Est!! Est!!! di Montefiascone DOC
Frascati DOC
Genazzano DOC
Marino DOC
Montecompatri-Colonna (Colonna, Montecompatri) DOC
Nettuno DOC
Orvieto* DOC
Roma DOC
Tarquinia DOC
Terracina (Moscato di Terracina) DOC
Velletri DOC
Vignanello DOC
Zagarolo DOC

Liguria (8 DOC)

Cinque Terre (Cinque Terre Sciacchetrà) DOC
Colli di Luni* DOC
Colline di Levanto DOC
Golfo del Tigullio–Portofino (Portofino) DOC
Pornassio (Ormeasco di Pornassio) DOC
Riviera Ligure di Ponente DOC
Rossese di Dolceacqua (Dolceacqua) DOC
Val Polcèvera DOC

Lombardy (5 DOCG, 22 DOC)

Franciacorta DOCG
Oltrepò Pavese Metodo Classico DOCG
Scanzo (Moscato di Scanzo) DOCG
Sforzato di Valtellina (Sfursat di Valtellina) DOCG
Valtellina Superiore DOCG
Bonarda dell'Oltrepò Pavese DOC
Botticino DOC
Buttafuoco dell'Oltrepò Pavese (Buttafuoco) DOC
Capriano del Colle DOC
Casteggio DOC
Cellatica DOC
Curtefranca DOC
Garda* DOC
Garda Colli Mantovani DOC
Lambrusco Mantovano DOC
Lugana* DOC
Oltrepò Pavese DOC

Oltrepò Pavese Pinot Grigio DOC
Pinot Nero dell'Oltrepò Pavese DOC
Riviera del Garda Bresciano (Garda Bresciano) DOC
San Colombano al Lambro (San Colombano) DOC
Sangue di Giuda dell'Oltrepò Pavese (Sangue di Giuda) DOC
San Martino della Battaglia* DOC
Terre di Colleoni (Colleoni) DOC
Valcalepio DOC
Valtellina Rosso (Rosso di Valtellina) DOC
Valtènesi DOC

Marche (5 DOCG, 15 DOC)

Castelli di Jesi Verdicchio Riserva DOCG
Cònero DOCG
Offida DOCG
Verdicchio di Matelica Riserva DOCG
Vernaccia di Serrapetrona DOCG
Bianchello del Metauro DOC
Colli Maceratesi DOC
Colli Pesaresi DOC
Esino DOC
Falerio DOC
I Terreni di Sanseverino DOC
Lacrima di Morro (Lacrima di Morro d'Alba) DOC
Pergola DOC
Rosso Cònero DOC
Rosso Piceno (Piceno) DOC
San Ginesio DOC
Serrapetrona DOC
Terre di Offida DOC
Verdicchio dei Castelli di Jesi DOC
Verdicchio di Matelica DOC

Molise (4 DOC)

Biferno DOC
Molise DOC
Pentro di Isernia (Pentro) DOC
Tintilia del Molise DOC

Piedmont (17 DOCG, 42 DOC)

Alta Langa DOCG
Asti DOCG
Barbaresco DOCG

Barbera d'Asti DOCG
Barbera del Monferrato Superiore DOCG
Barolo DOCG
Brachetto d'Acqui (Acqui) DOCG
Dogliani DOCG
Dolcetto di Diano d'Alba (Diano d'Alba) DOCG
Dolcetto di Ovada Superiore (Ovada) DOCG
Erbaluce di Caluso (Caluso) DOCG
Gattinara DOCG
Gavi (Cortese di Gavi) DOCG
Ghemme DOCG
Nizza DOCG
Roero DOCG
Ruchè di Castagnole Monferrato DOCG
Alba DOC
Albugnano DOC
Barbera d'Alba DOC
Barbera del Monferrato DOC
Boca DOC
Bramaterra DOC
Calosso DOC
Canavese DOC
Carema DOC
Cisterna d'Asti DOC
Colli Tortonesi DOC
Collina Torinese DOC
Colline Novaresi DOC
Colline Saluzzesi DOC
Cortese dell'Alto Monferrato DOC
Coste della Sesia DOC
Dolcetto d'Acqui DOC
Dolcetto d'Alba DOC
Dolcetto d'Asti DOC
Dolcetto di Ovada DOC
Fara DOC
Freisa d'Asti DOC
Freisa di Chieri DOC
Gabiano DOC
Grignolino d'Asti DOC
Grignolino del Monferrato Casalese DOC
Langhe DOC
Lessona DOC
Loazzolo DOC
Malvasia di Casorzo d'Asti (Malvasia di Casorzo or Casorzo) DOC
Malvasia di Castelnuovo Don Bosco DOC
Monferrato DOC

Nebbiolo d'Alba DOC
Piemonte DOC
Pinerolese DOC
Rubino di Cantavenna DOC
Sizzano DOC
Strevi DOC
Terre Alfieri DOC
Valli Ossolane DOC
Valsusa DOC
Verduno Pelaverga (Verduno) DOC

Puglia (4 DOCG, 28 DOC)

Castel del Monte Bombino Nero DOCG
Castel del Monte Nero di Troia Riserva DOCG
Castel del Monte Rosso Riserva DOCG
Primitivo di Manduria Dolce Naturale DOCG
Aleatico di Puglia DOC
Alezio DOC
Barletta DOC
Brindisi DOC
Cacc'è Mmitte di Lucera DOC
Castel del Monte DOC
Colline Joniche Tarantine DOC
Copertino DOC
Galatina DOC
Gioia del Colle DOC
Gravina DOC
Leverano DOC
Lizzano DOC
Locorotondo DOC
Martina (Martina Franca) DOC
Matino DOC
Moscato di Trani DOC
Nardò DOC
Negramaro di Terra d'Otranto DOC
Orta Nova DOC
Ostuni DOC
Primitivo di Manduria DOC
Rosso di Cerignola DOC
Salice Salentino DOC
San Severo DOC
Squinzano DOC
Tavoliere delle Puglie (Tavoliere) DOC
Terra d'Otranto DOC

Sardinia (1 DOCG, 17 DOC)

Vermentino di Gallura DOCG
Alghero DOC
Arborea DOC
Cagliari DOC
Campidano di Terralba (Terralba) DOC
Cannonau di Sardegna DOC
Carignano del Sulcis DOC
Girò di Cagliari DOC
Malvasia di Bosa DOC
Mandrolisai DOC
Monica di Sardegna DOC
Moscato di Sardegna DOC
Moscato di Sorso-Sennori (Moscato di Sennori, Moscato di Sorso) DOC
Nasco di Cagliari DOC
Nuragus di Cagliari DOC
Sardegna Semidano DOC
Vermentino di Sardegna DOC
Vernaccia di Oristano DOC

Sicily (1 DOCG, 23 DOC)

Cerasuolo di Vittoria DOCG
Alcamo DOC
Contea di Sclafani DOC
Contessa Entellina DOC
Delia Nivolelli DOC
Eloro DOC
Erice DOC
Etna DOC
Faro DOC
Malvasia delle Lipari DOC
Mamertino di Milazzo (Mamertino) DOC
Marsala DOC
Menfi DOC
Monreale DOC
Noto DOC
Pantelleria DOC
Riesi DOC
Salaparuta DOC
Sambuca di Sicilia DOC
Santa Margherita di Belice DOC
Sciacca DOC
Sicilia DOC
Siracusa DOC
Vittoria DOC

Tuscany (11 DOCG, 41 DOC)

Brunello di Montalcino DOCG
Carmignano DOCG
Chianti DOCG
Chianti Classico DOCG
Elba Aleatico Passito (Aleatico Passito dell'Elba) DOCG
Montecucco Sangiovese DOCG
Morellino di Scansano DOCG
Rosso della Val di Cornia (Val di Cornia Rosso) DOCG
Suvereto DOCG
Vernaccia di San Gimignano DOCG
Vino Nobile di Montepulciano DOCG
Ansonica Costa dell'Argentario DOC
Barco Reale di Carmignano DOC
Bianco dell'Empolese DOC
Bianco di Pitigliano DOC
Bolgheri DOC
Bolgheri Sassicaia DOC
Candia dei Colli Apuani DOC
Capalbio DOC
Colli dell'Etruria Centrale DOC
Colli di Luni* DOC
Colline Lucchesi DOC
Cortona DOC
Elba DOC
Grance Senesi DOC
Maremma Toscana DOC
Montecarlo DOC
Montecucco DOC
Monteregio di Massa Marittima DOC
Montescudaio DOC
Moscadello di Montalcino DOC
Orcia DOC
Parrina DOC
Pomino DOC
Rosso di Montalcino DOC
Rosso di Montepulciano DOC
San Gimignano DOC
San Torpè DOC
Sant'Antimo DOC
Sovana DOC
Terratico di Bibbona DOC
Terre di Casole DOC
Terre di Pisa DOC
Val d'Arbia DOC

Val d'Arno di Sopra (Valdarno di Sopra) DOC
Valdichiana Toscana DOC
Val di Cornia DOC
Valdinievole DOC
Vin Santo del Chianti DOC
Vin Santo del Chianti Classico DOC
Vin Santo di Carmignano DOC
Vin Santo di Montepulciano DOC

Trentino–Alto Adige (8 DOC)

Alto Adige (Südtirol) DOC
Casteller DOC
Lago di Caldaro (Caldaro, Kalterer, Kalterersee) DOC
Teroldego Rotaliano DOC
Trentino DOC
Trento DOC
Valdadige (Etschtaler)* DOC
Valdadige Terradeiforti (Terradeiforti)* DOC

Umbria (2 DOCG, 13 DOC)

Montefalco Sagrantino DOCG
Torgiano Rosso Riserva DOCG
Amelia DOC
Assisi DOC
Colli Altotiberini DOC
Colli del Trasimeno (Trasimeno) DOC
Colli Martani DOC
Colli Perugini DOC
Lago di Corbara DOC
Montefalco DOC
Orvieto* DOC
Rosso Orvietano (Orvietano Rosso) DOC
Spoleto DOC
Todi DOC
Torgiano DOC

Valle d'Aosta (1 DOC)

Valle d'Aosta (Vallée d'Aoste) DOC

Veneto (14 DOCG, 28 DOC)

Amarone della Valpolicella DOCG
Asolo Prosecco DOCG
Bagnoli Friularo (Friularo di Bagnoli) DOCG
Bardolino Superiore DOCG
Colli di Conegliano DOCG

Colli Euganei Fior d'Arancio (Fior d'Arancio Colli Euganei) DOCG
Conegliano Valdobbiadene Prosecco DOCG
Lison* DOCG
Montello Rosso (Montello) DOCG
Piave Malanotte (Malanotte del Piave) DOCG
Recioto della Valpolicella DOCG
Recioto di Gambellara DOCG
Recioto di Soave DOCG
Soave Superiore DOCG
Arcole DOC
Bagnoli di Sopra (Bagnoli) DOC
Bardolino DOC
Bianco di Custoza (Custoza) DOC
Breganze DOC
Colli Berici DOC
Colli Euganei DOC
Corti Benedettine del Padovano DOC
Gambellara DOC

Garda* DOC
Lessini Durello (Durello Lessini) DOC
Lison-Pramaggiore* DOC
Lugana* DOC
Merlara DOC
Montello–Colli Asolani DOC
Monti Lessini DOC
Piave DOC
Prosecco* DOC
Riviera del Brenta DOC
San Martino della Battaglia* DOC
Soave DOC
Valdadige (Etschtaler)* DOC
Valdadige Terradeiforti (Terradeiforti)* DOC
Valpolicella DOC
Valpolicella Ripasso DOC
Venezia DOC
Vicenza DOC
Vigneti della Serenissima (Serenissima) DOC

Answers to Unit Exercises

Answers to the exercises (or in some cases, directions on where to find the answers) are listed below. The answers in this section are good ones based on the course material, but other correct answers are possible in some instances. If your response is not shown but you think it is correct, check the course material or the Italian Wine Central website to see if it is a correct alternative to the one(s) shown.

Unit 1

1. See the maps on page 5.
2. France, Switzerland, Austria, and Slovenia (as well as the enclaves of San Marino and Vatican City)
3. See the maps on page 5.
4. Compare your results with the topographic map on page 5. The Alps are the mountains along the entire northern border, and the Apennines are the mountains that run from Liguria south down the peninsula. The Po Valley is the light green area that starts in Piedmont and runs east to the Adriatic Sea.
5. See the list of regions on page 8.
6. See the map on page 9.
7. Northwest to northeast: Liguria, Tuscany, Lazio, Campania, Basilicata, Calabria, Basilicata again, Puglia, Molise, Abruzzo, Marche, Emilia Romagna, Veneto, Friuli–Venezia Giulia.
8. Valle d'Aosta, Piedmont, Lombardy, Trentino–Alto Adige, Umbria
9. Liguria, Piedmont, Valle d'Aosta, Piedmont again, Lombardy, Trentino–Alto Adige, Veneto, Friuli–Venezia Giulia
10. See the map on page 5.
11. Ancient Greeks
12. Primarily by establishing vineyards and a winemaking culture throughout the southern half of Europe
13. French in the northwest, Germans/Austrians in the north central and northeast, and Spanish in Sardinia and other parts of the south, among others
14. EU: three; Italian: four. Italy has two levels, DOC and DOCG, that are equivalent to the EU's single PDO (DOP) level.
15. Compare with the quality pyramids on page 13 and 15.
16. Highest quality wines: PDO/DOP; highest production quantities: Wine/Vino; lowest prices: Wine/Vino; least restrictions: Wine/Vino
17. DOCG: Denominazione d'Origine Controllata e Garantita; DOC: Denominazione d'Origine Controllata; DOP: Denominazione d'Origine Protetta; IGP: Indicazione Geografica Protetta; IGT: Indicazione Geografica Tipica
18. Classico: Historical center of wine production in an area; Riserva: Higher quality category with longer aging before release; Superiore: Higher quality category with a higher minimum alcohol requirement (from riper grapes at harvest)

Unit 2

1. Liguria, Piedmont, Valle d'Aosta, Lombardy, Trentino–Alto Adige, Veneto, Friuli–Venezia Giulia
2. Liguria: France; Piedmont: France, Switzerland; Valle d'Aosta: France, Switzerland; Lombardy: Switzerland; Trentino–Alto Adige: Switzerland, Austria; Veneto: Austria; Friuli–Venezia Giulia: Austria, Slovenia
3. Table completion possibilities:
    *   Amarone della Valpolicella DOCG; Corvina; Veneto
    *   Barolo DOCG; Nebbiolo; Piedmont
    *   Dogliani DOCG; Dolcetto; Piedmont
4. In southern Lombardy next to Piedmont, south of the Po River
5. Barbera: Piedmont, Lombardy; Corvina: Veneto; Croatina: Lombardy; Dolcetto, Freisa, and Grignolino: Piedmont; Lagrein: Trentino–Alto Adige; Nebbiolo: Piedmont, Lombardy; Refosco: Veneto, Friuli–Venezia Giulia; Rondinella: Veneto; Schiava and Teroldego: Trentino–Alto Adige
6. Possibilities are listed in the "Dolcetto-based DOPs" and "Large Multipurpose DOCs in Piedmont" sections on pages 22–30.

7. IGP delle Venezie (Friuli–Venezia Giulia, Trentino–Alto Adige [part], Veneto); IGP Veneto (Veneto)
8. DOCGs: Piedmont; DOCs: Piedmont
9. 100% Nebbiolo
10. Table completion possibilities:
    - Alto Adige DOC; Various; Trentino–Alto Adige
    - Dolcetto d'Alba, Dolcetto d'Acqui, Dolcetto d'Asti, Dolcetto di Ovada; DOC; Dolcetto; Piedmont
    - Friuli Grave DOC; Various; Friuli–Venezia Giulia
    - Gattinara DOCG; Nebbiolo; Piedmont
    - Roero DOCG; Nebbiolo; Piedmont
    - Valpolicella DOC; Corvina; Veneto
11. Alto Adige/Südtirol DOC, Trentino DOC, Valdadige DOC, and IGP delle Venezie are the ones mentioned in the unit.
12. Piedmont: Nebbiolo; Veneto: Corvina
13. Alba and Asti: Piedmont; Verona: Veneto
14. Table completion possibilities:
    - Barbera d'Asti DOCG, Nizza DOCG, Barbera d'Alba DOC; Barbera; Piedmont
    - Garda DOC; Various; Lombardy and Veneto
    - Valdadige DOC, Delle Venezie IGP; Various; Trentino–Alto Adige and Veneto
    - Valtellina Superiore DOCG, Sforzato di Valtellina DOCG, Valtellina Rosso DOC; Nebbiolo; Lombardy
15. See the maps on pages 28–30.
16. Barbaresco, Barolo, Gattinara, Ghemme, Roero, Sforzato di Valtellina, Valtellina Superiore
17. Milan (Milano)
18. Alto Adige: Südtirol; Lombardy: Lombardia; Piedmont: Piemonte; Valle d'Aosta: Vallée d'Aoste
19. Schiava
20. Veneto
21. A DOC in eastern Friuli along the Slovenian border

Unit 3

1. Calabria, Basilicata, Campania, Lazio, Tuscany, Liguria
2. Sangiovese (#1), Montepulciano
3. Emilia Romagna (#2), Veneto (#1)
4. DOC and DOCG are Italian quality wine categories, with DOCG the higher level of the two; both are equivalent to the DOP quality wine category under EU law.
5. S = Emilia Romagna, Lazio, Marche, Tuscany, Umbria; M = Abruzzo, Marche, Molise
6. Corvina: Veneto; Dolcetto: Piedmont; Freisa: Piedmont; Lagrein: Trentino–Alto Adige; Lambrusco: Emilia Romagna; Nebbiolo: Piedmont, Lombardy; Sagrantino: Umbria; Schiava: Trentino–Alto Adige

7. Tuscany (#2), Piedmont (#1)
8. The course definition is "a very high quality wine [from Tuscany, naturally] that does not meet the requirements for a prestigious DOP."
9. Cònero DOCG, Rosso Cònero DOC, Offida DOCG, Rosso Piceno DOC
10. Table completion possibilities:
    - Morellino di Scansano DOCG; Sangiovese; Tuscany
    - Lambrusco Grasparossa di Castelvetro DOC; Lambrusco; Emilia Romagna
    - Valtellina Superiore DOCG; Nebbiolo; Lombardy
    - Carmignano DOCG; Sangiovese; Tuscany
    - Langhe DOC; Various; Piedmont
    - Cerasuolo d'Abruzzo DOC; Montepulciano; Abruzzo
11. Brunello di Montalcino, Carmignano, Chianti, Chianti Classico, Morellino di Scansano, Vino Nobile di Montepulciano
12. Tuscany: Toscana; Le Marche: (The) Marches
13. Rome (Roma)
14. Umbria; Montefalco Sagrantino DOCG
15. Emilia Romagna
16. Table completion possibilities:
    - Cesanese del Piglio; DOCG; Cesanese; Lazio
    - Diano d'Alba, Dogliani, Ovada; DOCG; Dolcetto; Piedmont
    - Valle d'Aosta, Vallée d'Aoste; DOC; Various; Valle d'Aosta
    - Rosso di Montalcino, Rosso di Montepulciano; DOC; Sangiovese; Tuscany
    - Bolgheri, Maremma Toscana, Sant'Antimo; DOC; Cabernet, Merlot, Syrah; Tuscany
    - Cònero, Offida/Montepulciano d'Abruzzo Colline Teramane; DOCG; Montepulciano; Marche/Abruzzo
17. Entire region of Tuscany
18. Colli Aretini, Colli Fiorentini, Colline Pisane, Colli Senesi, Montalbano, Montespertoli, Rufina (Colli Senesi and Rufina most commercially important)
19. Montepulciano
20. See the maps in the "Sangiovese-based DOPs" section on pages 46–48
21. Most prestigious: Brunello di Montalcino. Other possibilities: Rosso di Montalcino DOC, Sant'Antimo DOC, IGP Toscana (Chianti DOCG Colli Senesi, too, if the question didn't say "not at the DOCG level")

Unit 4

1. Puglia, Molise, Abruzzo, Marche, Emilia Romagna, Veneto, Friuli–Venezia Giulia; Slovenia; Adriatic Sea
2. See map on next page.

3. Either Sicily or Puglia, depending on the harvest, produces the highest volume of wine in southern Italy every year. Veneto (#1), Emilia Romagna (#2)
4. Table completion possibilities:
   - Bardolino Superiore; DOCG; Corvina; Veneto
   - Castel del Monte Nero di Troia; DOCG; Uva di Troia; Puglia
   - Etna; DOC; Nerello Mascalese; Sicily
   - Morellino di Scansano; DOCG; Sangiovese; Tuscany
   - Offida; DOCG; Montepulciano; Marche
   - Isola dei Nuraghi; IGP; Various; Sardinia
   - Taurasi; DOCG; Aglianico; Campania
   - Valtellina Rosso; DOC; Nebbiolo; Lombardy
5. Aglianico: Campania, Basilicata; Barbera: Piedmont, Lombardy; Bovale: Sardinia; Croatina: Lombardy; Gaglioppo: Calabria; Lambrusco: Emilia Romagna; Monica: Sardinia; Nerello Mascalese: Sicily; Piedirosso: Campania; Primitivo: Puglia; Teroldego: Trentino–Alto Adige; Uva di Troia: Puglia
6. Tuscany
7. Sardinia: Sardegna; Sicily: Sicilia
8. *Other correct denominations are possible.* Abruzzo: Montepulciano (Montepulciano d'Abruzzo DOC); Basilicata: Aglianico (Aglianico del Vulture DOC); Calabria: Gaglioppo (Cirò DOC); Campania: Aglianico (Taurasi DOCG); Piedmont: Nebbiolo (Barolo DOCG); Sardinia: Cannonau (Cannonau di Sardegna DOC); Sicily: Nero d'Avola (Cerasuolo di Vittoria DOCG); Umbria: Sagrantino (Montefalco Sagrantino DOCG); Veneto: Corvina (Amarone della Valpolicella DOCG)
9. Protected Designation of Origin (PDO)/ Denominazione d'Origine Protetta (DOP); Protected Geographical Indication (PGI)/Indicazione Geografica Protetta (IGP); Wine/Vino
10. Bombino Nero: Puglia; Cannonau: Sardinia; Carignano: Sardinia; Frappato: Sicily; Freisa: Piedmont; Grignolino: Piedmont; Negroamaro: Puglia; Nero d'Avola: Sicily; Rondinella: Veneto
11. The Anglicized name for Puglia
12. Table completion possibilities:
    - Cerasuolo di Vittoria; DOCG; Nero d'Avola and Frappato; Sicily
    - Barbera d'Alba; DOC; Barbera; Piedmont
    - Aglianico del Vulture; DOC; Aglianico;

Basilicata
- Terre Siciliane; IGP; Various; Sicily
- Salice Salentino; DOC; Negroamaro; Puglia
- Rosso di Montalcino, Rosso di Montepulciano; DOC; Sangiovese; Tuscany
- Primitivo di Manduria; DOC; Primitivo; Puglia
- Cannonau di Sardegna; DOC; Cannonau; Sardinia
13. Naples (Napoli)
14. Brunello (Montalcino), Morellino (Maremma, Scansano), Prugnolo Gentile (Montepulciano)

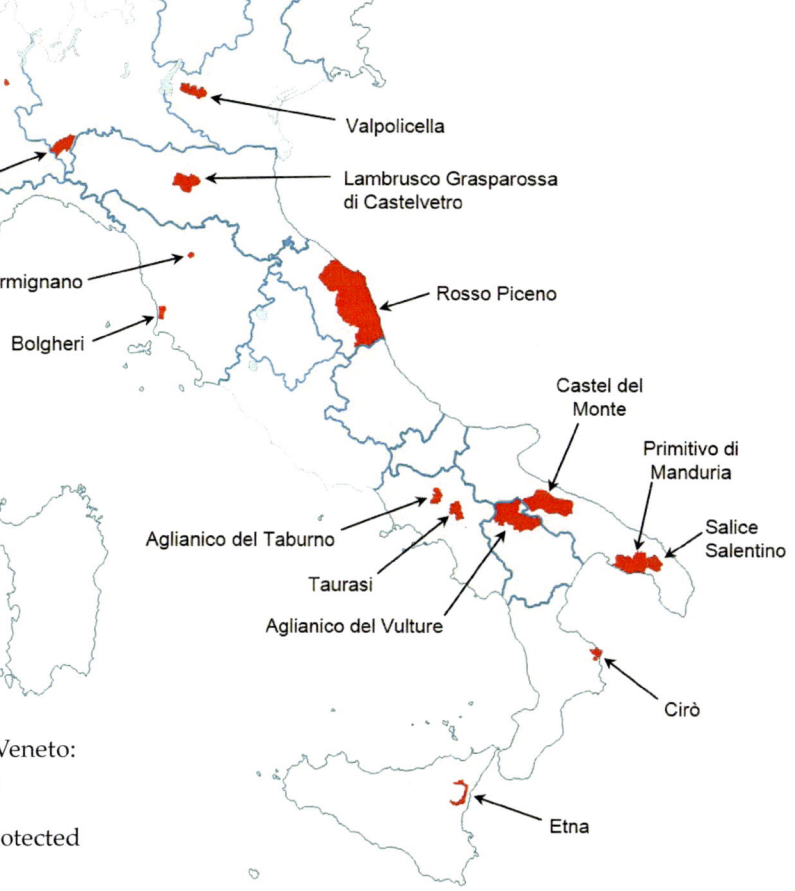

15. Nero d'Avola, Frappato, Nerello Mascalese
16. Alto Adige/Südtirol DOC, Trentino DOC, Valdadige DOC
17. Cerasuolo di Vittoria DOCG; Sicilia DOC

Unit 5

1. Trebbiano, Sangiovese; central Italy
2. Tuscany: Vernaccia; Sardinia: Vermentino; Abruzzo: Trebbiano; Marche: Verdicchio

3. *Best answers:* Ansonica, Grillo, Grecanico Dorato, Carricante; *other possibilities:* Zibibbo, Catarratto, Trebbiano, Chardonnay; Sicilia DOC, IGP Terre Siciliane

4. Table completion possibilities:
   - Fiano di Avellino; DOCG; Fiano; White; Campania
   - Salice Salentino; DOC; Negroamaro; Red; Puglia
   - Vernaccia di San Gimignano; DOCG; Vernaccia; White; Tuscany
   - Dolcetto d'Alba, Dolcetto d'Acqui, Dolcetto d'Asti, Dolcetto di Ovada; DOC; Dolcetto; Red; Piedmont
   - Trebbiano d'Abruzzo; DOC; Trebbiano; White; Abruzzo
   - Greco di Tufo DOCG, Cirò DOC; Greco; White; Campania, Calabria
   - Vermentino di Sardegna, Nuragus di Cagliari; DOC; Vermentino, Nuragus; White; Sardinia

5. Pecorino: Marche, Abruzzo; Fiano: Campania; Zibibbo: Sicily; Nuragus: Sardinia; Coda di Volpe: Campania; Grillo: Sicily; Passerina: Marche; Vermentino: Sardinia, Tuscany, Liguria; Greco: Campania, Calabria

6. The Superiore, made with riper grapes, should be richer, fuller bodied, and generally of higher quality.

7. Trebbiano: Trebbiano d'Abruzzo DOC; Negroamaro: Salice Salentino DOC; Pecorino: Offida DOCG; Frappato: Cerasuolo di Vittoria DOCG; Vermentino: Vermentino di Gallura DOCG, Vermentino di Sardegna DOC, etc.; Montepulciano: Montepulciano d'Abruzzo DOC, Cerasuolo d'Abruzzo DOC, Offida DOCG, Cònero DOCG, Rosso Cònero DOC, Rosso Piceno DOC, etc.; Vernaccia: Vernaccia di San Gimignano DOCG; Barbera: Barbera d'Asti DOCG, Nizza DOCG, etc.; Sangiovese: Chianti DOCG, Chianti Classico DOCG, Brunello di Montalcino DOCG, etc.

8. Lombardy

9. Review the maps for units 3 through 5.

10. Aglianico del Taburno DOCG; Chianti Classico DOCG; Fiano di Avellino DOCG; Cesanese del Piglio DOCG; Falanghina del Sannio DOC; Verdicchio dei Castelli di Jesi DOC; Montepulciano d'Abruzzo DOC; IGP Terre Siciliane; Offida DOCG; Maremma Toscana DOC; Vermentino di Gallura DOCG; Etna DOC; Salice Salentino DOC; Taurasi DOCG

11. Piedmont (#1), Tuscany (#2)

12. Table completion possibilities:
    - Vesuvio; DOC; Coda di Volpe; White; Campania

- Verdicchio di Matelica; DOC; Verdicchio; White; Marche
- Vino Nobile di Montepulciano; DOCG; Sangiovese; Red; Tuscany
- Cirò; DOC; Gaglioppo; Red; Calabria
- Valdadige; DOC; Various; White or Red; Trentino–Alto Adige, Veneto
- Greco di Tufo; DOCG; Greco; White; Campania

13. PGI is the English-language designation for the midlevel quality wine category under EU law; IGP is the same thing in Italian. IGT is an equivalent quality wine category under Italian law that may be used in lieu of the EU terms.

14. Insolia/Inzolia

15. Barbaresco DOCG, Barolo DOCG, Gattinara DOCG, Ghemme DOCG, Roero DOCG, Sforzato di Valtellina DOCG, Valtellina Superiore DOCG, Langhe DOC, Piemonte DOC, etc.

Unit 6

1. Alps and Apennines; Po River Valley

2. Veneto: Garganega; Marche: Verdicchio; Piedmont: Cortese; Sardinia: Vermentino; Friuli–Venezia Giulia: Pinot Grigio; Umbria: Grechetto

3. By expanding the extent of grape growing and winemaking to new areas throughout the empire.

4. Table completion possibilities:
   - Orvieto; DOC; Grechetto; White; Umbria and Lazio
   - Collio Goriziano, Friuli Grave, Friuli Colli Orientali; DOC; Various; Red; Friuli–Venezia Giulia
   - Vernaccia di San Gimignano; DOCG; Vernaccia; White; Tuscany
   - Vesuvio; DOC; Coda di Volpe; White; Campania
   - Cerasuolo di Vittoria; DOCG; Blend of Nero d'Avola and Frappato; Red; Sicily
   - Trentino; DOC; Various; White; Southern province of Trentino–Alto Adige
   - Frascati Superiore; DOCG; Malvasia; White; Lazio

5. Tai; Veneto

6. Piedmont, Valle d'Aosta

7. Arneis: Piedmont; Ribolla Gialla: Friuli–Venezia Giulia; Veneto; Falanghina: Campania; Grecanico Dorato: Sicily; Cortese: Piedmont; Teroldego: Trentino–Alto Adige; Erbaluce: Piedmont; Catarratto: Sicily; Garganega: Veneto; Gaglioppo: Calabria; Vermentino: Sardinia, Tuscany, Liguria; Greco: Campania, Calabria

8. The Riserva, aged longer than the other wine, should be more mature, possibly fuller bodied, and generally of higher quality

9. Falanghina, Fiano, Greco, Coda di Volpe
10. Emilia Romagna (Pignoletto DOC, Colli Bolognesi Pignoletto DOCG); Umbria (Orvieto—only a small amount is grown in the Lazio portion of Orvieto)
11. Chardonnay, Pinot Grigio, Pinot Bianco, Riesling, Sauvignon Blanc, Traminer (Gewürztraminer)
12. Review the maps in units 2 and 6.
13. Oltrepò Pavese DOC; Barbaresco DOCG; Delle Venezie IGP; Barbera d'Asti DOCG; Valpolicella DOC (Amarone della Valpolicella is DOCG); Gavi DOCG; Barolo DOCG; Collio DOC; Custoza DOC; Soave DOC (Soave Superiore is DOCG); Südtirol DOC; Dolcetto d'Alba DOC
14. Rome, Lazio
15. 85%
16. Cònero, because it is a DOCG, with higher requirements
17. Montepulciano d'Abruzzo DOC, Cerasuolo d'Abruzzo DOC, Offida DOCG, Cònero DOCG, Rosso Cònero DOC, Rosso Piceno DOC, etc.
18. Table completion possibilities:
    • Erbaluce di Caluso; DOCG; Erbaluce; White; Piedmont
    • Soave Superiore; DOCG; Garganega; White; Veneto
    • Rosso di Montalcino; DOC; Sangiovese (Brunello); Red; Tuscany
    • Lugana; DOC; Trebbiano (specifically Trebbiano di Lugana; Verdicchio would also be technically correct); White; Veneto and Lombardy
    • Roero; DOCG; Arneis; White; Piedmont
    • Aglianico del Vulture; DOC; Aglianico; Red; Basilicata

Unit 7

1. Trentino–Alto Adige (specifically Alto Adige); (Red) Lagrein, Merlot, Pinot Nero, Schiava, Teroldego; (White) Chardonnay, Pinot Bianco, Pinot Grigio, Sauvignon Blanc, Traminer (Gewürztraminer)
2. It ferments very slowly for a period of years in small, sealed wooden barrels.
3. A common visual representation of the quality levels of wine. The small segment of wines at the top of the pyramid generally have higher production standards, smaller production volume, and higher prices than the larger segments of wine at lower levels.
4. Vendemmia tardiva: Late harvest; Liquoroso: Fortified; Spumante: Sparkling (wine); Muffa nobile: Noble rot, botrytis; Passito: Wine made from dried grapes; Occhio di pernice: "Eye of the pheasant," a sweet rosato dried-grape wine
5. Table completion possibilities:
    • Alta Langa; DOCG; Chardonnay, Pinot Nero;

Classic Method; White, rosato; Piedmont
    • Roero; DOCG; Nebbiolo for reds & Arneis for whites; Still; Red & white; Piedmont
    • Brachetto d'Acqui; DOCG; Brachetto; Tank Method; Red; Piedmont
    • Trento; DOC; Chardonnay, Pinot Bianco, Pinot Nero; Classic Method; White, rosato; Trentino–Alto Adige
    • Castel del Monte Nero di Troia DOCG, Castel del Monte Rosso Riserva DOCG, Castel del Monte DOC; Uva di Troia; Still; Red; Puglia
    • Oltrepò Pavese Metodo Classico, Franciacorta; DOCG; Chardonnay, Pinot Bianco, Pinot Nero; Classic Method; White, rosato; Lombardy
    • Conegliano Valdobbiadene Prosecco, Asolo Prosecco; DOCG; Glera; Tank or Classic Method; White; Veneto
6. Vermouth is a *wine* flavored with herbs and other botanical ingredients, amaro is distilled spirits flavored with herbs and botanicals, and grappa is a distilled spirit made from grape pomace.
7. Second fermentation takes place in bottle for Classic Method, in large tanks for Tank Method. *Advantages:* Classic Method has finer bubbles and often a yeasty character and ages better; Tank Method can have better aromatics and is less expensive to carry out. *Grape varieties:* Glera, Moscato, Brachetto, Lambrusco.
8. Harvest later, allow botrytis to form, dry the grapes after harvest (there are several other methods not discussed in the course as well). Most often used: Drying the grapes.
9. Frizzante wines are "fizzy," with less bottle pressure and fewer bubbles; spumante wines are fully sparkling.
10. Prosecco
11. Asti is a spumante (sparkling) wine, while Moscato d'Asti is always frizzante (slightly sparkling). Asti is packaged in a sparkling wine bottle with a mushroom cork, while Moscato d'Asti comes in a standard bottle with a standard cork.
12. Table completion possibilities:
    • Diano d'Alba; DOCG; Dolcetto; Still; Red; Piedmont
    • Oltrepò Pavese Metodo Classico; DOCG; Chardonnay, Pinot Bianco, Pinot Nero; Classic Method; White, rosato; Lombardy
    • Asti; DOCG; Moscato; Tank Method; White; Piedmont
    • Barbaresco; DOCG; Nebbiolo; Still; Red; Piedmont
    • Prosecco; DOC; Glera; Tank Method; White; Veneto, Friuli–Venezia Giulia
    • Lambrusco di Sorbara; DOC; Lambrusco; Tank Method; Red; Emilia Romagna

13. Brut nature (aka Brut zero, Dosaggio zero), Extra brut, Brut, Extra dry, Secco (Dry), Abboccato (Demisec), Dolce (Sweet)

14. Table completion possibilities:
    - Vino Nobile di Montepulciano; DOCG; Prugnolo Gentile (aka Sangiovese); Dry Still; Red; Tuscany
    - Recioto della Valpolicella; DOCG; Corvina; Sweet Still; Red; Veneto
    - Primitivo di Manduria; DOC; Primitivo; Dry Still; Red; Puglia
    - Primitivo di Manduria Dolce Naturale; DOCG; Primitivo; Sweet Still; Red; Puglia
    - Fiano di Avellino; DOCG; Fiano; Dry Still; White; Campania
    - Marsala; DOC; Various; Sweet Still; White, Rosato, Red; Sicily

15. Seven subzones: Colli Aretini, Colli Fiorentini, Colline Pisane, Colli Senesi, Montalbano, Montespertoli, Rufina

16. Carbon dioxide (CO_2)

17. Nebbiolo; 100%

18. No. Skins of red grapes in contact with the juice during the vinification process provide the coloration. Pinot Nero (Pinot Noir)

Unit 8

1. Piedmont, Tuscany, Veneto
2. Answers will vary.
3. Barolo, Barbaresco, Chianti Classico, Brunello di Montalcino, and Amarone della Valpolicella; Chianti Classico; Bolgheri
4. Table completion possibilities:
    - 1 year; Not required; Bolgheri Rosso and Chianti Classico
    - 2 years; Not required; Amarone and Chianti Classico Riserva
    - 2 years; 9 months; Barbaresco
    - 2 years; 1 year; Bolgheri Superiore
    - 2½ years; Not required; Chianti Classico Gran Selezione
    - 3 years; 18 months; Barolo
    - 4 years; Not required; Amarone Riserva
    - 4 years; 9 months; Barbaresco Riserva
    - 4 years; 2 years; Brunello di Montalcino
    - 5 years; 18 months; Barolo Riserva
    - 5 years; 2 years; Brunello di Montalcino Riserva
5. *Require* 100%: Barolo (Nebbiolo), Barbaresco (Nebbiolo), Brunello di Montalcino (Brunello/Sangiovese). *Allow* 100%: Chianti Classico (Sangiovese); Bolgheri

(Sauvignon Blanc, Vermentino, Cabernet Sauvignon, Cabernet Franc, Merlot)

6. One (Bolgheri); Sauvignon Blanc and Vermentino
7. Barbaresco: Barbaresco; Barolo: Barolo; Castagneto Carducci: Bolgheri; Castellina: Chianti Classico; Castelnuovo Berardenga: Chianti Classico; Castiglione Falletto: Barolo; Fumane: Amarone della Valpolicella; Gaiole: Chianti Classico; Greve: Chianti Classico; La Morra: Barolo; Monforte d'Alba: Barolo; Montalcino: Brunello di Montalcino; Negrar: Amarone della Valpolicella; Neive: Barbaresco; Radda: Chianti Classico; San Casciano in Val di Pesa: Chianti Classico; San Pietro in Cariano: Amarone della Valpolicella; Sant'Ambrogio: Amarone della Valpolicella; Serralunga d'Alba: Barolo; Treiso: Barbaresco
8. "Additional geographical definitions"—named parcels of land within the denomination that are considered in some way unique from the rest of the area; Barolo and Barbaresco
9. Amarone della Valpolicella; 45–95% Corvina, 5–30% Rondinella
10. Riserva requires a higher minimum alcohol level and therefore riper grapes than basic Chianti Classico; Gran Selezione requires a still higher level. In addition, the grapes for Gran Selezione must be estate grown; the other two categories do not have that requirement.
11. Amarone della Valpolicella; Classico and Valpantena. Bolgheri (Sassicaia)
12. Amarone della Valpolicella. As a dried-grape wine, the minimum alcohol level is high to ensure that the grapes have been dried to a sufficient extent.
13. Brunello di Montalcino (Rosso di Montalcino DOC) and Amarone della Valpolicella (Valpolicella DOC)
14. Table completion possibilities:
    - Amarone della Valpolicella; DOCG; Veneto; Corvina; 14.0%; 2 years
    - Barbaresco Riserva; DOCG; Piedmont; Nebbiolo; 12.5%; 4 years, including 9 months in wood
    - Barolo; DOCG; Piedmont; Nebbiolo; 13.0%; 3 years, including 18 months in wood
    - Bolgheri Rosso; DOC; Tuscany; Usually Cabernet Franc, Cabernet Sauvignon, or Merlot; 11.5%; 1 year
    - Brunello di Montalcino Riserva; DOCG; Tuscany; Sangiovese; 12.5%; 5 years, including 2 years in wood
    - Chianti Classico Gran Selezione; DOCG; Tuscany; Sangiovese; 13.0%; 2½ years

Credits

All photos, maps, and illustrations apart from those listed below are either licensed by or original to Italian Wine Central.

Index

About Italian Wine Central

As the leading English-language source of accurate, up-to-date information about Italian wine worldwide, Italian Wine Central (IWC) is recognized as a key spokesmedium for Italian wine in the United States.

Online at **ItalianWineCentral.com** since January 2014, the website features a wealth of information on every Italian wine denomination, including clear, concise summaries of the primary rules and regulations; details about more than 200 of the grape varieties used in Italian wines; statistics about the global and Italian wine trade; and topical articles and educational features. IWC is organized in a powerful, searchable database that is optimized for mobile devices. With readers in more than 120 countries, Italian Wine Central serves as a central network for wine professionals wanting to learn and teach about Italian wines.

The **Italian Wine Professional** (IWP) certification program was developed by Italian Wine Central to help those in the global wine trade—and by extension, those who buy and enjoy wine—to widen and deepen their knowledge of Italian wines in order to more confidently and professionally buy, sell, and consume these enchanting wines. The IWP program includes both online and in-class courses, this book, and a certification exam, with certified graduates and enrolled students around the world.

About the Authors

Jack Brostrom
Cofounder and Editor in Chief, Italian Wine Central

Jack is a former naval flight officer and intelligence officer with a master's degree in National Security Studies from Georgetown University. During his career in the Navy and as an intelligence and security analyst, his responsibilities often involved training and instructional systems design. His duty tours in such locations as New Zealand, Spain, and South America also allowed him an early exposure to wine while he was serving. After transitioning from government service, Jack became a book editor and writer with more than 300 titles in his repertoire, editing everything from travel books to medical texts. His personal interest in wine led to much crossover between his editing and wine education. Among other things, Jack wrote the seminal 2009 edition of the Society of Wine Educators' *Certified Specialist of Wine Study Guide* and introduced the SWE Workbook. He also coedited the Greenwood Press book *The Business of Wine: An Encyclopedia.* He holds the Level III Award in Wines and Spirits with distinction from the WSET. Focusing increasingly on Italian wine, Jack decided to put his computer science degree and his analysis expertise to work by creating Italian Wine Central in a culmination of a lifetime of interests.

Geralyn Brostrom, CWE
Cofounder and Education Director, Italian Wine Central

A 25-year veteran of the wine industry, Geralyn has held positions in multiple channels, from wineries to retail operations. Building on a lifelong love of education, she enjoyed taking on the role of wine educator early on. Along the way, she became a member and later director of education and executive director of the Society of Wine Educators. Just prior to starting Italian Wine Central, Geralyn was vice president of education for the importer-distributor Winebow, where her deep interest in Italian wines was forged. When not focusing on things Italian, she lectures on wine business topics in the Wine MBA program at Sonoma State University and teaches at the Napa Valley Wine Academy. Her professional wine credentials include the Certified Wine Educator from SWE, the Level III Award in Wines and Spirits with distinction from the WSET, and of course the Italian Wine Professional. A dual citizen of the United States and the Italian Republic, Geralyn holds a BS in Management and an MBA in Marketing, which she put to good use in coediting *The Business of Wine.* The Italian Wine Professional represents the synergy between two of her passions: helping others learn and the allure of Italy—its language, culture, food, wine, and people.

Made in the USA
San Bernardino, CA
27 October 2017